Political Realism and International Morality

D0068954

About the Book and Editors

It is always appropriate to ask whether an expedient foreign policy is morally justifiable, just as it is always appropriate to ask whether a morally defensible policy is consistent with the national interest. The ongoing dialogue between morality and realpolitik gives much of foreign policy debate its characteristic bite. In this collection of essays, a distinguished group of philosophers, political theorists, and lawyers— including Russell Hardin and Marshall Cohen—explore these contrasting themes.

In essays that are at once insightful and accessible, noted political thinkers examine the tension of the conflicting demands of morality and national self-interest in the context of the foundations of international order, the possession and use of nuclear weapons, recourse to war, and the prospects for peace. A final postscript addresses the question of the responsibility of intellectuals in the national foreign policy debate.

This book will appeal to scholars and students in any discipline dealing with international affairs as well as to lay readers who wish to explore the implications of taking morality and reason seriously in foreign policy.

Kenneth Kipnis is a member of the philosophy department at the University of Hawaii. **Diana T. Meyers** is a member of the philosophy department at the University of Connecticut. They are coeditors of *Economic Justice.* Kipnis is the author of *Legal Ethics,* and Meyers is the author of *Inalienable Rights: A Defense.*

Political Realism and International Morality

Ethics in the Nuclear Age

edited by
Kenneth Kipnis and
Diana T. Meyers

Consulting Editor: William Nelson

An AMINTAPHIL Volume

Westview Press / Boulder and London

Copyright © 1987 by Westview Press, Inc.

Published in 1987 in the United States of America by Westview Press, Inc.; Frederick A. Praeger, Publisher; 5500 Central Avenue, Boulder, Colorado 80301

Library of Congress Cataloging-in-Publication Data
Political realism and international morality.
    Chiefly papers presented at Tenth Plenary Conference
of American Section of International Association for
Philosophy of Law and Social Philosophy, 1984, University
of Notre Dame.
    Includes index.
    1. International relations—Moral and ethical aspects
—Congresses. 2. Nuclear weapons—Moral and ethical
aspects—Congresses. I. Kipnis, Kenneth. II. Meyers,
Diana T. III. International Association for Philosophy
of Law and Social Philosophy. American Section. Plenary
Conference (10th : 1984 : University of Notre Dame)
JX1255.P65 1987   172'.4   87-10109
ISBN 0-8133-0456-3
ISBN 0-8133-0457-1 (pbk.)

Printed and bound in the United States of America

The paper used in this publication meets the requirements of the American National
Standard for Permanence of Paper for Printed Library Materials Z39.48-1984.

10   9   8   7   6   5   4   3   2   1

Contents

Preface

Although it is not always acknowledged, there is a characteristic tension within foreign policy debates between realpolitik, on the one hand, and the moral approach to international relations, on the other. For it seems always relevant to ask whether effective policies are morally justified or, alternatively, whether morally defensible policies can be reconciled with the national interest, especially where security is involved.

Although the opposition between these two perspectives has a long history, there can be no question that the proliferation of nuclear weaponry has generated, along with its familiar anxieties, a new vitality in the old debate. For just as the unprecedented threat posed by the nuclear age cries out for a hard-nosed realism in international relations, so the unconscionable atrocity implicit in the use of these weapons summons us to new understandings of responsibility.

In its three parts and postscript, *Political Realism and International Morality: Ethics in the Nuclear Age* explores these themes in several ways. Part 1, "Morality and the International Order," initially raises questions about political realism, a movement that is ascendant in the field of political science. Here the questions concern the application of ethics to the structural foundations of the international order; issues involving international intervention and, in particular, the bombing of civilian populations receive particular attention. Part 2, "The Ethics of Nuclear Deterrence," takes up a range of concerns regarding the possession and use of nuclear weapons. Part 3, "Nationalism and the Prospects for Peace," examines the impetus to war among nations and their loyal citizens. The Postscript surveys the contributions to the book and considers the role and responsibility of intellectuals in these momentous international debates.

Although the chapters assembled here are for the most part drawn from more than forty presented at the Tenth Plenary Conference of the

American Section of the International Association for Philosophy of Law and Social Philosophy (AMINTAPHIL), held at University of Notre Dame in November 1984, this volume is *not* intended as that conference's proceedings. No attempt has been made to capture the orientation and tone of those meetings. Instead we have tried to display in this book something of the diversity of contemporary efforts to come to grips with the issues. We have included advocates of armament, mutual disarmament, and unilateral disarmament. Commentaries on several of the chapters serve to enliven the debate. The book includes well-known authors as well as promising young scholars.

The editors are grateful to President Albert J. Simone of the University of Hawaii and to the University of Hawaii Foundation for help at crucial stages of the editorial process.

Kenneth Kipnis
Diana T. Meyers

Introduction: Moral Principles and Moral Theory

William Nelson

From the 1930s to the early 1950s, the dominant mood in Anglo-American moral philosophy was skepticism. The common opinion among philosophers as well as theorists in other disciplines was that no moral truths exist. People had moral opinions, but such opinions could not have *validity*. The pronouncements of moralists had no authority, for there were no real facts that these pronouncements were about, and religious or metaphysical conceptions of authority had been abandoned.

During the 1950s a reaction set in, and by the end of the 1960s, the standard arguments in support of these skeptical views had been thoroughly discredited. Then progress slowed. It became clear that refuting skeptics' arguments is not the same as showing that their conclusions are false. Philosophers did not come up with a generally accepted account of the nature or source of moral truth, nor did they agree on what morality, whatever its nature, requires or permits.

Still, there has been since the late 1970s some original and exciting philosophical work about the foundations of morality. Some philosophers, rather tentatively, began to put forward theories identifying morality with certain natural facts about human beings and human societies. According to these theories, there are moral truths, and true moral beliefs are beliefs about natural facts.[1] At the same time, however, a number of other philosophers, most of whom would not accept the arguments of the earlier skeptics, offered new arguments against the idea that morality can have any objective validity or binding authority.[2]

Just as theorists have long doubted the objectivity or validity of morality in general, they also have doubted morality's place in international relations. Many of these latter theorists, generally called "realists," have come to their conclusions as a result of a more general skepticism about morality. Others, however, have accepted the possibility of moral truths in some spheres, within a settled polity for example, but have denied morality among nations. Still others have granted the possibility of moral truths in both spheres, but have claimed that morality has a different, and more limited, content when applied internationally.

In the first chapter in this book, Marshall Cohen undertakes an exhaustive investigation of different forms of realism, and he shows, decisively I think, that its defenders' arguments fail. Although there is a widespread belief that moral considerations have no validity when applied to the conduct of nations vis-à-vis one another, this belief has never been given an adequate foundation. But here the debate has reached the same stage as the debate about general moral skepticism once the skeptics' arguments had been refuted. We know the realists' position has not been established, but those of us who view the conduct of international relations in moral terms cannot complacently assume that no further arguments for realism are forthcoming.

I do not record this observation because I want to defend skepticism. Indeed, I believe morality is objective in a sense sufficient to make rational moral discussion both possible and necessary; and I believe the fundamental principles that apply within nations apply to relations between them. Still, I think it is important to be aware of the prevalent theoretical situation in moral philosophy. We do not have *proofs* that either realism or general skepticism is false, and we do not have a generally accepted account of what morality requires. Moreover, as Cohen notes, even if we agreed about the fundamental principles of morality, and agreed that they applied to international relations as well as more locally, it would not follow that they give rise to the same requirements in the very different *circumstances* of domestic relations and international relations.

This is worth mentioning, for a theme that runs through more than one of the chapters in this book (for example, those by Hardin and Bobbitt) is that standard conceptions of what morality requires, both deontological and utilitarian, fail when applied to issues of nuclear strategy. The scale of the problems, the sophisticated technology, and the role of institutional structures and cultural and ideological conflict make common moral categories somehow irrelevant. Not everyone agrees, of course. And if we are tempted to agree, that does not put us in the realist camp. To reject realism is not to be committed thereby to the strong, deontological principles these authors reject. It leaves us with a lot of theoretical flexibility.

What is central to realism itself also is not always clear. Theorists in the realist tradition, while denying that moral categories apply to international relations, nevertheless have, with doubtful consistency, put forward very definite ideas about how nations should conduct themselves. The proper aim of policy, realists argue, is simply to promote the national interest and to bolster national security. But if the skeptical premises of realism constitute a dubious foundation for normative prescriptions, even self-interested ones, it is equally true that a commitment to the relevance of morality does not necessarily preclude a concern for national security and for legitimate national interests. Whether morality requires a concern for security is itself a substantive moral question. Insofar as we associate realism with advocacy of national interest and not with skepticism about morality or with simple amoralism, it is quite possible that some elements of realism will reappear within theories explicitly inspired by a concern with morality.

There are different aspects to realism, and people have been led to realist conclusions by a variety of considerations. Some theorists begin with a general skepticism about morality or with an overly narrow conception of its scope. But even those who reject these starting points can arrive consistently at substantive conclusions not unlike those of the realists on the basis of moral argument. There is, however, a further source of the realist impulse I find in some ways more interesting. This is the idea that although there is no problem about the existence of morality—and perhaps even no problem about knowing some of its requirements—what it requires, at least in the conduct of international relations, is simply too costly, too risky. When so much is at stake— the survival of a way of life or even of the world—to demand that we be bound by the requirements of morality is to demand too much.

The attitude I have just described, it seems to me, is not an uncommon attitude toward morality in international relations. Defenders of morality, of course, will object that it rests on simple confusions. Either, they will say, the attitude is mistaken in assuming that morality rules out the kind of action necessary for national and human survival or it rests on mistaken evaluations of outcomes—it regards as disastrous outcomes that really are not.

Surely there is something to this reply. When people claim they *need* to violate the requirements of morality, it is always appropriate to question whether their aims are truly urgent. All of us, and perhaps nations more than individuals, are liable to exaggerate the importance of our ideals and interests. Moreover, it may often be possible, as Sterba argues in his chapter, to reconcile the demands of morality with the requirements of, for example, a credible deterrent. Sometimes morality puts limits on what we can legitimately seek, but sometimes it simply forces us to adopt one means over another.

Still, I think a defender of morality should not be completely satisfied with this reply. What I, at least, would like to be shown is that it is *possible* to attain goals, such as peace and security, consistent with the requirements of morality and that respect for these requirements is instrumental in bringing about these and other good ends. If respect for morality does not actually promote good ends, or if it is not consistent with protection of legitimate national and political interests, then it is not clear that morality deserves the respect it demands. The objection that morality is just an expensive and risky luxury then would be justified. (For an argument that moral institutions actually contribute to peace and prosperity, see the chapter by Doyle. See also the article by Railton cited in note 1.)

On what basis can moral requirements be recommended to persons and nations, and what principles can be so recommended? There is something to be said for requirements of nonaggression and nonintervention. If all nations respect these requirements, and it is known they are respected, then each enjoys the fruits of peace and security. Assuming that each benefits from others respecting these requirements, they can be recommended to people who care about being able to justify the conduct of their country to others. What cannot be said of these requirements, however, is that they are effective *strategies* for achieving peace and security in the sense that by following them, a given nation automatically promotes peace and security. Or, at least, it is not obvious that this is so.

Thus, the requirement just described is of limited applicability. There are two problems with this requirement. First, where some nations do not respect the principle of nonaggression, it is doubtful that we can reasonably recommend nonbelligerence to their victims. At least we cannot do so if we assume they value national survival at least as much as self-justifiable conduct. Some room must be made for effective self-defense, and, indeed, if a nation has a genuinely effective strategy for promoting general peace and security, that strategy cannot reasonably be ruled out even if it violates principles like nonintervention.

A second problem is that both people and nations have many interests and goals over and above the interests in peace and security I have mentioned so far. Indeed, the foregoing discussion has been misleading insofar as it suggests that the main issue is the justification of morality to self-interested persons and nations. In one sense, nations are motivated more than individuals by moral concerns. National rhetoric bristles with moral fervor and righteous indignation, and nations' behavior, although often more controlled, nevertheless is colored by these attitudes. Nations pursue goals, like economic justice, protection for human rights, and the spread of democratic political arrangements. It is only a prejudice that these are mere masks for self-interest;[3] neither citizens nor governments see such goals that way. But this is a problem, for nations differ in their conceptions of what goals are desirable; often, principles of the kind I have emphasized (for example, nonintervention or prohibitions against war or certain methods of fighting wars) prevent nations from pursuing what they see as morally compelling goals. If these principles are not necessarily effective strategies for promoting peace and security, and if they actually limit the pursuit of what some see as moral ideals, what kind of rationale can be given for them?

Among the most powerful metaphorical rationales for morality is the metaphor of the contract. Moral principles are viewed as rules everyone could agree to, given individual ends and at least a minimal, basic interest in finding some system of mutually beneficial rules.[4] When I suggested earlier that everyone might benefit from compliance with certain minimal principles and that these would need to be supplemented by principles permitting self-defense, I had a contractualist justification in mind. But the more nations and peoples are divided by deeply conflicting ideals, the more difficult it will be to find principles all can reasonably be expected to accept. Or, to put the same point differently, any attempt to defend a system of principles will involve a prior decision about which ideals or goals should take priority, and this kind of decision, although it may sometimes be justified objectively, will be difficult to justify in practice to some parties.

Some think that where people have conflicting ends, it is at least possible to agree on procedures (such as majority rule) or on arrangements demanding mutual forebearance and respect for local spheres of autonomy (such as property rights). According to this view, these procedures are neutral and make possible the effective pursuit of individual goals and ideals, either within spheres of autonomy or through the neutral political process. But I am inclined to think that where these arrangements really can be rationally justified to each, there already is considerable basis for mutual trust and an agreement in values. Democracy is desirable where shared assumptions provide the basis for constructive dialogue; respect for individual rights is desirable where there is some common understanding as to how, within broad limits, these rights will be exercised.

The problem is that it is just these kinds of agreement that we often find lacking in international politics, in, for example, the religiously based conflicts in areas like the Middle East. This does not mean that there are no rationally justifiable moral limits on how states can behave; but it does cast doubt, I think, on the idea that principles of nonintervention and the like, given the present conflict of ideals and lack of mutual trust, will be found mutually acceptable. Nevertheless, I want to propose that the contractualist ideal suggests a way of viewing these principles, suitably qualified, as effective strategies for pursuing the ends of morality.

Contractualism is a democratic conception of morality that enjoins us to act in ways that can be justified to others. Contractualism enjoins nations to act this way vis-à-vis other nations, and it enjoins them to govern in accordance with principles that can be justified to their citizens. It requires an honest respect for the interests, ideals, and opinions of others. But, in practice, we cannot expect to find consensus on ideals or on the relative urgency of conflicting interests. The best we can do is to pursue the policy of seeking consensus while acting in ways that we hope others will be persuaded to find acceptable. This does not require denying our own ideals and interests, but it does require looking for an accommodation with those who have conflicting ideals and interests. When others threaten our security, our interests, or our ideals, this does not rule out a response, but it calls for a measured response, a response that leaves room, as far as possible, for a mutually acceptable resolution of the conflict.

According to this way of thinking about morality, the most fundamental moral demand is that we seek to *find* a mutually acceptable conception of the more specific requirements that constitute morality in the ordinary sense. This enterprise is less a matter of following specific rules or respecting specific prohibitions than of adopting an attitude. It requires and permits flexibility in response to changes in the situation with which we are confronted. Still, if I am not mistaken, there is an important place within this conception for the principles and maxims often associated with the morality of international relations. Rules of nonintervention, for example, or the rules of proportionality and just cause in just-war theory, are plausible guides to the kind of conduct that is compatible with the underlying moral aim I have described. They fit into morality in two ways. First, these rules represent a potentially rational accommodation, in the sense that if all nations followed them, each would be able to attain its justifiable goals and aspirations, and each therefore would be required, in fairness, to comply. Second, even in the absence of general compliance and cooperation, a given nation, by following these rules, invites and lays the groundwork for future accommodation without having to sacrifice its own essential interests. They counsel the *prudent* pursuit of a limited but important kind of moral goal.

Consider some examples: Although we can imagine (indeed, we can find) situations in which foreign governments violate the fundamental rights of their citizens and resident aliens, and although this may look like good cause for intervention, many forms of intervention are unlikely to be effective to the end of reconstituting a just and viable political community. Yet it is this that should be our aim, and so nonintervention constitutes simple good advice. Again, when we must resort to force, if we formulate clear, reasonable, and attainable aims and adopt proportional means (as just-war theory requires), we leave our adversaries with alternatives they can accept, without losing face or sacrificing their vital interests. This is an essential first move in the development of the moral dialogue I suggest we take as the first goal of morality.

Notes

I wish to thank the American Council of Learned Societies for fellowship support during the time this chapter was written.

1. See, for example, Nicholas Sturgeon, "Moral Explanations," in D. Copp and D. Zimmerman, eds., *Morality, Reason and Truth* (Totowa, NJ: Rowman and Allenheld, 1984), pp. 49–78; and Peter Railton, "Moral Realism," *Philosophical Review* 95, no. 2 (April 1986):163–207.

2. See John Mackie, *Ethics: Inventing Right and Wrong* (Hammondsworth, Eng.: Penguin, 1977). See also three works by Gilbert Harman: "Moral Relativism Defended," *Philosophical Review* 84, no. 1 (January 1975):3–22; "Relativistic Ethics: Morality as Politics," *Midwest Studies in Philosophy* vol. 3 (University of Minnesota at Morris, 1978); and *The Nature of Morality* (New York: Oxford University Press, 1977); and R. B. Brandt, *A Theory of the Good and the Right* (New York: Oxford University Press, 1979); Alan Gibbard, "Moral Judgment and the Acceptance of Norms," *Ethics* 96, no. 1 (October 1985):5–21. (See also, in the same issue of *Ethics*, the comments by Nicholas Sturgeon and the reply by Gibbard.)

3. For the classic, and perhaps still best, argument against egoism as a general theory of motivation, see Joseph Butler, *Fifteen Sermons Upon Human Nature*, Sermon 11 (London, 1726, 2nd. ed. 1729). For a sophisticated, modern critique of the assumption of egoism in the social sciences, see Howard Margolis, *Selfishness, Altruism and Rationality* (Chicago: University of Chicago Press, 1982).

4. For a good discussion of the kind of contractualist theory I have in mind, see T. M. Scanlon, "Contractualism and Utilitarianism," in A. Sen and B. Williams, eds., *Utilitarianism and Beyond* (New York: Cambridge University Press, 1982), esp. p. 110f.

PART ONE

Morality and the International Order

Introduction to Part One

Diana T. Meyers

The chapters in this part address the question of how morality applies to international relations. Although the adage "All's fair in love and war" reflects the pervasiveness of the assumption that morality has no part in international affairs, these chapters argue that morality should control relations among states, and the authors debate the particulars of international morality. Marshall Cohen takes up the fundamental question of whether an ethics of international relations is intelligible and urges that it is. Russell Hardin, James Child, and Jefferson McMahan assume Cohen's conclusion and inquire into the form that an ethics of international relations should take. Hardin rejects an agent-centered, deontological international ethics in favor of a strategy-based, consequentialist approach. Child resurrects the individual point of view and contends that even in mass society individuals are responsible for seeing to it that their governments comply with moral requirements. McMahan considers international morality from the standpoint of nation-states and affirms that morality imposes limits on nation-states' intervention in one another's domestic affairs.

Marshall Cohen begins his chapter, "Moral Skepticism and International Relations," with a reminder that the history of international relations is one of such appalling greed, cruelty, and duplicity that some commentators have doubted that moral standards apply in this realm. Nevertheless, Cohen's aim is to assess the cogency of moral skepticism in regard to international relations, and he argues that foreign policy should be governed by moral constraints. Cohen examines two forms of moral skepticism:

1. Realist skepticism—the view that power is the controlling force in international relations and that promoting the national interest

must be the overriding goal of national leaders in conducting foreign policy
2. Hobbesian skepticism—the view that independent states remain in a state of nature in which no moral law is binding and that each state is entitled to promote its national interest as best it can

He maintains that both positions are open to fatal objections.

Cohen diagnoses the problem in the realist view as a tendency to conflate morality with moralism—judging and acting on the basis of "utopian ideals and sentimental slogans"—coupled with a yearning for absolutism—judging and acting on the basis of a set of exceptionless moral rules. However, neither moralism nor absolutism is morality, and states often conform to morality properly construed. The trouble with the Hobbesian view is that moral constraints do not presuppose the existence of a coercive institution to enforce them and that the state's duty to protect its citizens cannot justify an unlimited right to pursue the national interest. On the basis of this critique, Cohen argues that the "primary obligation of the nuclear age is to abstain from the first nuclear strike and to adopt policies that . . . reduce the temptation to make such a strike."

Russell Hardin agrees that moral considerations do have a place in international relations. But whereas Cohen's project is to show that moral theory must inform public policy, Hardin's is to show how public policy issues affect moral theory. In "Deterrence and Moral Theory," Hardin maintains that "because nuclear weapons may bring about the most grievous outcome imaginable, they elevate concern with outcomes over concern with actions." He defends this shift toward teleology by pointing out the inadequacies of a series of deontological doctrines in the setting of the nuclear deterrence debate. Hardin contends that the institutional nature of deterrence (that is, retaliation must be virtually automatic for deterrence to work) must color all moral discussion of this policy.

On the basis of this view, Hardin argues that it is a mistake to frame the issue of deterrence in terms of individual responsibility for choice and action. Likewise, to understand policy alternatives in terms of outcomes as opposed to strategies is not to grasp the context in which decisions about nuclear policy are made. Hardin takes issue with the doctrine of the double effect—its distinction between letting something happen and causing it to happen is irrelevant when the outcome being contemplated is the destruction of a large part of humanity. He takes issue with just-war theory—its distinction between the justice of a state's *reasons for going to war* and the justice of a state's *conduct in war* collapses where a deterrence policy requires action in advance of the occasion for it, that is, arranging for a retaliatory strike before a first strike has occurred. Finally, he takes issue with intuitionism, which fails before the novelty and awesome power of nuclear weaponry.

James Child's chapter, "Political Responsibility and Noncombatant Liability," takes exception to Hardin's rejection of the individual point of view in contemporary discussions of defense policy. Invoking a series of legal concepts, Child holds that individual citizens in a democracy bear a considerably greater burden of responsibility for their government's conduct than is ordinarily thought.

Using a pair of hypothetical states—one the aggressor that cynically puts its citizens at risk and the other the defender that must decide whether it can risk the lives of its attacker's noncombatants in order to defend itself—Child asks whether citizens bear sufficient responsibility for their country's foreign policy to have any complaint if they are killed accidentally by the defending state when it is seeking to destroy military targets. Child varies political institutions and first considers a democratic aggressor state that holds a referendum in which the majority votes to wage war. In this case, the state evidently acts as the agent of the majority when it attacks; those who voted for the attack are responsible for the acts they authorized their agent to perform. Thus, they are not entitled to immunity from risk. But what of the citizens who voted against the attack? Just as a corporate officer is obligated to blow the whistle on the illegal or immoral plans of his or her corporation, so opponents of the war can claim no immunity unless they protest the war, for example, through civil disobedience or emigration. Furthermore, Child denies that an aggressive dictatorship would absolve its citizens from responsibility for its wars. Most dictatorships have come to power through the traditions and institutions of their people and with the passive acquiescence if not the active support of their people. Moreover, because the dictatorship claims to act as the agent of its citizens, citizens have an affirmative obligation to distance themselves from their leaders. Even in a dictatorship, noncombatants who are killed collaterally may have no complaint against those who have taken their lives.

The focus of Child's chapter is the way in which entrenched political power, if not legitimacy, can render its citizens responsible for its acts and vulnerable to retaliation. In other words, Child considers the moral consequences that political association imposes on individuals. In contrast, Jefferson McMahan explores the moral prerogatives of states and, specifically, the ways in which political establishments gain moral protection from intervention. "The Ethics of International Intervention" addresses a twofold problem in the morality of international relations— what is international intervention, and when is international intervention justified? Starting from the claim that international intervention involves "coercive external interference in the affairs of a population that is organized in the form of a state," McMahan goes on to consider various refinements of this definition that would be necessary in order to hold that such intervention is always wrong. He then points out that the U.N. position on this matter is that intervention against the state is always wrong, although intervention on behalf of the state can be permissible.

Several arguments have been advanced in support of the U.N. view, and McMahan critically examines each of them. The paternalistic argument regards states as analogous to persons and maintains that, like persons, states cannot be forced to do things for their own good. However, this argument would prevent intervention on behalf of an oppressed minority. The communal autonomy argument maintains that the inviolability of the state protects the collective self-determination of its citizens, provided that the state is a legitimate one. Although it is notoriously difficult to provide workable criteria of legitimacy, McMahan grants that there is a presumption against intervention when states are clearly legitimate but notes that, in this view, there may be an obligation to intervene when states are blatantly illegitimate. Nevertheless, intervention is rarely justified, for it may interfere with the evolution of a tradition of communal self-determination. A final argument against intervention is the stability argument. One version of this argument rejects intervention on the grounds that it instigates counterintervention and leads to war. A second version rejects intervention on the grounds that it undermines the world order, which rests on a plurality of sovereign states. But a principle allowing intervention could be qualified to prohibit intervention that threatened to escalate; history does not bear out the claim that intervention will destroy the system of sovereign states. In synthesizing the lessons of his inquiry, McMahan concludes that an overridable presumption against intervention protects legitimate states and that intervention can be justified only at the lowest effective level.

1

Moral Skepticism
and International Relations

Marshall Cohen

To an alarming degree the history of international relations is a history
of selfishness and brutality. It is a story in which spying, deceit, bribery,
disloyalty, ingratitude, betrayal, exploitation, plunder, repression, sub-
jection, and genocide are all too conspicuous. And it is a history that
may well culminate in the moral catastrophe of nuclear war. This situation
has elicited a number of very different reactions from those who discourse
on international relations. For some the moral quality of international
relations from the Athenians at Melos to the Soviets in Poland is so
deplorable that they question whether moral standards in fact apply to
the international realm. George Kennan remarks, for instance, that the
conduct of nations is not "fit" for moral judgment.[1] This ambivalent
way of putting the matter betrays a nostalgia for moral assessment while
announcing a skepticism about its very possibility. Benedetto Croce is
beyond ambivalence or nostalgia. This self-professed disciple of Machiavelli
boldly proclaimed that in the realm of international politics lies are not
lies, or murders murders.[2] Moral categories and judgments are simply
out of place in the realm of international affairs. The first task of this
chapter will be to examine this extreme form of moral skepticism about
international relations, first in its realist, and then in its Hobbesian,
form.

The realists argue that international relations must be viewed under
the category of power and that the conduct of nations is, and should
be, guided and judged exclusively by the amoral requirements of the

Marshall Cohen, "Moral Skepticism and International Relations." *Philosophy and Public
Affairs* 13, no. 4 (Fall 1984). Copyright © 1984 by Princeton University Press. Reprinted
with permission of Princeton University Press and the author.

national interest. Sometimes they argue, as writers since Spinoza have argued, that if a statesman fails to pursue the national interest (and submits to some other, perhaps ethical, standard) he acts improperly and violates his contract with those he represents.[3] On this view, the only proper question to ask of him is whether his actions and policies advance the national interest and increase his nation's power. But the suggestion that the statesman has a moral obligation to do for his constituency whatever he has implicitly undertaken to do (on a contract, or as trustee or agent) is no better than the argument that the corporation president has an overriding obligation to sell thalidomide for the benefit of his shareholders, or that the Mafia hitman has an overriding obligation to kill for his employers.[4] And, in any case, these are not the terms a responsible constituency can be understood to have exacted from those who conduct its affairs. Often a democratic people will wish its affairs to be conducted in a morally acceptable fashion and it is, in any case, entirely appropriate to judge both a nation's, and its statesmen's, conduct by pertinent moral standards. A more tempting argument for the realist view that international conduct is improperly guided or judged by moral standards supposes that actions which seem to be politically acceptable in the international realm appear to be condemned by morality, and that morality must, therefore, be irrelevant to the judgment of international conduct. I argue that this view of the realists is founded on an overly simple conception of the structure of morality, one that they share with the naive moralists who are the main object of their attack. Once a more complex account of morality is provided, the realist view that international relations can only be measured against political standards of power and the national interest loses its plausibility. The substance of that more complex morality is, I believe, nonutilitarian, and I employ it to provide a moral assessment of the realist doctrine of the balance of power.

Hobbesian skepticism about international relations also rests on an inadequate view of morality. But here the problem is less with the Hobbesian account of the structure of morality than with the Hobbesian view of the conditions under which morality applies. For, in Hobbes's view, issues of justice and injustice do not arise in the state of nature even as, in the view of Treitschke and Bosanquet, ethical issues do not arise in the absence of "community" or outside the realm of Hegelian *Sittlichkeit*.[5] I argue, however, that ethical principles apply in the state of nature even as they apply in the absence of the common life that allegedly characterizes national communities. Besides, the actual situation of states is very different from that of individuals in the state of nature.

Realism and Power Politics

Realist writings display many serious misunderstandings of the nature of morality and, as I have suggested, these misunderstandings contribute to the realists' skepticism about the role of morality in international affairs. The post–World War II realists, for instance, often fail to distinguish between the moral and the "moralistic" or between the legal and the "legalistic." All too often the realists suggest that because "moralistic" or "legalistic" attitudes and policies are irrelevant, and even dangerous, in international affairs, morality and law are irrelevant and dangerous as well. This is, of course, a non sequitur. There is no reason why the genuine moralist cannot agree with the realist that "moralistic" politicians often claim to discern moral issues where doing so is inappropriate and self-defeating. The moralist may acknowledge, for instance, that the diplomatic recognition of a Communist regime does not imply moral approval and that it is often both permissible and politically prudent to extend such recognition to regimes whose moral principles we nevertheless reject.[6] Again, the genuine moralist can agree with the realist that a "moralistic" foreign policy, one founded on utopian ideals and sentimental slogans designed to win elections or to galvanize the passions of a democratic populace in time of war, is often hypocritical, obtuse, and self-defeating. But the moralist is not required to endorse a foreign policy because it invokes moral-sounding formulas that call on us to conquer the forces of evil, to exact war "reparations" because justice requires it, or to make the world safe for democracy come what may. He can agree, for instance, that morality did not require the Allies to demand total victory or to impose a humiliating peace on Germany after World War I. Even if Germany's actions gave the Allies the right to impose such a peace, morality did not require them to exercise it. We do not think we are morally obliged to punish children or criminals as severely as their conduct justifies if giving them another chance, issuing a moderate rebuke, or devising a rehabilitative regime is likely to produce better results. When Kennan condemns the vindictive reparation requirements imposed on Germany, or criticizes the humiliating attitude of the Western powers toward the Weimar Republic, he is not deploring something that morality or a moral attitude requires.[7] Indeed, the sensible moralist will doubtless agree with the realists that imposing a moderate peace of the sort Metternich and Castlereagh imposed on France after the Napoleonic wars would have been better than the Versailles approach. Similarly, morality did not require that we pursue a policy of unconditional surrender during World War II. Kennan himself admits that faced with an enemy like Hitler there may have been no practical alternative to this policy.[8] However that may be, the moral, as distinguished from the purely strategic, arguments against inviting the Red Army into the heart of Europe would surely have outweighed the argument that Germany must be rendered helpless and put utterly at our mercy.

The realist's critique of "moralism" is, then, often politically acute and salutary. But "moralism" is not morality, and showing that "moralistic" attitudes and policies have a pernicious influence on foreign policy does not show that morality itself must be banished from the realm of international affairs. Certainly, it does not show that a moral point of view must be replaced by a realistic one that takes the national interest to provide what Morgenthau calls "the one guiding star, one standard of thought, one rule of action" in the international sphere.[9] Power politics is not the only alternative to a muddled moralism.

If the confusion of "moralism" with morality provides one source of skepticism about the role of morality in international affairs, confusions about the structure of morality provide others. For many who speak in favor of a moral approach to international politics identify morality with the simple rules that in their opinion govern the conduct of ordinary life. R. W. Mowat, for instance, sees the Ten Commandments and the Golden Rule as central and remarks that they are "universal propositions without reservations, without exceptions."[10] Mowat's book is entitled *Public and Private Morality* and it is characteristic of writers of his persuasion to insist that the rules and principles which apply in private life apply in the public realm as well. Often, like Mowat, and like the realists' *bête noire*, Woodrow Wilson, they deplore the standard of conduct that prevails in the relations of states and look forward (in the words of Wilson's address to Congress on declaring war in 1917) to "the beginning of an age in which it will be insisted that the same standards of conduct and of responsibility for wrong shall be observed among nations and their governments that are observed among the individual citizens of individual states."[11]

But we do not need to invoke the special circumstances of international life to see that Mowat's position is untenable. Breaking a promise in order to aid the victim of an accident, lying to the Gestapo about the Jew in the attic, or killing a ruthless attacker in self-defense or to save a third party all constitute justifiable exceptions to the rules that Mowat and other simple moralists have in mind. If this is the case in domestic life, it is reasonable to expect that there will be exceptions to the rule forbidding promise breaking, lying, and killing in the circumstances of international life as well, and on occasion, at least, we can share Treitschke's scorn for the statesman who warms his hands over the smoking ruins of his fatherland comforting himself with the thought that he has never lied.[12] As Treitschke's remark suggests, the realists are correct in thinking that at least some of the actions simple moralists deplore are in fact necessary, defensible, and even admirable. But since realists all too often share the simple moralist's view that these actions are proscribed by morality, they are compelled to adopt the untenable position that international conduct cannot and should not be judged by moral standards. We have here the familiar phenomenon of the skeptic or realist who is a disappointed absolutist. But this inversion of the simple moralist's view is theoretically unsound and encourages a cynicism that is, if anything, even more dangerous than the naiveté and utopianism it is meant to supplant. It is necessary, therefore, to question this inadequate view of morality and to replace it with a more complex conception that will dissipate some of the tension between the often reasonable political positions of the realists and the demands of morality as the simple moralist sees them.

We must agree, then, that any reasonably accurate account of our moral view will acknowledge that moral rules often have exceptions and that we do nothing wrong when we act within an exception. (This is, indeed, what we mean when we speak of an exception.) But we need to complicate our conception of morality still further if we are to guard against more sophisticated skepticisms that feed on what is, even with this amendment, an overly simple view of morality.

For a more sophisticated realist may argue that even a morality which admits exceptions to its rules (as his does) will not be able to accept as legitimate actions that he (and sometimes that we) nevertheless consider legitimate. For many such actions, far from falling within the recognized exceptions to moral rules, actually require us to default on our moral obligations, to violate the rights of others, or to do other things that are objectionable from a moral point of view. For instance, Britain and France unquestionably defaulted on their legal (and in this case on their moral) obligations under the Covenant of the League of Nations when they failed to impose sanctions on Italy in response to her invasion of Abyssinia.[13] And the Jews violated the right of the Palestinian people to live where and how they reasonably wished when they established the State of Israel. But these more sophisticated realists may argue that despite these moral infractions, what Britain and France did, and what the Jews did, was legitimate. And, since these actions were legitimate they must have been legitimate from a "political," even if they were illegitimate from a "moral," point of view. Therefore, the realists conclude once again that in international affairs the political point of view is the appropriate or, at least, the overriding one.

But analyses of this sort are nevertheless misguided. They are flawed by their failure to appreciate the phenomenon of moral conflict. And this is a phenomenon that any adequately complex morality must acknowledge.[14] For it is often the case, and many would argue it is the case in the examples just mentioned, that those who violate a moral obligation do so in obedience to a weightier or a more compelling moral obligation. Thus, Britain and France failed to fulfill their duties under the League Covenant but they did so because they feared that honoring them would seriously impair their ability to defend either themselves or the fundamental values of a liberal civilization in what they could see was the coming struggle against fascism. In acting on these weightier obligations Britain and France acted not simply with political realism but in what was, from a moral point of view, the better way. Similarly, it can be argued, the Jews in asserting their religious and historical rights, and in doing what was required to secure the very existence of the Jewish people, acted on morally justifiable grounds. It is because the realist fails to appreciate the fact of moral conflict, or to understand that we are sometimes morally justified in defaulting on our obligations, in violating the rights of others, or, more generally, in doing dark and terrible things, that he develops a "political" justification for doing them. From this "realistic," political point of view he often criticizes the naiveté of the moralist's political thinking. But the fault lies rather in the simplicity of his own view of morality. For, as we have seen, that view fails to provide an adequate account of moral conflict and lacks an adequate understanding of moral tragedy.

But while stressing complexity we must avoid complicity, and it is therefore important to emphasize that many of the wrongs which so unhappily disfigure the history of international relations are wholly unjustifiable from a moral point of view. We must resist those theorists (and apologists) who discern imponderable moral conflict or inescapable moral tragedy in every act of aggression or exploitation. If the British and the French were justified in defaulting on their legal obligations to the League, the same cannot be said of the German failure to honor Belgian neutrality. If the Jews were justified in violating the rights of the Palestinians, the same cannot be said of the Italian assault on the rights of the Abyssinians. All too often the atmosphere of international relations is precisely as objectionable as the simple moralist says it is. The actions of a Kaiser Wilhelm or a Mussolini must not be rationalized from a "political" point of view or romanticized as cases of "tragic" necessity.

Although we cannot accept the simplicities of a moral theory like Mowat's, we should endorse his view that the history of international conduct is to an alarming degree the history of unconscionable insolence, greed, and brutality. Napoleon addressing his troops suggests what is all too often its moral atmosphere: "Soldiers, you are naked, [and] ill nourished. . . . I will lead you into the most fertile plains in the world. Rich provinces, great cities, will be in your power. There you will find honour, glory, riches."[15] On sentiments like these it is not difficult to pass moral judgment. If the realist is to persuade us that such judgments are inappropriate or impossible, this will require more forceful arguments or considerations than we have so far examined.

Many realists would claim that the tradition of political theory which stretches from Machiavelli to Croce and culminates in the main line of present-day thinking about international relations provides arguments and considerations of the required sort. According to this tradition, international relations occupies an autonomous realm of power politics exempt from moral judgment and immune to moral restraint. Unquestionably, this ubiquitous school of thought displays an amazing vitality, but a systematic presentation of its views is not easy to find. Perhaps the most notable in recent times is Hans Morgenthau's classic work, *Politics Among Nations*, and it will be useful to examine it here.

A main objective of Morgenthau's book, and of the realist school, is to show that Wilsonian hopes for a moral alternative to power politics is at very least naive and sentimental. Morgenthau asserts, for example, that it is an illusion to think that "men have the choice between power politics and its necessary outgrowth, the balance of power, on the one hand, and a different, better kind of international relations on the other."[16] It is, therefore, surprising to discover that Morgenthau does not argue directly that this better kind of international politics is impossible. Rather, he argues more generally that since all politics is ultimately power politics the desire for a better kind of international politics is, at best, utopian.[17]

In defending the claim that all politics is "power" politics Morgenthau illicitly stretches this phrase beyond its traditional meaning and offers implausible biopsychological and quasi-Marxist arguments to show that domestic politics, and even that family relations, are really disguised forms of the struggle for power. It is unnecessary to examine these arguments here because even if Morgenthau were correct of thinking that all politics is power politics, these argumentative strategies would not help him. If the operation of power politics is compatible with the felicities of family life and the moderation and legal character of the most fortunate national communities, then the operation of power politics does not preclude the possibility of that "better kind" of international politics that the liberal hopes for and works toward. To the contrary, showing that all relations are infected with power politics in this sense shows that international relations do not present a unique problem or an impossible terrain for ethical conduct or ethical judgment.

If Morgenthau wishes to demonstrate that this better kind of international politics is impossible, he will have to show that international politics is power politics in a narrower sense—one that fails to characterize at least some forms of municipal politics and family life. Power politics in the required sense must be incompatible with ethical conduct and impervious to ethical judgment.

Morgenthau tries to make plausible the claim that international politics is power politics in this appropriately narrower sense by suggesting, to begin with, that at least some international activities are not political at all.[18] Since they are nonpolitical he does not need to show that they characteristically display a struggle for power. The fact is, however, that if (as he says) the exchange of scientific information, famine and disaster relief, cultural and trade relations, and even much diplomatic activity are free from the struggle for power, the thesis that all international politics is power politics, opaque to moral assessment, loses much of its bite. Indeed, the claim threatens to reduce to the uninformatively circular observation that the aspect of international relations which is pure power politics is the aspect of international relations which is pure power politics—assuming there is one. But what, if anything, is that aspect? Morgenthau further dilutes the claim that all international politics is power politics by conceding that some nations, like Monaco, are politically inactive on the international scene or are, like Switzerland, only minimally active. Morgenthau insists, however, that unlike Monaco and Switzerland some nations, in particular, the United States and the USSR are maximally active and their relations (again, he does not say which of their relations) constitute the paradigm of international political relations. These nations are engaged in a straightforward struggle for power, and their conduct confirms the view that international politics is best understood as an autonomous realm of power in which the actions of nations are neither motivated by ethical considerations nor subject to ethical judgment. But even Morgenthau's paradigm case is far from persuasive, and no one has stated the main objection to it more forcefully than Morgenthau himself. In another, less theoretical work, he writes that "Washington and Moscow are not only the main centers of power, they are also the seats of hostile and competing political philosophies. . . . [We have here] a conflict between two kinds of moral principles, two types of moral conduct, two ways of life."[19] This is, in a sense, quite true, but it suggests that we shall not understand even Morgenthau's paradigm case of international politics unless we acknowledge that the parties involved are in part ethically motivated and that their actions are subject to moral assessment. I would argue that despite alarming lapses Washington often acts in conformity with moral requirements, even in its conflicts with Moscow. After all, Washington refrained from attacking Moscow at a time when the United States enjoyed a monopoly of nuclear weapons. And, surely, moral restraint, and sometimes something more attractive, often characterizes Washington's political relations with many other, more amicable nations. Whether or not this is so, however, the way of life we are defending is founded on moral principles that are plainly incompatible with the amoral pursuit of power, for any such policy must systematically ignore the rights and fundamental interests of others. If in certain extreme circumstances a struggle for power can be justified on grounds of, say, self-defense, this will itself be a morally grounded defense. In other circumstances an unrestrained pursuit of power will be condemned by the moral principles we ourselves acknowledge.

Morgenthau might argue that, while this seems to be so, the moral principles that nations announce are simply ideological counters employed in the struggle for power. But Morgenthau has given no reason to think this is true of moral language in its international applications alone, and if the claim is meant to follow from an account of the ideological nature of moral discourse in general, it implies a broader moral skepticism than Morgenthau wants to embrace, or than we are examining here. Morgenthau also suggests that from the point of view of the political scientist seeking to predict the behavior of nations they are best viewed as entities inhabiting an autonomous realm of power. But even if this were plausible (as I think it is not), it would not follow that statesmen and citizens should view themselves as occupying an autonomous realm in which the only appropriate grounds for action and judgment are assessments of power. In Morgenthau's view

the political realist maintains the autonomy of the political sphere, as the economist, the lawyer, and the moralist maintain theirs. He thinks in terms of interest defined as power, as the economist thinks in terms of utility; the lawyer, of the conformity of action with legal rules; the moralist, of the conformity of action with moral principles. The economist asks: "How does this policy affect the welfare of society, or a segment of it?" The lawyer asks: "Is this policy in accord with the rules of law?" The moralist asks: "Is this policy in accord with moral principles?" And the political realist asks: "How does this policy affect the power of the nation?" . . . The political realist is not unaware of the existence and relevance of standards of thought other than the political one. As a political realist, he cannot but subordinate these other standards to the political one. And he parts company with other schools when they impose standards of thought appropriate to other spheres upon the political one. It is here that political realism takes issue with the "legalistic-moralistic approach" to international politics.[20]

Plainly, however, morality has no discrete sphere of its own (a sphere of moral "fact") parallel to, but separate from, the main areas of human activity. It is not only appropriate, but characteristic and necessary, to apply its standards to economic, legal, and political phenomena. If the economist asks which of two policies produces greater utility, the moralist should ask of those policies, is the distribution of utility they propose morally acceptable? If the lawyer asks of an action, does it conform to the legal rules, the moralist should ask, are those rules just? Similarly, then, if the political realist asks, how does this policy affect the power of the nation, the moralist must ask of that policy, does this increase in the nation's power, or the method of achieving it, violate the rights of others, or unfairly threaten their security, or is it, rather, within the permissible limits of autonomous action? Moral standards can and must be applied to the same phenomena that are also judged by economic, legal, and political standards. Often, too, moral standards will have to prevail over those more special standards. As we cannot accept the extreme realist view that moral concepts and judgments do not apply in the political realm, so we must also reject the less extreme, but still insupportable, view that these judgments must always be subordinated to political ones. For this requires that the decisive considerations always be considerations of power, and even its most celebrated proponents like Morgenthau cannot adhere to that deplorable doctrine unambiguously, consistently, or plausibly.

Hobbes and the State of Nature

Hobbes's doctrines are open to many interpretations, and every major interpretation has had its influence on the theory of international relations. According to one view, Hobbes is a moral subjectivist and a moral authoritarian. In the state of nature individuals can employ moral language only to signify their own appetites and desires as, in the view of contemporary political realists, nations can employ language only "ideologically."[21] In Hobbes's view, as in the view of the realists, this subjective use of language only exacerbates the difficulties of endeavoring peace. The realists often suggest, therefore, that we abandon the use of moral language altogether when we speak in the international state of nature. If we confine ourselves to speaking the language of the national interest, we are more likely to achieve sensible accommodations. In Hobbes's system instituting a sovereign provides the remedy, for he can endow moral language with objectivity. Sovereigns "make the things they command just by commanding them and those which they forbid unjust by forbidding them."[22] If we accept Hobbes's account of the sovereign's commands, or his laws, as the source of justice and injustice, we shall have to concede that in the absence of an international sovereign, perhaps in the form of an effective, law-giving world government, the use of moral language in international contexts is nothing more than ideology, or in Hobbes's terms an expression of "appetites and aversions" that encourage "disputes, controversies, and at last war."[23] Hobbes's view of moral appraisal is, however, unpersuasive. If acts and omissions are just or unjust only when they are commanded or permitted by the sovereign, acts and omissions to which the sovereign's law does not speak could be neither just nor unjust. Yet we often consider harsh actions, chilly responses, and accusing words unjust although the law does not forbid them, even as we consider acts of restoration or recompense to be demanded by justice although the law does not require them. More importantly, if justice is what the sovereign commands and injustice what he forbids, it would make no sense to judge the sovereign's own acts and rules just or unjust. Yet the criticism of law and government on moral grounds is one of the central moral activities.

We cannot identify justice and injustice with the sovereign's commands and our refusal to do so suggests one of our reasons for enduring the perils of international society as we know it. We fear that a world sovereign might become an invincible international tyrant or disclose himself as our deadliest enemy invested with enhanced political legitimacy. We cannot concede that what such a sovereign deemed just would in fact be just (or that his command made it so). Nor can we acquiesce in Hobbes's view that in the absence of a sovereign our judgments about the international realm are mere expressions of appetite and aversion. Like much moral skepticism about the international realm, this view is one manifestation of a far more pervasive and unacceptable moral skepticism.

In the absence of a law-giving and law-enforcing sovereign, Hobbesian individuals inhabit a state of nature, a realm of intense competition and insurmountable insecurity in which the life of man is solitary, poor, nasty, brutish, and short. It is, in fact, a realm in which the main objective must be self-preservation and in which we enjoy what Hobbes called the right of nature, the right "by all means we can, to defend ourselves."[24] In the state of nature Hobbes thinks this requires seeking "power after power," and in this situation "to have all, and do all, is lawful to all."[25] Those who believe that the international arena is itself a state of nature often argue that states also have a right to act on what Morgenthau calls "the moral principle of self-preservation" which, in the state of nature not only permits them, but (going beyond Hobbes) may actually require them, to pursue the national interest and maximize national power (to seek "power after power") without regard to other moral considerations. As Raymond Aron says, "The necessity of national egoism derives from what philosophers called the state of nature which rules among states."[26]

We may concede that in the state of nature individuals have a right to defend themselves against physical attack. Indeed, we may think they act justly when they do so, and argue that this in itself insures the notion of justice application in the state of nature. By the same token, it seems clear that (other things being equal) it would be unjust to attack others when doing so was not required for self-preservation. Even in the individual state of nature it is questionable whether this principle of self-preservation permits us to "do all."

Hobbes claims, for instance, that in the state of nature men are equal in the sense that even the weakest can kill the strongest.[27] But, in fact, young children, and those who are seriously incapacitated by injury or disease, will often constitute no threat even in the Hobbesian state of nature. To rape or kill them would clearly be unjust.[28] Not even for all practical purposes does the right of self-defense yield a right of universal aggression. This right comes into play only in certain circumstances and incorporates principles of parsimony and proportionality.

If individuals are prohibited from attacking those who do not threaten them, so are nations. Even in the international state of nature it will not be permissible to attack the young or the unwell intentionally or, more generally, those who do not constitute a physical threat. In addition, attacks must be repelled, and offensives conducted, by appropriate means. These principles support the doctrine of civilian immunity and find expression in the laws of war. Insofar as this body of law fails to reflect such principles, it is itself open to criticism. Here law is not the source of criticism as it must be in Hobbes. Rather, it is the object of criticism.

Even in the state of nature, then, the use of violence cannot be justified on every occasion or in every degree. In particular, not every interest can be defended by an appeal to self-preservation. The implications of this fact are especially important in the international realm. For Hobbesian theorists of international relations often claim that states possess a "moral right of self-preservation" or enjoy a right to "national security." Hobbes himself called the Leviathan an "Artificial Man" and believed that like individual men it possessed a right of self-preservation. For he writes that "the same elements of natural law and right . . . being transferred to whole cities and nations, may be taken for the elements of the laws and right of nations."[29] But it is far from obvious that because individual men have a natural right of self-preservation, states do so as well. Certainly we do not think that all collective entities enjoy a right to "do all" to preserve themselves. This is not true of the Mafia or the Sierra Club, of General Motors or the Ethical Culture Society, of the Comintern or the Roman Catholic Church. Or if such a right is claimed for one or another of these institutions, the right will have to be defended. This is true of the state as well. Unquestionably, there are many ways in which such a right might be defended. A right to property might be invoked, or a right of people to live together under political institutions of their own choice, or even a right to live in close association with those who share the same language and cultural aspirations. There is something to be said for (and against) each of these suggestions, but they are far from Hobbesian in spirit. For I take it that a Hobbesian defense of the state's right of self-preservation would attempt to draw its justification from the individual's natural right of self-preservation. Perhaps this is what Hobbes is suggesting in his far from lucid observation that "every Sovereign hath the same right, in procuring the safety of his people, that any particular man can have, in procuring the safety of his own body."[30]

The scope of this right is by no means clear and Arnold Wolfers, among others, has complained of a similar "ambiguity" in the concept of national security.[31] For some, the right of self-preservation permits the state to defend any of its interests including, perhaps, its ideological influence and its economic advantages. For others the right of self-preservation permits the state to defend only its legal rights. This still very expansive conception has been central to international law up to the 1930s (and has, in the questionable judgment of some, been given renewed support by the opinion of the International Court of Justice in the Corfu Channel Case). But Article X of the League of Nations Covenant and Article 2(4) of the United Nations Charter suggest a much narrower conception.[32] The right of self-defense (as it is now called to distinguish it from the broader conception of self-preservation) is the right to defend what for many are the essential features of the state: its territorial integrity and political independence. Some have argued that the right of self-defense permits a state to employ force solely in defense of its territorial domain. In this spirit, Article 51 of the United Nations Charter defines self-defense by reference to the concept of "armed attack."[33]

Hobbesians may claim that a defense of some, or even of all, these readings of the state's right to self-preservation can be founded on the individual's right of self-preservation. For it can be argued that the defense of all, or at least of some, of these interests is necessary if the state is to guarantee the physical security of its citizens. But this is implausible. A state's failure to defend its ideological influence, its economic advantages, or even many of its treaty rights, may in no way decrease its ability to provide for the physical security of its population. The argument may seem more persuasive when the state's territorial integrity and political independence are at issue. But even here the argument is not compelling. The state may actually improve its ability to guarantee the physical security of its citizens by surrendering territory (as Israel has done) or by extinguishing its sovereignty (as the American colonies and the German principalities did). The death of the state does not require the loss of a single life. Indeed, it may even save some.

Hobbesians may then attempt a less ambitious argument. They may concede that a defense of its economic advantages, or even of its territorial integrity, is not necessarily required if a state is to protect its citizens. They may insist, however, that the defense of these interests increases the likelihood that the state will be able to provide that security. In view of this fact we should concede that the state has a right to defend these interests when it believes that doing so will enhance security. But this line of argument is also unpersuasive.[34] We do not have a right to increase our security by working injustices on others or by endangering their security to an unacceptable degree. Perfect security might require, but could not in itself justify, world domination. And incremental improvements in one nation's security do not, as a matter of course, justify the violation of the right of others to live in communities of their choice, to reform unfair economic arrangements, or to enjoy a reasonable measure of security themselves. As with other goods in limited supply, individual and national security are themselves subject to a principle of distributive justice. The requirements of natural justice, and the political rights of others, place strict limits on the pursuit of the "national interest" and on the striving for "power after power" in the search for national "security." Certainly, they do not allow those who are internationally well placed "to do all and have all."

A weaker claim may nevertheless succeed. While the state may not always need to defend its territory, or maintain its independence, in order to provide for the physical security of its population, often it will. It is, therefore, reasonable to provide a legal right to do so. Of course, legal rights cannot always conform exactly to the contours of the moral rights they protect, but they can nevertheless draw strong moral support from them. A legal right to state self-preservation will lack moral justification to the extent that it permits the use of force against others simply to increase state security (as did the traditional right of "self-preservation," an easily penetrated disguise for a right of war). The best formulation of the rule is an enormously difficult matter. But to be equitable and to protect the rights of the innocent any reasonable version must (with very few exceptions) confine the right to situations in which an attack, the threat of an attack, or preparations for an attack can be established. A narrowly drawn rule like the one announced in Article 51 of the United Nations Charter is probably very desirable. But if the rule is understood to forbid "preventive" attacks it may, in certain situations, conflict with the natural right of self-defense that underlies it. Although the fact that this rule is a rule of law itself carries moral weight (how much will depend in part on the degree to which it is observed in international life), the rule may have to give way in these circumstances to deeper moral considerations. Often, however, the plea of self-defense will have little plausibility. Authoritative pronouncements assure us that the plea was without justification in such cases as the Japanese invasion of Manchuria, the Italian invasion of Abyssinia, and the German invasion of Norway.[35] Certainly, any morally tenable account of the right of self-defense, individual or collective, requires that a distinction between aggression and self-defense be maintained.

Hobbesian theorists of international relations will protest that these remarks fail to take seriously Hobbes's contention that the state of nature is inevitably a state of war. From their point of view it is pointless to speak of moral constraints on the pursuit of interests other than the security interest. For the nation-state is in fact overwhelmingly and inescapably preoccupied with the provision of security, and the logic of international relations is the logic of individuals in the Hobbesian state of nature writ large. As the Hobbesians see it, the "competition" for goods and resources brings nations into direct conflict with one another and in this conflict one nation's gain is, or will appear to be, another nation's loss. Still worse is the effect of what Hobbes calls "diffidence." Even where nations are content with the status quo and do not wish to threaten others, they have no assurance of one another's present intentions, not to mention future ones. Out of fear nations will therefore seek "power after power" in order to increase their security. But in doing so they inspire fear in others and decrease, or appear to decrease, their security. In this "security" dilemma, nations whose intentions are fundamentally pacific appear aggressive. They will be forced to strengthen themselves in ways that alarm others and out of fear may "anticipate" or engage in preventive attack. Thus, even nations whose intentions are basically defensive and cooperative will act in ways that are indistinguishable from those who are in fact hostile and aggressive. Of course, some nations will in fact be hostile and aggressive and this further aggravates everyone's fears. Then, too, like Hobbesian men some nations seek "glory." If they sought glory in a reputation for peacefulness and generosity, this would be one thing, but nations have often understood glory to consist in the display and exercise of military power. For them, an increase in glory must always come at the expense of another.

In one degree or another these features characterize many international situations. Europe on the eve of World War I may have been one example. But Hobbes himself observed that the state of war among nations does not create the same degree of misery as the state of war among individuals,

and it is important to notice the differences between them because they
have important moral consequences. To begin with, nations are not as
vulnerable as individuals in the state of nature and it is not true that
they and their citizens invariably live in fear of violent death. Nations
in the state of nature are better able to defend themselves than individuals
are. As Spinoza observed, states are not overcome by sleep every day,
they are not afflicted with diseases of mind and body, and they are not
prostrated by old age.[36] Even in the state of war, as Hobbes observed
"particular Sovereigns are able to uphold the industry of their subjects."[37]
If nations do not share the vulnerability of individuals, neither do they
share their equality. It is not true of them that the weakest can kill the
strongest. The nineteenth-century United States, because of its size, its
location, and the protection of the British navy, enjoyed a high degree
of security. Large and well-armed nations, and nations protected by
oceans and mountain ranges, are often in a similarly secure situation
and do not live in a condition of Hobbesian fear. They are in a position
to show restraint, to calm the fears of others, and even to create the
conditions of peace. Often it is their duty to do so. It is also important
to note that in contrast to Hobbesian individuals, nations can often
improve their security in ways that need not alarm others. Their best
defense is not always an attack, and they can often give evidence of
their peaceful intentions by choosing weapons and strategies that do not
threaten others. They can build forts, mount fixed guns, mine harbors
or, like the Russians, build wide gauge railway tracks that are useless to
invaders. They can also train civilian militias, study guerrilla warfare,
and prepare themselves for passive resistance. To be sure, there are
circumstances in which these defensive choices could be aspects of a
fundamentally aggressive design, but this is not invariably the case and
will not always seem to be.[38]

Individuals in the Hobbesian state of nature are anonymous and
ahistorical. But nations have names and reputations, geographies and
histories, principles and purposes, and these allow others to judge their
intentions with considerable confidence. Sometimes these intentions will
be cooperative and even friendly. For nations have allies, belong to
regional blocs, engage in mutually beneficial trade, and support larger
cultural enterprises. They will often have strong moral reasons to
perpetuate these relationships. Hobbes's suggestion that because nations
retain their sovereign independence they must be in a state of war in
which every nation has a "known disposition" to attack every other and
in which no "assurance" can be obtained flies in the face of the evidence
and suggests the presence of a stubborn philosophical thesis that its
proponents are unwilling or unable to submit to empirical test.

Some have argued that the advent of nuclear weapons brings the international realm closer to the Hobbesian state of nature than it has ever been before. As David Gauthier observes, "Each new effort we undertake to increase our security merely increases the insecurity of others, and this leads them to new efforts which reciprocally increase our own insecurity. This is the natural history of the arms race—a history which bids fair to conclude, later if not sooner, in mutual annihilation."[39] But some of the observations we have made about the prenuclear period are relevant to the nuclear era as well, and they show that while we may get ourselves into the situation Gauthier describes, this is by no means inevitable even in the absence of a world sovereign.

The Hobbesian situation is most closely approximated when both sides rely on vulnerable weapons that are capable of destroying weapons on the other side (highly accurate missiles in unhardened silos).[40] As in the classic Western gun duel, the obvious strategy in such circumstances is to "anticipate," to shoot and shoot first. Any nation that can mount a successful first strike without using all of its weapons is free to destroy entire enemy populations. But if the first strike does not succeed in taking out the other side's retaliatory force, both may be destroyed utterly. Nevertheless, the existence of nuclear weapons does not make a situation of this sort inevitable. By confining themselves to second-strike weapons, nuclear powers can make clear that they do not intend to initiate nuclear war. If both sides acquire invulnerable, second-strike weapons then neither side can, by shooting first, destroy the other side's deterrent, its capacity to strike back. If a nuclear nation shoots, it must be prepared to pay the penalty. In this situation there is far less reason to jump the gun, and less reason to fear that others will do so.

It is not true that in the nuclear world "each new effort we take to increase our security merely increases the insecurity of others, and [that] this leads them to new efforts which reciprocally increase our own insecurity." We can increase our second-strike capacity without increasing the insecurity of others. And to the extent that they are likely to strike out of fear of being struck, we can, as Oskar Morgenstern has suggested, increase our own security by helping our adversaries make their own second-strike forces invulnerable. Their insecurity increases our insecurity, but we can increase our security by increasing theirs. The fact that nuclear nations can destroy one another's populations unquestionably strengthens the analogy between the individual, and the international, state of nature. But the fact that nuclear nations—unlike Hobbesian men or gun duellers—can respond in kind after they have been hit undermines it. The balance created by the equality of Hobbesian men, or by the "equalizer" of the Old West, is unstable, but the nuclear balance is capable of stability if one nation cannot, by "anticipating," prevent the other from striking back.[41] In these circumstances there is no advantage in striking first and, if they are rational, nuclear nations will see that it is irrational to strike at all.

This stability will, of course, be lost if either side believes that the invulnerability of its retaliatory forces is endangered. There is a strong obligation, therefore, to eschew the development of a first-strike capacity if a nation can achieve reasonable assurance that the other side is not developing one. In appropriate circumstances, then, it will be morally inexcusable to reject measures (like adequate inspection schemes) that will reassure one's opponent, or perhaps to retain weapons whose uses are ambiguous. For these are precisely the weapons that can return us to a Hobbesian dilemma in which what one side believes, or claims to believe, are defensive, or in this case deterrent, weapons appear to the other side to be offensive, first-strike weapons. The primary obligation of the nuclear age is to abstain from the first nuclear strike and to adopt policies, especially as regards adequate conventional strength, that reduce the temptation to make such a strike. A more general obligation in situations of serious conflict is to try to see ourselves as others see us. This is always a weighty consideration for those in Hobbesian situations. But it is a supremely weighty one in the nuclear situation where the acquisition of ambiguous weapons can easily be misinterpreted by others and with disastrous effects. Moral blindness in this area may bind us all to the final wheel of fire. The Hobbesians could not be more wrong. It is precisely in what they regard as a state of nature that men and nations must acknowledge their most awesome moral responsibilities.

Neither the realist nor the Hobbesian forms of skepticism concerning the role of morality in international relations can plausibly be maintained. They are intellectually indefensible and morally pernicious. From a practical point of view they may well prove disastrous.

Notes

1. George Kennan, *American Diplomacy 1900–1950* (New York: New American Library, 1951), p. 87.

2. Benedetto Croce, *Politics and Morals*, trans. Salvatore J. Castilione (New York: Philosophical Library, 1945), pp. 3–4.

3. Benedict de Spinoza, "Tractatus Theologico-Politicus," in *The Political Works of Spinoza*, ed. A. G. Wernham (Oxford: Clarendon Press, 1958), p. 141.

4. Thomas Nagel, "Ruthlessness in Public Life," in *Public and Private Morality*, ed. Stuart Hampshire (Cambridge: Cambridge University Press, 1978), p. 80.

5. Thomas Hobbes, *Leviathan*, ed. C. B. McPherson (Middlesex, England: Penguin Books, 1968), p. 188; Heinrich von Treitschke, *Politics*, trans. Blanche Dugdale and Torben de Bille (London: Constable, 1916), p. 94; Bernard

Bosanquet, *The Philosophical Theory of the State* (London: Macmillan, 1958), p. 325.

6. Hans J. Morgenthau, *Politics Among Nations*, 2nd ed. (New York: Alfred A. Knopf, 1959), pp. 11–12.

7. Kennan, *American Diplomacy*, pp. 57–71.

8. Ibid., p. 76.

9. Hans J. Morgenthau, *In Defense of the National Interest* (New York: Alfred A. Knopf, 1951), p. 242.

10. R. B. Mowat, *Public and Private Morality* (Bristol: Arrowsmith, 1933), p. 40.

11. Quoted by Morgenthau in *Scientific Man vs. Power Politics* (Chicago: University of Chicago Press, 1974), p. 180.

12. Treitschke, *Politics*, p. 104; R. M. Hare, "Reasons of State" in Bernard Williams, ed., *Applications of Moral Philosophy* (Berkeley and Los Angeles: University of California Press, 1972), p. 19.

13. I owe the example to Michael Howard.

14. Bernard Williams, "Ethical Consistency," in R. M. Hare, ed., *Problems of the Self* (Cambridge: Cambridge University Press, 1973), pp. 166–186; Ruth Barcan Marcus, "Moral Dilemmas and Consistency," *Journal of Philosophy* 17 (March 1980):121–136.

15. Quoted by Mowat in *Public and Private Morality*, p. 59.

16. Morgenthau, *Politics Among Nations*, p. 155.

17. Ibid., p. 155ff.

18. Ibid., p. 26.

19. Morgenthau, *In Defense of the National Interest*, p. 62.

20. Morgenthau, *Politics Among Nations*, pp. 10–11.

21. J.N.W. Watkins, *Hobbes's System of Ideas* (London: Hutchinson University Library, 1973), p. 110.

22. Thomas Hobbes, *De Cive*, ed. Sterling Lamprecht (New York: Appleton-Century-Crofts, 1949), p. 129.

23. Hobbes, *Leviathan*, p. 216.

24. Ibid., p. 190.

25. Hobbes, *De Cive*, p. 28.

26. Raymond Aron, *Peace and War*, Richard Howard and Annette Baker Fox, trans. (Garden City, N.Y.: Doubleday), p. 580.

27. Hobbes, *Leviathan*, p. 183.

28. Marcus Singer, "State of Nature Situations," in A. I. Melden, ed., *Essays in Moral Philosophy* (Seattle: University of Washington Press, 1958), p. 157.

29. Hobbes, *De Cive*, p. 158.

30. Hobbes, *Leviathan*, p. 394.

31. Arnold Wolfers, "National Security as an Ambiguous Symbol," in *Discord and Collaboration* (Baltimore: The Johns Hopkins Press), pp. 147–167.

32. Ian Brownlie, *International Law and the Use of Force by States* (Oxford: Clarendon Press, 1963), p. 256.

33. Ibid., pp. 256, 264–268.

34. Charles Beitz, *Political Theory and International Relations* (Princeton, N.J.: Princeton University Press, 1979), p. 52ff.

35. Brownlie, *International Law*, pp. 242–243, 311.

36. Spinoza, "Tractatus Politicus" in *The Political Works*, p. 295.

37. Hobbes, *Leviathan*, p. 188.

38. Robert Jervis, "Cooperation Under the Security Dilemma," *World Politics* 30, no. 2 (January 1978):167–214. Most of this paragraph and much else in my discussion is drawn from this article.

39. David Gauthier, *The Logic of Leviathan* (Oxford: Oxford University Press, 1969), p. 208. This quotation needs to be considered in the context of Gauthier's full discussion.

40. Jervis, "Cooperation," p. 212.

41. Thomas C. Schelling, *The Strategy of Conflict* (Oxford: Oxford University Press, 1971), p. 232.

2

Deterrence and Moral Theory

Russell Hardin

Issues in public policy have been challenging and remaking moral theory for two centuries. Such issues force us to question fundamental principles of ethics while these same issues cast doubt on our ability to generalize from traditional intuitions. No issue poses more remarkable difficulties for moral theory than nuclear weapons policy. Because the consequences of their deployment and possible use could be grievous beyond those of any previously conceivable human action, these weapons frame the conflict between outcome-based, especially utilitarian, and action-based deontological moral theories more acutely than perhaps any other we have faced. Because nuclear weapons may bring about the most grievous outcome imaginable, they elevate concern with outcomes over concern with actions. More generally, they wreak havoc with a focus on the morality of individual choices and actions, set limits to the notion of intention and the doctrine of double effect, call into question the so-called just-war theory, and overwhelm the intuitionist basis of much ethical reasoning.

Of course, utilitarians have their own massive difficulties with deterrence, as they do with any major policy issue, because their moral assessment of the policy requires objective assessments of the likelihood that deterrence will fail and that the weapons will be used. Likewise, utilitarians require an assessment of the damage the weapons will cause. The only progress that has been made toward providing credible assessments of these is the dismal progress of coming to recognize that the scale of damage that would result from a serious nuclear war has become so awesome as possibly even to obliterate humanity.

Reprinted by permission of the *Canadian Journal of Philosophy* and the author from *Nuclear Weapons, Deterrence and Disarmament*, ed. D. Copp, *Canadian Journal of Philosophy* Supplementary Volume 12 (1986). Copyright 1986 *Canadian Journal of Philosophy*.

I do not think a utilitarian can assert confidently what is the morally best policy on nuclear weapons, but I will not pursue such calculations here.[1] Rather, I wish to discuss several problems that nuclear deterrence poses for action-based deontological moral theories. In all of these problems, it is remarkable how radically the utilitarian and the deontological perspectives come into conflict; the usual trick of showing how deontological rules for action are really utilitarian does not work. Despite apparent differences, the problems I wish to discuss—in intention, the doctrine of double effect, just-war theory, and intuitionist reasoning— are not entirely separable. Their chief points of commonality are that they all involve relationships between actions and consequences and are complicated by the institutional nature of the nuclear deterrence system.

Although there is virtually unanimous agreement among moral theorists on nuclear weapons that the weapons should not be used deliberately, there is widespread disagreement about whether their use may meaningfully be threatened in order to deter awful actions by another state. I wish not to argue for or against deterrence but only against certain kinds of argument about it. Even more than did Nazi genocide for an earlier generation, deterrence poses for us a unique moral problem. Against Nazi genocide the only moral dilemma was not whether it was right or wrong but what to do about it. Nuclear deterrence, however, belies the commonplace claim that all moral theorists generally agree on what is right or wrong, that they merely have different bases for making their judgments.

Consequences are so grievous in this context that consequentialist considerations should dominate all others in anyone's reasoning about the morality of nuclear weapons policies. At the very least, consideration of consequences should be given some force even in the most action-based or deontological arguments about nuclear weapons. A purely principled argument made without considering whether it implied the likely destruction of a large part of humanity cannot count plausibly as a moral argument, no matter where the principles come from.

My purpose, however, is not to defend this view, which I will assume is accepted, but to show how it, the strategic nature of actions, and the institutional nature of nuclear policies and actions complicate reasoning about nuclear weapons from moral theories that are largely action based. It is plausible that the current revival of philosophical interest in nuclear arms policies will stimulate reconsideration of metaethical issues simply because the possibility of nuclear war is so stark and because the choice of policies to prevent it shows up central difficulties in the two major traditions in Western moral philosophy.

Deterrence

It is not surprising that action-based theorists should have difficulty with deterrence, which is an inherently consequentialist program. But there is another problem with nuclear deterrence that may more perversely confuse action-based deontological reasoning: Deterrence is an inherently institutional, not a personal, program. If deterrence is to work it must be made credible. Hence, retaliation must be massively organized in advance; it cannot be left wholly to the discretion of a moral chooser who may or may not be available to act when the time comes. What we must judge is not actions taken when the time comes so much as the policy taken in advance.

Oddly, this point in another context has been the focus of a commonplace critique of utilitarianism—that is, that utilitarianism, at least Act-utilitarianism, leaves it up to individuals to choose on the ground of the best outcome on the whole. But this undercuts the whole point of such institutions as that of, say, justice. John Rawls's discussion of the institution of punishing is an effort to rescue the morality of officers in institutions, such as McCloskey's sheriff in a southern town who must decide whether to let an innocent man be lynched or to let a race riot tear the town apart.[2] In this respect, the system of nuclear deterrence, if it is to be meaningful and effective, must be as embedded in an institution as is the system of justice. The system would not be desirable if it depended on the autonomous commitments of a single actor.

Hence, much of the discussion of the morality of retaliating once deterrence has failed is remarkably wrong-headed or beside the point. Retaliation will not be left up to a philosophically grounded moral chooser in the relevant moment; it will have been arranged almost fully in advance in the complex sense that all the institutional and physical requirements for it will be in place. Therefore one cannot reasonably separate the issue of retaliation from the larger policy of deterrence. If there are decisions to be made, they are all one, which is whether to deter at the risk of retaliating. Certainly this is the issue for citizens as policymakers who will not themselves be in control of events at possible moments of retaliation. This is the heart of the moral problem of deterrence, and it may not become fully clear without much of the following discussion.

Understanding often may be led astray by the persuasive misdefinition of "threat" in this context. Curtis Lemay and Nikita Khrushchev were well known for asserting that their nations would retaliate and destroy the other side if provoked. Khrushchev, however, proclaimed his threat well before the Soviet Union was capable of carrying it out. To one who knew better, therefore, Khrushchev's "threat" was meaningless. The meaningful threats that both sides pose today require no proclamations; they gain their meaning and therefore their force from the clear existence of physical capability and apparent organizational will. Because of these, a U.S. president probably could not successfully retract a U.S. threat. The U.S. deterrent has a life of its own that is not subject simply to anyone's will or action, although it may be that its misuse could be subject to someone's will.

It is a standard move in utilitarianism to consider a whole package of actions and their implications, typically in comparison to alternative whole packages. In action-based moral theories it generally is not. Rather, each separate action is judged as though it were independent of any other. Hence, action-based theorists all too often argue against the system of deterrence in a way that is analogous to the way they think utilitarians must argue against the system of justice. Action-based theorists suppose that individual choosers cannot morally carry out the decisions that might fall to them and that therefore the system of deterrence is morally wrong. A utilitarian can reach such a conclusion only after comparing the expected results of the system of deterrence to the expected results of plausible alternatives. Or perhaps a utilitarian would wish to argue that it is both right to set up the deterrence system and wrong of relevant individuals to carry out some of the actions it requires.

The Focus on Individuals

Action-based moral theories are concerned with what an individual does, with the natures of actions and individuals, with the relationship of actions to character rather than to consequences.[3] In some ways such theory seems self-indulgent and egocentric, and in its focus on clean hands it is egocentric when it concludes that what matters is what *I* do rather than what happens. Some of this concern in the work of non-theological moral theorists may be a residue of Christian concern with salvation, for which what *I* do may be of paramount interest. But traditionally the concern with what *I* do governed choices very different from those we face with nuclear weapons.

Most of contemporary action-based theory is generally Kantian in its content but often intuitionist rather than rationalist in its arguments. Kantian theory is paralleled, even overlapped, by Catholic theory. Contemporary Kantian and Catholic philosophers have contributed massively to the debate about the morality of nuclear weapons. The action-based quality of Catholic theory is somewhat ambiguous, especially in the just-war theory, which is rather more institutional than individual.

Presumably because their prescriptions are typically for individual action, many deontological accounts of deterrence tend to focus on decisionmakers and their actions at relevant moments. Jefferson McMahan argues that certain of these accounts are misguided in their interpretation of the wrongness of certain contingent intentions, and he goes on to suggest that the relevant issue for these deontological critics of deterrence is what policy citizens of a democratic polity should want their nation to adopt.[4] This is an artful effort to make a moral theory for individuals relevant to institutions. Given the plausible structure of an institution for deterrence—and many other public policies—action-based theories will be lost without such an artful effort.

The only alternative to McMahan's kind of effort would be to argue about what one might do if one happened into a significant role in the deterrent system. Even this will be irrelevant to the morality of the U.S. and Soviet deterrent systems, however, because it is implausible that any one individual roleholder could make a significant difference in preventing the use of weapons in retaliation. Hence, a deontological argument against nuclear deterrence must focus on the large number of prior decisions by all those who might influence whether a deterrent system is put in place or maintained. On the U.S. side, at least, this leads in part to McMahan's concern with democratic citizens.

As a citizen what is it right for me to do? Alas, the individualist focus of action-based theories leaves me in a quandary here. It might be right for me qua individual not to participate in retaliation for an attack on my nation. But in the collective decision would it be right for me to impose on my fellow citizens the risk that we not participate in deterrence of such an attack?

For what am I as a citizen in a representative democracy responsible? Very indirectly and conditionally I may be responsible in part for whatever policy my nation adopts. If the issue when I vote or participate in politics were solely whether I should defend my own life by threatening to kill millions of innocent Soviet citizens in a nuclear retaliation in order to deter Soviet leaders from killing me,[5] debate would not last long. But that, of course, is not the issue, which is whether millions of other innocent people should be protected by such a threat at the risk that it be carried out. My vote whether my nation should erect or maintain a system of nuclear deterrence is inherently other-directed in large part. If I believe that not having a system of nuclear deterrence invites the destruction of some of my fellow citizens much more than having such a system invites destruction of them as well as of many Soviet citizens and others, how am I to decide what an action-based morality demands of me in the polling booth or in political activity? Both these groups are innocent. In plumping for or against deterrence,

I am plumping for the risk of killing innocents, merely different innocents at different risks. The only questions at issue are which innocents and at what relative risks.

This conclusion cuts both ways in current policy debates. Many critics of deterrence suppose that certain new ostensibly defensive weapons systems are morally preferable to current systems for massive retaliation against innocents.[6] This conclusion cannot follow from the fact that the weapons are directed against weapons rather than against cities. One also must be able to assert that the new weapons would lead to fewer expected deaths and other harms overall. But this is, of course, a fundamentally utilitarian calculus. It is impossible to escape the task of consequentialist calculation here. Given the inherently institutional and interactive nature of the deterrent system, we cannot consider the problem of killing innocents as simply the problem of one or the other policy.

More generally, the problem of fixing responsibility for various outcomes in a large polity makes action-based arguments very complicated. For example, one might ask what my responsibility is for racism in the United States. Suppose I have done something toward solving that problem but have not dedicated my whole energies to it. Just how much must I do?[7] Independently of this question, which seems to plague much hortatory moral theory including utilitarianism and many deontological theories, deterrence poses another that particularly plagues recent deontological accounts. Supposing responsibility for any policy my nation adopts is partly mine, we then may ask, Toward whom am I acting when I support or oppose a U.S. deterrent? My action is necessarily directed at Americans and Russians as well as many others.

It is a peculiar fallacy of composition to argue as though I were acting only toward Russians and to judge my action on the basis of analogies to how I should act toward another. My own interest counts as nothing in the face of potential nuclear war. Although my concern for my family actually might motivate me to take a stand one way or the other on certain nuclear weapons issues, I doubt that my own direct interest even matters to me in this context. Beyond the interests of my family, I will be motivated exclusively by fairly general sympathy and reasoned generalization from sympathy. If this is true, as I suspect it is of almost all who are grievously concerned with the threat of nuclear war, then a direct assessment of my actions will be misguided if it is posed in the typical manner of action-based moral theories.

Intention

The notion of intention runs afoul of institutional and strategic considerations in the context of nuclear deterrence, for two reasons.

First, it often is hard to know what it means for a nation, an institution, or a collectivity to have intentions at all. Second, it is hard to know what is intended in the contingent future of a strategic interaction in which one party's action is defined as dependent on another's. The latter consideration applies to individuals as well as to institutions. Let us consider each of these issues in turn and then bring them together briefly.

Institutions and Intentions

First let us consider the institutional problem of what it means to say that the intention behind the U.S. nuclear weapons is, say, to deter the Soviet Union from attacking. There is no one person whose intentions matter in this issue. Nor can we easily read from legislative and administrative records just what the weapons are intended by anyone to do. This is a problem common to governmental institutions. In the common law there is a special term, now obsolete in all other uses, for the intention of the law: The *intendment* of a law is not the intention that went into its design but rather the interpretation the courts read out of its words as embodied in legislation or past cases dealing with it. As Lon Fuller notes, "Any private and uncommunicated intention of the draftsman of a statute is properly regarded as legally irrelevant to its proper intepretation."[8] If we have an understanding of what it means for an individual to have an intention (and we may not), we cannot immediately translate this understanding into a notion of collective or institutional intention.

We probably can safely read from the actual institutional arrangements that U.S. nuclear weapons are intended to retaliate in part because they are virtually certain to do so. Whether they also are intended to be used by agents making active choices in other circumstances is much less clear. It seems likely that it will be hard for any agent to use more than a handful of the weapons without a rather massive and prior popular expression of support. But it is possible for a provocative agent to launch a handful of warheads and thereby stimulate a counterattack that would motivate "retaliation." That such a sequence of events is counted as an accidental war suggests how far from the actual intendment of the weapons anything but retaliation is.

Much of the discussion of nuclear weapons may have been colored by the fact that their initial use in wartime is widely supposed to have been by the decision of President Truman. Not since the early days of the Eisenhower administration, however, has such a choice been faced by anyone with the autonomy to initiate nuclear war.[9] Once the weapons were sufficiently numerous and diverse and were faced by a credible threat from the Soviet Union, they necessarily came under increasingly articulated institutional control.

It is a morally painful fact that the first use of nuclear weapons in war was perhaps a fully intentional act. There may eventually be more such acts. But a full-scale nuclear war between the superpowers cannot easily be such an act. Richard Nixon, as president, is supposed to have said, "I can go into my office and pick up the telephone and in twenty-five minutes seventy million people will be dead."[10] If he actually believed that, then, as was all too often true, his judgment was poor. He could not have initiated a full-scale nuclear attack on the Soviet Union without massive, persistent, willful effort and perhaps not even then. If Watergate could bring him down in slow agony, nuclear macho would have brought him down instantly.

Someone in Nixon's position is not entirely irrelevant to what happens, but the world is not so simply organized as to respond instantly to a U.S. president's whim in so important a matter. It would take long effort for a nascent Caligula or Hitler to pervert the system of institutional control of nuclear weapons. On the other hand, if the conditions for nuclear war came about, a U.S. president probably could not stop its happening either. A president most assuredly could not stop retaliation for a massive attack on the United States.

Intentions and Strategic Interaction

The fundamental question of intention in contexts of strategic interaction is, What do we want when we want deterrence? Recall the foregoing discussion of the nature of individual choice in setting national policy. All morally relevant action takes place prior to the moment of retaliation. For citizens it takes place more or less continually as we try to influence or we ignore weapons policies.

What do I intend when I support a national policy of nuclear deterrence against nuclear attack on my nation? Primarily I intend to influence or support my nation's institutions in striving to protect a large number of innocent people from horrible consequences. I cannot plausibly intend myself to bring about their protection, and I cannot plausibly intend myself to carry out retaliation in the event deterrence fails. Should the relevant moment come, there may be people who do intend the latter and who will do it, but they will be people who have been selected to be reliable in doing so. If I thought the consequences of the deterrent system were likely to be better than those of abandoning it and if there were a way to secure retaliation without dependence on actual people, I would prefer it if I thought it posed the lesser risk of harming anyone, East or West. Hence, the morality of the action in the moment it is

TABLE 2.1: Prisoner's Dilemma Game

		Column	
		C	D
Row	C	2,2	4,1
	D	1,4	3,3

taken is of little interest to our policy choice because the "action" could be an automatic result that, like cancer, simply happens in the relevant moment. That is the kind of expectation we want in order to make our deterrent credible enough to be most effective. (Of course, we might want a probability of less than certainty of retaliation. If, say, a 50 percent probability of retaliation against a full-scale strike would be nearly as effective as a virtual certainty of retaliation in deterring such a strike and if it were no more likely to be used when it should not be, it would be a less harmful and therefore morally better system. We would want this system to be credibly sure to respond with the relevant probability insofar as its likelihood of working that way would secure its deterrent effect.) In short, our intention is systemic and, as argued earlier, other directed. We want to protect one set of innocents at the risk of harming another set of innocents. What we want overall is to harm as few as possible.

The clearest way to pose this issue analytically is to put it into game-theoretic terms and to ask, What counts as the action I take in a game? In a game in which one party is in strategic interaction with another, choices are of strategies, not outcomes. Of course, particular strategies are chosen for the purpose of influencing the joint determination of outcome. Nevertheless, it is simply false and misleading to say that I choose an outcome.

For example, in the ubiquitous prisoner's dilemma game (Table 2.1), I as the row player can choose one of two strategies, C or D, and you as the column player can choose between your C and D. The outcomes are abstractly represented by the values we each place on them. In the usual RC (or *R*oman *C*atholic) convention, the *r*ow player's valuation of each outcome is given first and the *c*olumn player's valuation is given second, after the comma. In either case, 1 is the most preferred outcome, 4 the least preferred. It is obvious in the game that I cannot choose an outcome. If I tried to obtain the outcome that I value most highly, I could be relatively sure you would want to prevent that outcome by choosing your D strategy. Whatever the outcomes are in the way of objective events or states of affairs, I am powerless to decide which happens beyond narrowing down the set of possible outcomes. For example, if I choose my strategy D, the set will be narrowed down to the two outcomes we jointly value at (1,4) and (3,3).

Philosophical discussions of action generally do not deal with the problem of strategic interaction except by treating specific cases in an ad hoc way. For example, Alan Donagan discusses a poker player's effort to maximize his winnings by betting in such a way as to lead others in the game to bet more than they would have done if he had accurately tipped the strength of his hand.

> Smith is playing stud poker with Jones and Robinson. His hole cards give him a hand that is probably stronger than Jones's, whose face-up cards are stronger than his. At the second round of betting, he checks [that is, he passes on this round of betting], foreseeing that Jones will raise heavily and that Robinson, who has marked Jones as a bluffer, will stay in the game. Jones does raise, and Robinson stays, enabling Smith to achieve his purpose, of winning a large pot.

Donagan concludes that "an agent can intend, not only to cause certain events to come about, but to create situations in which others will act as he foresees, even though he neither can cause their reactions nor believes that he can."[11] This is, in Donagan's discussion of intention, merely an aside to show that responsibility can be established even though cause cannot. In the usual context of social choices, however, this is not merely a side issue—it is the central problem.

Action in social contexts often is inherently interactive. I cannot cause the outcome—(1,4) in the prisoner's dilemma of Table 2.1—that I want; I can hope only to restrict the set of likely outcomes. If I can do as well as Donagan's poker player at foreseeing the reactions of another to my own actions, I may be able to make myself or both of us better off. My action, however, will be a choice of strategies, not of outcomes.

Where does this leave us in the superpower dilemma? Each side only can choose a strategy that will include the relevant range of responses to the other side's strategy choices. What is chosen is an *expected* outcome, that is, some probabilistic mixture of various potential outcomes. Neither side alone can choose a simple outcome because the outcome that results from one side's strategy choice is necessarily contingent on the other side's strategy choice. To treat one side's strategy choice as though it were the cause of just one of the possible outcomes in that strategy would be unintelligible. Yet that is what much of the recent philosophical discussion of deterrence does. What each side does is choose either a strategy of nuclear disarmament or a strategy of deterrence (this latter can be at any of many possible levels of armament, but let us simplify for the moment). Suppose we choose the strategy of deterrence. What is our moral responsibility?

Return for a moment to Donagan's poker players. Smith took advantage of his knowledge of his fellow players to select the strategy that would maximize the pot he was likely to win. When U.S. leaders follow a strategy of nuclear deterrence against the Soviet Union, they do something quite similar to what Smith does. They suppose that Soviet leaders are relatively rational and therefore would not undertake any action that would guarantee their nation's destruction. Hence, the U.S. leaders suppose that the policy of deterrence very likely will deter Soviet leaders from attacking the United States. In words analogous to Donagan's, the U.S. leaders will have created a situation in which others will act as they foresee, even though they could neither cause Soviet reactions nor believe they could. The result will be mutual deterrence.

It is a necessary part of the rationality of creating the institutional arrangements to retaliate as a way of deterring the other side that each side assumes the rationality of the other and therefore foresees the other side's response. If this assumption were not credible, deterrence would be largely pointless. If it is credible, then it is an error to judge the action of retaliating *tout court* and to infer the morality of deterrence from that judgment. It is, of course, also a necessary part of the rationality of creating a system for deterrence that we suppose the likelihood of its failing for any reason at all is very low. Utilitarian criticism of deterrence policy often focuses on the factual validity of this supposition. Such criticism also might focus on the validity of the assumption that enough of the relevant actors on both sides are sufficiently rational as not to use the weapons. I think the latter issue is relatively easily settled in favor of the system of deterrence whereas the former is far harder to assess. Unfortunately, certain policymakers and advisers in the United States during the Reagan administration have given us to wonder about the latter assumption. But if it is valid, as in the action of Donagan's poker-playing Smith, the choice to maintain a system of nuclear deterrence must be judged as the complex action it is, an action that includes certain expectations of how others will react to U.S. readiness to retaliate for a nuclear attack. To ignore this consideration and to look solely at part of the larger set of possible outcomes of U.S. strategy is to make a mistake analogous to that of many economic actors who suppose that only they will be smart enough to react to others' actions while all others simply will act without reflection on how anyone else will react to their actions. Assuming that others will not react to one's own actions makes sense in a market context with very large numbers of equivalent actors but not in contexts in which the number of those with whom one interacts is very small.

Philosophers writing on deterrence from a deontological perspective typically focus not on strategies as actions but on contingent outcomes of strategy choices as actions. As with other fallacies discussed, this move cannot be assumed to yield results consistent with the usual accounts of action theorists or moral philosophers. It may yield a correct result in a particular case, but if so, the correctness of the result desperately wants argument. But the focus on contingent outcomes is wrong in principle because action theory for social choice is inherently more complex than much philosophical action theory typically is. Failure to deal with this complexity makes many moral accounts of nuclear deterrence irrelevant. (Of course, the issue is far more general than this; it arises in principle in all complex social choice contexts.)

It is interesting that the fallacy of reasoning from contingent outcomes of strategy choices in interactive social contexts is typically not treated as a general problem but is only addressed in such asides as Donagan's. It would be wrong to claim that it has not been recognized as a problem, but its general significance seems to be overlooked. In a similar vein one may note that the problem of strategic interaction in general had not been well analyzed until very recently with the advent of game theory. Ryle notes that "there is, anyhow at the start, an important sort of unfamiliarity about such generalizations of the totally familiar. We do not yet know how we should and how we should not operate with them, although we know quite well how to operate with the daily particularities of which they are the generalizations."[12] Theoretically, perhaps the most distressing aspect of a new generalization about the totally familiar is that eventually it must remake many of our other understandings, even those that have been extensively and articulately developed. The theory of games, even in its merely verbal grasp of the nature of strategic interaction, has been undoing and remaking our understandings for a generation, but clearly the work is far from done.

One can only hope that the slow entry of game-theoretic reasoning into social and moral philosophy will be accelerated. Unfortunately, however, game theory seems to smack enough of consequentialism that it does not appeal to many deontological moral theorists. But deontological theory will be the loser if it cannot be made to address more rigorously the issue of what counts as an action in social choice contexts.

Institutional Intentions and Strategic Interaction

Finally, consider just how complex the notion of intention is in a context of strategic interaction especially when complicated by institutional considerations. A system of deterrence requires a command and control structure to do two things: to ensure retaliation in a relevant moment and to prevent launch of missiles at all other times. Unfortunately, these two tasks must be handled by one structure, which therefore must be a compromise between those that best accomplish the one and the other.

To loosen central control in the future is to increase *present* control of future events in one way and to decrease it in another. It increases control in that it makes wanted retaliation more likely when central command structures fail or are destroyed. It decreases control in that it makes unwanted attack more possible. The value of the increased control of wanted retaliation is that it makes the deterrent threat more credible and therefore reduces the likelihood that there ever would be ground for retaliation.

These two effects cannot be separated fully. To reduce the likelihood of unintended attack is to decrease the likelihood of wanted retaliation and quite possibly therefore to increase the likelihood of there ever being occasion for retaliation. This is a problem that has long worried U.S. strategic planners.[13] In the early years of relatively primitive Soviet weapons, the more worrisome prospect was unintended attack, so that tight control was perhaps the easy choice. In recent years, the capacity of Soviet strategic weapons to decapitate U.S. command and control has become increasingly worrisome, and control presumably has become much looser.

This is a general problem of many control and enforcement systems. How do we prevent such enforcers as police and tax collectors from intimidating those who are honest while encouraging the enforcers to track down all who are dishonest? In the system of deterrence we accomplish both positive and negative control by building in redundancy as though to achieve regression toward the mean. We set up land-based missile controls so that action by each of two people is necessary but not sufficient to launch. And coordinated action may have to occur at two or more levels *each* of which is sufficient but not necessary to launch. No one person has much control either positively or negatively. Even if several people acted wrongly in helping to launch missiles, there would be only a limited number they could launch. In a variant of this system, each submarine in the strategic force has enough warheads by itself to devastate the Soviet Union, but no submarine's missiles can be launched without the concurrent actions of several officers, any one of whom might block the launching.

In relevant moments those who set up this system, including, of course, the general populace insofar as their democratic participation has mattered, would be unable to affect its behavior significantly. In certain moments, the president and the Joint Chiefs of Staff could not stop it. Although dozens of people acting morally might refuse to assist in retaliation once deterrence had failed and retaliation seemed useless to their own fellow citizens but grievously harmful to others, we probably can confidently expect that enough others would act to cause substantial retaliation. Indeed, the system is sufficiently large and involves enough people that it could not be credible without guaranteeing retaliation under certain circumstances. Too many people would have to participate in subterfuge for the system not to work to a substantial degree and still be credible.

How tight should we want our control to be? This is not a question that admits of a deontological or action-based answer. But if we want deterrence at all, we have to answer this very question. Hence, either we have no deterrence or we choose the level of control of unwanted and wanted attacks according to the likely effects of that level on the success of the deterrent system and of the damage it risks. Even if we want deterrence for deontological reasons, then we must be consequentialist in constructing the system for it.

The Doctrine of Double Effect

One way the nature of the "action" of nuclear deterrence has been addressed recently is by supposing that deterrence is somehow a complex action that either does or does not run afoul of the doctrine of double effect. The principle that underlies the doctrine of double effect is Aquinas's assertion that "moral actions are characterized by what is intended, not by what falls outside the scope of intention, for that is only incidental."[14] "Double effect" refers to the intended good effect of an action and the unintended bad effect. The two may or may not be causally inseparable.

Under this doctrine, I am exonerated from blame for, say, accidentally running over and killing a child while driving my car so long as it was no part of my intention to run over the child and I was driving with due care. My intention was only to get from home to a restaurant to enjoy a good meal. Now if I am to be held responsible for every causal result of what I do, I am as guilty of killing that child as would be a child murderer. The doctrine of double effect not only exonerates me from culpability in this case; it more fundamentally permits me to undertake such simple actions as driving my car even though I can be quite sure that there is a realistic chance that doing so will cause great harm—I may drive so long as doing such harm is not my intention in driving my car. We also need to include the condition that, in general, driving is not likely to be massively injurious, that the good that comes from doing it outweighs the bad. As Aquinas stipulates, "An action beginning from a good intention can become wrong if it is not proportionate to the end intended."[15] Hence, the doctrine involves a mixture of deontological and consequentialist principles; some actions are prohibited merely on the ground of their intentions, and others are prohibited despite good intentions on the ground of their disproportionate bad effects.

Elizabeth Anscombe gives the doctrine a particularly strong role. Without it, she says, "anything can be—and is wont to be—justified, and the Christian teaching that in no circumstances may one commit murder, adultery, apostasy (to give a few examples) goes by the board . . . and without them the Christian ethic goes to pieces." The doctrine is a "necessity" to buck up our resolve to pass up an opportunity to "do evil that good may come."[16] Unfortunately, she does not take up the complicating character of deterrence but addresses only such actual actions in war as obliteration bombing, actions that many supporters of deterrence also would condemn. Her rationales for the doctrine often are theological and not relevant to the present discussion.

Here again we find that a traditional view does not address the fundamental nature of the problem of deterrence. In order to generalize the traditional concern to our present problems, Grisez speaks of "the unity of action" and cites several instances of actions that necessarily include evil effects with the intended good effects, actions that cannot be separated into two "distinct human" acts. For example, he supposes that committing adultery to gain the release of one's child would constitute two distinct acts, while interposing one's own body in the path of a ravaging animal to protect one's child would constitute a single act.[17] Grisez supposes that "only the definite intention to act at the last . . . stage can make" the nuclear deterrent threat effective, so that the deterrent inherently entails a dual action.[18]

To speak of "double actions" rather than of "double effects" of a single action probably confuses the issue. The program of nuclear deterrence does not involve so clearly two separate actions, one evil and one good. It does not entail deterring on the one hand and retaliating on the other. Our system of deterrence, as devised by many people over many years, involves a disciplined response or even a nearly automatic electronic response to certain events. Is it two distinct acts if the system leads eventually to an actual retaliation, or is the creation or maintenance of this system inherently unitary even if it leads to retaliation? The U.S. threat to counterattack that deters the Soviet Union from attacking the West is not simply an action in its own right. What deters is the existence of a credible system for counterattacking. Its deterrent effect depends on its credibility, which in turn depends heavily on its likely actuality. One cannot meaningfully separate the threat from the potential retaliation. (That is why various bluff strategies proposed by clean-hands moral theorists are irrelevant to the problem of nuclear deterrence.) Institutionally speaking, there is only one action at issue: maintaining the deterrent force.

Where does the Thomistic doctrine come in? Unfortunately, it is not clear. That doctrine is applied by Aquinas in an example in which the use of force takes its traditional form in defeating the attacker upon actual attack.[19] A defender of deterrence may suppose sensibly that the purpose of creating the system of deterrence is only to deter attack—if that were not the purpose, it would be pointless to create the system. Then if, as in the case of my driving, the likelihood that the system will go awry is small enough, so that the deterrent system is proportionate to the end intended, its creation is morally permitted under the doctrine of double effect. For deterrence to be rational requires that its risk of failure be very small; for it to be utilitarian presumably requires that this risk be even smaller; for it to pass the test of Aquinas's doctrine may require that it be still smaller. The first two assessments have to be relative to the risks of alternative policies, as might Aquinas's assessment also if we interpret his concern with proportion and measured force reasonably.

Against the defender of nuclear deterrence, Grisez, Anscombe, and many others also may sensibly insist that maintaining a deterrent system implies a conditional intention to kill millions of people. One may well wish to conclude with them that this system is evil because it threatens and arranges for an evil result under certain contingencies. But then one should argue why that is distinctively wrong in this case despite its complexity as compared to usual cases in which one actually *does* evil that good may come. At that point, we seem to be up against a plausibly irresolvable problem in the notion of an intention in the context of complex strategic interaction.

One other way the doctrine of double effect has been generalized in contemporary moral theory is to distinguish letting something happen and causing it to happen, as in letting someone die versus killing someone.[20] This distinction might seem compelling for many of the problems to which it has been applied. But no matter where it stands on the issue of cases of individual killing versus letting die, a moral theory that is centrally concerned with the difference between letting a large part of humanity be destroyed and causing it to be destroyed seems beside the point. The polity or person who would knowingly do either is beyond the moral pale. As Robert Tucker says, "The prospect held out by nuclear war threatens to make of the issue of intent a grotesque parody."[21]

If we bring our analysis to the level of the individual voter in deciding on a policy, the very distinction between causing certain deaths from nuclear war and letting others happen collapses. Which of my possible actions as a voter is passive and which active: supporting the maintenance or supporting the elimination of the U.S. deterrent force? In which case do I cause and in which do I let a result potentially occur? Oddly, the doctrine of double effect with its focus on individual actions—with a consequentialist constraint on proportionality—loses its meaning in an account of the morality of individual citizens in their choice of public policies.

Just-War Theory

The Pauline injunction that we not do evil that good may come has spawned, in addition to the Thomistic doctrine of double effect, the Augustinian just-war theory. As does the doctrine of double effect, just-war theory builds from a combination of consequentialist and deontological concerns. The traditional doctrine of the just war, of *bellum justum,* deals with two distinct issues: first, with *jus ad bellum,* or with when it is just to engage in war; second, with *jus in bello,* or with what it is just to do while engaged in a war. As Tucker notes, earlier notions of when it is just to enter war have given way in our time to only one generally plausible justification: "War is no longer a means generally permitted to states for the redress of rights that have been violated. . . . Armed force remains a means permitted to states only as a measure of self-defense against a prior and unjust attack."[22] Hence, in contemporary concern, the doctrine of just war is almost exclusively a matter of *jus in bello* after an unjust attack.[23]

It should be clear immediately that the doctrine of *jus in bello* cannot apply simply to the system of nuclear deterrence without considerable casuistry about why our insights or intuitions regarding warfare once underway translate into valid insights about deterrence of war. After such casuistry one might conclude that deterrence is indeed unjust, but without such casuistry there is no reason for us to suppose simply from traditional *jus in bello* arguments that it is unjust. These traditional arguments are about what it would be just to do once attacked.

The peculiar difficulty of deterrence is that it is a move taken in advance of any attack that might justify warlike action, but what it threatens would no longer make sense after the fact. Indeed, unthreatened retaliation clearly would be immoral in virtually any moral theory. To justify deterrent moves in advance of any attack, supporters might argue that these moves respond to a reciprocal threat, whether explicit or implicit, made in advance. This would be analogous to a *jus ad bellum* argument for responding to "attack."

To discuss the morality of actually retaliating to a nuclear attack, however, is seemingly to be concerned with *jus in bello*. If we were faced with the simple decision whether to retaliate with a nuclear attack, the issue would be clear and easy: If it were not part of a larger program of deterrence, retaliation after the fact would be immoral. But it would be facile to conclude from this that the system of deterrence is immoral. Given that almost any supporter of deterrence would agree—perhaps only after argument—that unthreatened retaliation would be immoral, critics of deterrence who base their opposition merely on what would happen if deterrence failed will not persuade supporters. Indeed, such critics will seem to fail to grapple with the relevant distinction.

What advocates of deterrence claim is that the prior threat, because of its effects, is what would make retaliation moral, but only as part of the whole system of deterrence. This is at first glance such an odd position that its point often does not even get across. A harmful action is rendered moral only if it is first threatened? Not quite: The whole system of threat and fulfillment if and only if the conditions of the threat are met by action on the other side is moral because that system is supposed to produce better results on the whole.

In this respect, the present system of nuclear deterrence is radically different from traditional forms of conventional deterrence. For practical purposes we already have taken whatever action we are going to take before action is necessary. Military preparedness presumably always has been a strong deterrent to attack. Hume writes of Edgar, one of the ancient kings of Anglo-Saxon England, that "he showed no aversion to war; he made the wisest preparations against invaders: And by this vigour and foresight, he was enabled, without any danger of suffering insults, to indulge his inclinations towards peace. . . . The foreign Danes dared not to approach a country which appeared in such a posture of defence."[24]

The conventional deterrence that Hume describes involved preparation for action, not action in advance. This deterrence required accurately directed action to stop particular aggressors; however, nuclear retaliation is likely to be massively directed against populations who have taken no recent aggressive steps. Nor did the morality of Edgar's preparations for defense require that he threaten the foreign Danes before responding to an attack. Had his forces been secretly hidden and ready for attack they would have been morally acceptable, although one might suppose that open declaration to deter attack would have been morally better. A secret arsenal of nuclear weapons for retaliation would be reprehensible; such an arsenal also would be stupid because it would not deter attack on one's own nation. Unlike Edgar's defense forces and plans, the superpower nuclear deterrents require open acknowledgment to make them effective and to make them putatively moral.

Etymologically, to deter is to provoke terror, which is to cause to tremble and flee. That is the purpose of the nuclear deterrent. Although traditional defense establishments might have provoked terror and caused Danes and others to tremble and flee, just-war theory is concerned with these establishments only at the point at which they have failed to deter, at which they are put to use against attacking forces.[25] The creation of a defense establishment for the purpose of deterrence, of provoking terror that enemies might flee without first attacking, is simply not a part of the theory.

In Hume's account of Edgar's reign, deterrence of the foreign Danes was not the purpose of preparations to defend against them but was a causal effect of those preparations. At least since the late 1950s, the superpower nuclear arsenals have been created principally (I wish one could say "entirely") for the purpose of deterring one another. It probably would be foolish to suppose that no one had ever thought of the idea before our time, but it probably also is true that any program of deterrence before nuclear weapons was an afterthought, a derivative realization from the principal purpose of defense systems, which was to defend against actual attacks. In the nuclear era, the afterthought has become forethought and principal intention or intendment.

One way to put this issue in current strategic jargon is to note that deterrence may take at least two forms. First, traditional or conventional deterrence is "based on *denial*, which requires convincing an opponent that he will not attain his goals on the battlefield." Second, "deterrence based on *punishment* is associated usually with nuclear weapons."[26] Hume may well have grasped this distinction: "The domestic Danes saw inevitable destruction to be the consequence of their tumults and insurrections."[27] Surely nothing deters so effectively as inevitable destruction, although the sense of this notion has now surpassed what Hume had in mind.

The strategic considerations that complicate the just-war analysis of nuclear deterrence need not confuse a just-war analysis of deterrence by denial if the latter, in the event of the failure of deterrence, would not entail *jus in bello* violations. In that case we could analyze the problem as though its parts—prior preparation, threat, and eventual retaliation— were decoupled. If neither part were wrong, then the two parts taken together would not be wrong. But analyzing the system of nuclear deterrence, in which denial of an attacker's objective is not possible, as though its parts were decoupled will not do. In this system, a moral analysis must address the fact that the parts are inherently coupled just as the consequentialist justification of the punishment of miscreants generally depends on the prior establishment of a criminal justice system.

Intuitionist Reasoning

Arguments in moral theory often are grounded in intuitions of rightness and wrongness and of goodness and badness, with actions counting as either right or wrong and outcomes as either good or bad. Because the issue of nuclear deterrence is so unlike anything we have faced previously, we are apt to find our intuitions not very well supported by experience in their application. Conspicuously, we have contrary intuitions about deterrence as we increasingly do for other new issues, such as those that arise from new medical technologies. The belief of many intuitionists, such as Prichard, that we share moral intuitions clearly is undercut by our debate about moral positions on these issues. It is useful to state cases for and against the reliance on intuitions in moral reasoning to see how we stand on nuclear deterrence.

As Prichard supposes, much of our moral knowledge or beliefs at the level of routine practice is quite secure, and to know whether we have an obligation we need merely let "our moral capacities of thinking do their work."[28] Contrast with this our highly contested knowledge of abstract moral principles, such as Kantian imperatives, the basic utilitarian intuition that utility is right-making, Alan Gewirth's principle of generic consistency, and so forth.[29] Therefore, one might suppose, we can be more confident of our direct apprehension of the moral rightness of an action or the goodness of a state of affairs than of any theoretical assessment of these. This is essentially the view of Butler and of those who follow what Sidgwick calls the method of intuitionism in ethics.

Against this quick conclusion, note that the principles that make sense of the physical universe are abstract and, to most of us, very insecurely held. Indeed, our commonsense knowledge at the level of practice seems to be violated by the abstract principles of theoretical physics. For example, the theoretical account of the structure of the table at which I now work sounds utterly lunatic to anyone but a physicist. Nevertheless, it would be foolish to conclude that the confidence of our commonsense intuitions about these matters should call into doubt our abstract principles.

Unfortunately, as Hume, Gilbert Harman,[30] and others argue, the abstract principles of physics can be supported by experimental tests, whereas our abstract moral principles stand on their own without the possibility of test. Hence, it is not clear that our abstract moral principles should trump our direct intuition of moral rightness and goodness. We are forced into a form of reasoning back and forth between practical and abstract principles with rigor only in tests for consistency. In this standard form of reasoning in moral theory, our effort is to achieve what Rawls, with his gift for apposite labels, calls reflective equilibrium, in which we test our abstract principles against our substantive intuitions and our substantive intuitions against our abstract principles.

How we weigh the intuitions and the principles is, of course, the fundamental issue. In a letter to Hume, Gilbert Elliot of Minto writes, "I often imagine to myself, that I perceive within me a certain instinctive feeling, which shoves away at once all subtle refinements, and tells me with authority, that these air-built notions are inconsistent with life and experience, and, by consequence cannot be true or solid." Hence, he concludes, there must be "something in the intellectual part of our nature" that determines the truth of the practical principles instinctively.[31] Hume's response to what he labels Elliot's "correcting subtlety of sentiment" is somewhat ambiguous because Hume allows sentiment a role in moral reasoning.[32] But, he notes, some have argued "that it was neither by reasoning nor authority we learn our religion, but by sentiment: and certainly this were a very convenient way, and what a philosopher would be very well pleased to comply with, if he could distinguish sentiment from education. But to all appearances the sentiment of Stockholm, Geneva, Rome ancient and modern, Athens and Memphis, have [not] the same characters."[33] Locke speaks of practical principles that are "borrowed," saying that one "may take up from his Education, and the fashions of his Country, any absurdity for innate principles."[34]

Although Sidgwick is generally critical of the method of intuitionism, he argues forcefully that utilitarianism is based on "a first principle—which if known at all must be intuitively known—that happiness is the only rational utimate end of action."[35] In essence he finds intuitions about goodness more acceptable than those about rightness. But then for him rightness is a characteristic of means and therefore is contingent on the relationship of various means to the end of goodness. Because even in the face of a very rich description any action could be a means to both good and bad, actions are not right or wrong *tout court*.

Despite all these contrary arguments, I think a consequentialist can make serious claims for intuitive apprehension of the rightness of actions, at least prima facie, that is, subject to rational criticism. One ground for accepting Rule-utilitarian principles as adjuncts of Act-utilitarianism is that our knowledge often comes directly at the level of rules or relatively abstract generalizations—it is not aggregated from numerous particular instances. This is perhaps especially true of social knowledge, that is, knowledge of social facts. But as Wittgenstein's discussion of our knowledge that Mont Blanc is, say, 4,000 meters high suggests,[36] even many everyday facts about the physical world are highly articulated deductions from abstractions that are grounded in a system of social construction so that no one individual may know such facts fully by direct observation. Nevertheless, the facts count as known by any reasonable canons.

All of us, most of the time, must begin from such facts without testing them. Wittgenstein remarks, "My life consists in resting content with many things."[37] His contentment may derive partly, as Hume says, from "a little indolence,"[38] but without indolence in certain quests, life could not go on. Similarly, my moral life consists in my resting content with many things, although as a moral theorist I may increasingly question these. Many of us could test the utilitarian beneficence of various moral rules by violating them and observing the consequences in a few circumstances. Or we could carry out relevant thought experiments. (The deontologist, of course, has no such recourse available because the deontologist's rules are not merely means.) But it is a mark of good sense that we generally follow many of these rules without seriously testing them in such fashion.

A deontological defense of moral rules will be different from this consequentialist justification, at least in large part. It might be simply that one can apprehend rightness directly. To that claim, I have nothing to say apart from an expression of disbelief and a suspicion that what is apprehended is little more than what Hume and Locke deride. Alternatively, the defense might be that one derives moral rules for action by reasoned argument from first principles, as Kant and Gewirth attempt to do.

Virtually all deontological arguments about deterrence seem to follow the first tack. As in the just-war theory, they simply assert that it is wrong to kill innocents and that this rule cannot be violated. Hence, Grisez writes, "when I say that the deterrent is morally evil, I do not mean that we ought to dismantle it if and when world amity is established. I mean that we ought to dismantle the deterrent immediately, regardless of consequences. The end simply does not justify the means."[39] This is the most extreme view one might take in asserting the inviolability of a deontological principle that stands on its own without foundation.

If the principle of not killing innocents were rationally derived, one would still want to say why it follows that deterrence as a system for protecting certain innocents is condemned in the interests of other innocents. If the principle is not rationally derived but is a directly apprehended intuition, however, it runs up against the problems of specifying who is the agent and what is being done when a deterrent system is maintained. It may be that one's directly apprehended intuitions would survive intact through all of these changes in circumstance from those in the ordinary life of an individual. But if one does not even acknowledge the difference in circumstances in this proscription and in that against ordinarily killing an innocent, one cannot expect to have one's intuition taken at face value. In Locke's rude term, the principle here seems "borrowed." It is at best assumed by analogy to the usual principle, but then the analogy wants spelling out. Or is it plausible that we have meaningful intuitions about something that was inconceivable only a generation or two ago?

Earlier generations could swear with impunity to do justice, although the heavens might fall—it was not conceivable that they would have to make the choice. We may be forced to make the choice. Alas, we may be caught with our slogans in the lurch and with the mistaken but firm belief that our inherited slogans are unshakable moral truths.

Notes

I wish to thank David Copp, Thomas Donaldson, J.L.A. Garcia, Richard Miller, Christopher W. Morris, Joseph S. Nye, Jr., Susan Moller Okin, Charles Silver, Steven Walt, students and faculty at the weekly lunch of the Divinity School of the University of Chicago in November 1984, and participants in the seminar on practical reason at the University of Chicago and in the 1984 *AMINTAPHIL* conference at Notre Dame University for comments on an earlier draft of this chapter.

1. Russell Hardin, "Unilateral Versus Mutual Disarmament," *Philosophy and Public Affairs* 12 (1983):236–254; and "Risking Armageddon," in Avner Cohen and Steven Lee, eds., *Nuclear Weapons and the Future of Humanity* (Totowa, N.J.: Rowman and Allanheld, 1986), pp. 201–223.

2. John Rawls, "Two Concepts of Rules," *Philosophical Review* 64 (1955):3–32; H. J. McCloskey, "An Examination of Restricted Utilitarianism," *Philosophical Review* 66 (1957):466–485. For further discussion, see Russell Hardin, "The Utilitarian Logic of Liberalism," *Ethics* 97 (Oct. 1986):47–74, especially the section "Institutionalization of Rights."

3. Unfortunately, our vocabulary is not as perspicuous as we might wish. I am not happy with the distinctions as I have drawn them. I wish to highlight the difference between judgments of actions as kinds *tout court* and judgments of outcomes. In the latter, what is of interest in motivating behavior is also actions, but the character of the action that matters to us is the effects it has, not its type as determined by some other criterion. In *The Rejection of Consequentialism: A Philosophical Investigation of the Considerations Underlying Rival Moral Conceptions* (Oxford: Clarendon Press, 1982), Samuel Scheffler speaks of agent-centered versus consequentialist moral theories.

4. Jeff McMahan, "Deterrence and Deontology," *Ethics* 95 (1985):517–536.

5. Ibid., p. 535.

6. James Turner Johnson, *Can Modern War Be Just?* (New Haven, Conn.: Yale University Press, 1984).

7. See further, James S. Fishkin, *The Limits of Obligation* (New Haven, Conn.: Yale University Press, 1982); and Martin McGuire, "The Calculus of Moral Obligations," *Ethics* 95 (1985):199–223.

8. Lon L. Fuller, *The Morality of Law*, rev. ed. (New Haven, Conn.: Yale University Press, 1969), p. 86. Fuller (p. 86n) illustrates his point with a lovely chastisement of Lord Nottingham, who said in a case, "I had some reason to know the meaning of this law; for it had its first rise from me." Campbell's *Lives of the Lord Chancellors of England*, vol. 3, 3rd ed., (1848), p. 423n, retorts, "If Lord Nottingham drew it, he was the less qualified to construe it, the author of an act considering more what he privately intended than the meaning he has expressed."

9. Eisenhower reputedly did face such a decision in the days just before the Soviet Union achieved the capacity to attack the United States with nuclear weapons. He considered making a preemptive attack but then rejected the "concept" by the fall 1954 (David Alan Rosenberg, "The Origins of Overkill: Nuclear Weapons and American Strategy, 1945–1960," *International Security* 7 [Spring 1983]:3–71, at pp. 33–34). Such an attack was similar to what Bertrand Russell had advocated earlier except that Russell rather more humanely proposed that the Soviet Union first be given an ultimatum not to develop nuclear weapons (Ronald W. Clark, *The Life of Bertrand Russell* [New York: Knopf, 1976], pp. 517–530).

10. John Krige, "The Politics of Truth: Experts and Laypeople in the Nuclear Debate," in Nigel Blake and Kay Pole, eds. *Objections to Nuclear Defence: Philosophers on Deterrence* (London: Routledge and Kegan Paul, 1984), pp. 67–68.

11. Alan Donagan, *The Theory of Morality* (Chicago: University of Chicago Press, 1977), pp. 123–124.

12. Gilbert Ryle, *Dilemmas* (Cambridge: Cambridge University Press, 1954), p. 30.

13. Paul Bracken, *The Command and Control of Nuclear Forces* (New Haven, Conn.: Yale University Press, 1983).

14. Germain Grisez, "Toward a Consistent Natural-Law Ethics of Killing," *American Journal of Jurisprudence* 15 (1970):64–96, at p. 73; cf. Donagan, *Theory of Morality*, p. 164. Donagan (p. 163) holds that the doctrine is either otiose or wrong in its implications for actual cases. H.L.A. Hart thinks the doctrine is legalistic theology that distinguishes cases in which "there seems to be no relevant moral difference . . . on any theory of morality" (*Punishment and Responsibility: Essays in the Philosophy of Law* [Oxford: Oxford University Press, 1968], p. 124). But here we need be concerned only with the doctrine's relevance and application to nuclear deterrence, not with its acceptability more generally.

15. Grisez, "Toward a Consistent Natural-Law Ethics of Killing," p. 73.

16. G.E.M. Anscombe, "War and Murder," in *Ethics, Religion and Politics* (Minneapolis: University of Minnesota Press, 1981), pp. 58–59. (This chapter originally was published in 1961.)

17. Grisez, "Toward a Consistent Natural-Law Ethics of Killing," p. 90.

18. Ibid., p. 92.

19. Moreover, Aquinas takes care to apply his principle only to actions by individuals, not by public authorities acting for the common good (ibid., p. 74), but we may choose not to follow him here.

20. Philippa Foot, "The Problem of Abortion and the Doctrine of the Double Effect," in *Virtues and Vices* (Berkeley, Calif.: University of California Press, 1978), pp. 19–32.

21. Robert W. Tucker, "The Morality of Deterrence," *Ethics* 95 (April 1985):461–478, at p. 472.

22. Ibid., p. 463.

23. For further defenses of this view, see David Hollenbach, S.J., *Nuclear Ethics: A Christian Moral Argument* (Ramsey, N.J.: Paulist Press, 1983), p. 39; John Courtney Murray, *Morality and Modern War* (New York: Council on Religion and International Affairs, 1959), pp. 9–11; and William V. O'Brien, *The Conduct of Just and Limited War* (New York: Praeger, 1981), pp. 19–27.

24. David Hume, *The History of England,* vol. 1 (Indianapolis, Ind.: Liberty Classics, 1983), Chap. 2, pp. 96–97.

25. Just-war theory originally was broader than this because the theory held that it was morally permissible for a state to attack another for reasons other than direct defense against prior attack.

26. John J. Mearsheimer, *Conventional Deterrence* (Ithaca, N.Y.: Cornell University Press, 1983), p. 15, emphasis added.

27. Hume, *The History of England,* vol. 1, p. 97.

28. H. A. Prichard, "Does Moral Philosophy Rest on a Mistake?" in *Moral Obligation and Duty and Interest* (London: Oxford University Press, 1968 [1912]), p. 17.

29. Alan Gewirth, *Reason and Morality* (Chicago: University of Chicago Press, 1978).

30. Gilbert Harman, *The Nature of Morality: An Introduction to Ethics* (New York: Oxford University Press, 1977), pp. 3–10.

31. John Hill Burton, *Life and Correspondence of David Hume,* vol. 1 (New York: Burt Franklin, undated reprint of original edition published in Edinburgh in 1846), pp. 323–324.

32. Ibid., p. 324. David Norton relies on this passage to support his claim that Hume is a "common-sense moralist" but a "sceptical metaphysician" (David Fate Norton, *David Hume: Common-Sense Moralist, Sceptical Metaphysician* [Princeton, N.J.: Princeton University Press, 1982], pp. 50–54).

33. Burton, *Life and Correspondence of David Hume,* vol. 1, p. 326. Hume continues thus: "and no sensible man can implicitly assent to any of them, but from the general principle, that as the truth in these subjects is beyond human capacity, and that as for one's own ease he must adopt some tenets, there is most satisfaction and convenience in holding to the Catholicism we have been first taught. Now this I have nothing to say against. I have only to observe, that such a conduct is founded on the most universal and determined scepticism, joined to a little indolence; for more curiosity and research gives a direct opposite turn from the same principles."

34. John Locke, *An Essay Concerning Human Understanding,* edited by Peter H. Nidditch (Oxford: Clarendon Press, 1975), I.III.26, pp. 83–84.

35. Henry Sidgwick, *The Methods of Ethics* (London: Macmillan, 1907 seventh edition, reprinted by Dover Publications, New York), p. 201.

36. Ludwig Wittgenstein, *On Certainty* (Oxford: Basil Blackwell, 1969), 170.

37. Ibid.,   344.

38. Burton, *Life and Correspondence of David Hume,* vol. 1, p. 326.

39. Grisez, "Toward a Consistent Natural-Law Ethics of Killing," p. 93.

3

Political Responsibility and Noncombatant Liability

James W. Child

To what extent are the noncombatant citizens of a country responsible for the aggressive wars their government may wage? More specifically, does the attacked country's right of self-defense extend to the killing of noncombatants in the attacking country? If so, under what conditions does this extension of the right of self-defense arise?

Noncombatant Immunity

Most of us believe World War II was a just war, viewed from the Allies' perspective. However, many also would hold that the massive fire bombing raids carried out with the sole purpose of killing civilians by RAF Bomber Command in Europe or by the U.S. Twentieth Air Force over Japan, or the two atomic bomb raids carried out by the United States, were morally wrong. If so, those raids would constitute a failure of *jus in bello*, justice in war, even while the Allies genuinely stood for *jus ad bellum*, justice of war.

Likewise, many people find morally abhorrent the doctrine of mutual assured destruction, which would require the United States to launch retaliatory, nuclear strikes, the sole purpose of which would be to kill millions of Soviet noncombatants in retribution for a Soviet first strike against U.S. strategic forces. Indeed, the entire moral foundation of nuclear deterrence has been challenged for just this reason. Is it moral to threaten to do what it is clearly morally monstrous to do?[1]

It is generally conceded by philosophers that there exist no cogent moral arguments, certainly none within just-war theory at least, that justify attacks whose objective is to kill noncombatants.[2] Thus, I will begin by assuming the principle of just-war theory known as noncombatant immunity. That is, noncombatants possess a strong presumptive right not to be attacked.[3] This inquiry, broadly put, will ask, What, if any, combinations of other principles and factual circumstances might overcome this presumptive right?

Note that I use the technical term *noncombatant*. This notion should not be confused with that of innocence. In the context of the theory of just war, the two terms have distinct meanings. To use Jeffrie Murphy's example, the octogenarian Nazi who helped promote his country's policy of aggressive war waging is not liable to your attack, for he does not threaten you.[4] He is not innocent, but that is irrelevant. The anti-Nazi, pacifist, German conscript is liable to attack because his bearing arms means that when you attack him you are acting to protect yourself under a right of self-defense. He well may be morally innocent, but that is irrelevant.

However, the thesis I propose changes the Nazi octogenarian's status somewhat. But Murphy, Fullinwider, and Nagel are surely correct; we possess no right to kill him as a matter of purpose, purely as punishment or in retribution for his country's aggressive war waging. Most certainly we may not kill innocents in his vicinity just to inflict punishment upon him.

Collateral Deaths

If the purposive killing of noncombatants in urban area bombing raids (countervalue attacks) in World War II was morally wrong, was the daylight "precision bombing" carried out by the U.S. Eighth Air Force over Germany also immoral? Eighth Air Force employed a doctrine and practice totally different from that applied by RAF Bomber Command or U.S. Twentieth Air Force. The only targets bombed were military or military/industrial in nature.[5] Considerable photo reconnaissance and analysis were done in choosing targets. Substantial efforts were made, sometimes at grave risk to bomber crews, to minimize civilian casualties. Indeed, merely flying in the daylight, in order to achieve greater accuracy, increased crew casualties manyfold.[6]

Nonetheless, Eighth Air Force caused thousands of noncombatant casualties by collateral damage. Try as the air force might, even daylight bombing with the famed Norden bombsight was far from genuinely precise. Was the United States morally wrong in carrying out these kinds of raids, knowing that large numbers of civilian casualties would occur?

A similar moral puzzle arises in modern nuclear strategy. Contrary to popular belief, the United States in recent years has held to a doctrine of *counterforce* (versus countervalue) deterrence. That is, we threaten, should the Soviets attack us, to attack *only* military targets.[7] Is there any theory that would morally justify the operations of Eighth Air Force?

Is it possible that such a theory might even justify a strategy of narrowly circumscribed counterforce second strikes?[8]

Double Effect

There is of course the time-honored doctrine of double effect, which holds that it may be morally acceptable to kill innocents as an unintended result of otherwise morally justified war making. Paul Ramsey has used the notion to justify civilian casualties in nuclear war waging (or perhaps only in *threatening* nuclear war waging; Ramsey is not clear on this point).[9] The use of double effect by Ramsey and others in a recent analysis of the morality of war has been subjected to powerful, and I believe dispositive, criticism.[10]

For the purpose of this chapter I shall assume simply that traditional double effect will not work when, as in the example of Eighth Air Force, the level of accuracy in targeting is so gross that you know, regardless of the care you exercise, the chances you will kill noncombatants in large numbers is somewhat greater than that you will destroy your target at all, let alone without killing many noncombatants. The overwhelming disproportionate gain in moral benefit over moral cost required by the doctrine of double effect simply is not there.

Is there any other way in which attacks upon targets, which cannot be justified by the traditional application of double effect, might be justified, particularly by a nation resisting aggression? I believe there is. It turns upon a notion of a limited noncombatant liability, and this chapter constitutes an effort to formulate such a theory.[11]

Liability with Political Participation

Let us image two nations, A and B. Both are armed with long-range, conventional missiles, rather like the German V-2. A and B each have a capital that is a major city, A-ville and B City, respectively. A has chosen to base its rockets in the middle of A-ville. In addition to the missiles, both A and B possess armies, artillery, and other conventional arms based near their common border.

A is a direct democracy. Its leaders call its citizens to a popular assembly to propose war against B. The leaders of A neither have, nor even claim to have, any moral justification for attacking B. This is an aggressive war, plain and simple. Among other things, the plan requires an explicit authorization to launch A's long-range missiles at B City in a pure countervalue attack, to kill civilians and destroy B's economy. The citizens of A vote, not unanimously, to make war. A then proceeds to launch missiles at B City as well as commencing an invasion of B.

A has reloadable launchers for its long-range missiles and missiles in reserve, all based at the center of A-ville. A intends, B has strong reason to believe, to continue launching missiles from A-ville upon B City.

The members of B's government, being philosophically inclined, ask, Do we have a moral right to attack A's long-range missile launchers? If we do so, we know that we will kill many of A's noncombatant citizens in the process. We do not want to kill them deliberately, even though A is doing that to our citizens. Killing them will not shorten the war or serve any other military purpose. We do not believe we have a right to punish them. But surely we have a right to protect our citizens by attacking those long-range missile launchers before they reload and attack us again. Does that right extend to imposing large (disproportionately large under traditional double effect), noncombatant casualties by collateral damage? The answer seems to me to be yes because the citizens of A are somehow morally liable for their government's action.

Note I am *not* claiming that the citizens of A are liable to direct attack in retribution or as punishment; nor am I following some gross and dubious application of the rule of proportionality, which says that Country B should "break the will" of A's citizens and shorten the war. The notion articulated by Murphy et al. seems quite correct here. Attacks upon combatants are justified on the basis of self-defense only. Here those noncombatant citizens cannot be directly and purposively attacked in self-defense. They do not threaten B's citizens. But those missiles and launchers certainly do! Attacking them and their crews is a direct application of the right of self-defense. Surely B can put A's citizens at risk, even large numbers at great risk, as it attempts to defend its citizens from subsequent attacks it knows are coming.

One must limit this right of risk-imposing counterattacks, however. Not only must B *not try* to kill noncombatants of A, B must *try not* to, within the means at B's disposal. This is a familiar concept to lawyers. B must *take care* not to gratuitously kill A's noncombatants. B must not be *negligent* and especially not *wanton* or *reckless* in how it attacks A's weapons. That limitation holding, however, B does seem to have such a right to counterattack in self-defense.

How might this intuitively felt right of B to attack A's missile launchers be justified? Remember, one cannot appeal to traditional double effect as a justification for the generalized violation of noncombatant immunity. How then? A first took a plebiscite. All citizens of A who voted for the attack certainly seem to be culpable. They actively approved. Surely a citizen acquires some level of responsibility for the actions of his or her government when that citizen, through the political machinery of a democracy, votes before the fact for the government's actions. The "aye" voting citizens of A *authorized* their government to do what it did. The legal notion of agency operates here as a strong guide to moral intuitions. A person is legally (and presumably morally) responsible when his or her agent acts in ways that have been *authorized explicitly*.[12]

What if the government of A has received only an open-ended authorization to wage aggressive war upon B, rather than explicit permission to launch missiles against B City? It would seem that the "aye" voting citizens remain liable. A principal is liable for the acts of an agent that are reasonably within the scope of the agent's authority even if not explicitly authorized by the principal.[13]

What of the citizens of A who voted against war upon B? It seems that in the absence of other stronger dissenting action on their part, they are as liable to be put at risk by B's counterattacks as are their compatriots who voted in favor of the aggressive war. How so? Let us again move to the law for an analogous situation, but now to corporate law. A company is thinking about engaging in some massively immoral and illegal activity, pouring large quantities of arsenic into the public water supply as a matter of ongoing operations, let us say. A member of the board of directors of the company, when the policy is before it, votes no, but does nothing else. Later, when charged in tort (or crime) with her transgressions she pleads that she voted no. What would our reaction be? The answer is obvious! We could say, "You are responsible as much, or almost as much, as your fellow board members who voted 'aye.' You should have blown the whistle, gone public or to regulatory authorities, or at the very least resigned from the board of so despicable a company." Mere formal dissent in this case does almost nothing to relieve her liability, legal or moral. In general, exculpation for the monstrous actions of institutions requires more than formal dissent.

Does similar liability exist for the dissenting citizens of A? It seems that it does. We impose a negligence-like standard of *failing* to do something they *should have* done. There exists a range of activities that tend to relieve that liability. Strong vocal dissent, continuing attempts to get the issue back before the assembly to defeat it, civil disobedience, emigration in protest, or even warning B of the attack all present themselves. At some point, the dissenting citizens' actions become strong and sustained enough to absolve them of responsibility or liability. Exactly where on the spectrum of dissident activity this occurs need not detain us here. It is sufficient merely to observe that in most polities the number of such dedicated dissidents on such issues will be few.

What of the apathetic person who did not attend the assembly, who did not know the issue of the war with B would be considered, and in general does not give much of a damn what his government does. He is too busy watching television game shows, perhaps. The strong temptation is to say, "Well, fellow, you *should have* given a damn. You should have skipped the game show on the day of the meeting. Your government claims to act for you, as well as for those who participated in the assembly, and it is your business to know what it is up to and to act as best you can to influence it." Indeed, I would go on to say to the apathetic citizen, "Don't blame B's citizens if their missiles, in a desperate effort to destroy your country's missile launchers, kill or maim you. There is something you should have done and failed to do, and that failure makes you liable to be at risk as B endeavors to save the lives of its citizens."

What of the children of A-ville? True innocents! A heart-wrenching situation that is faced in any war by any warring nation, no matter how just its cause. If there is any justification here it is by traditional double effect, and the ratio of moral benefit gained over moral cost paid must be high indeed. I am tempted to say to the government and citizens of A, "*You* brought death and injury upon your children. The citizens of B are defending *their* children from your rockets, and however terrible the collateral killing of children, it is you, not the citizens of B, who must bear the primary responsibility for it."[14]

I will gloss over the application of these standards to a representative democracy like the United States. Suffice it to say, there is nothing in the somewhat more gross controls U.S. citizens have over their government's behavior that would obviate their responsibility should their government launch an aggressive war.

Liability in Dictatorships

A moral puzzle arises here. If the citizens of a democracy are responsible for their government's actions to the degree that their absolute noncombatant immunity can be compromised, what of the citizens (or subjects) of a dictatorship? Let us suppose that country A is a dictatorship. Its citizens have no say at all in the decision of their leaders to wage war upon B or, more specifically, to launch long-range missiles against B City. Because of their inability to participate, do the citizens of A preserve their absolute noncombatant immunity, where the freedom to offer dissent without serious penalty in a free and open democracy would cause its loss? Put the question more fully from B's perspective. Are A's citizens innocent in so strong a sense that B cannot even put them at risk as it seeks to destroy A's missiles and launchers? Is B now morally prohibited from taking action in its own defense solely because of A's arrangements for political decisionmaking?

There is one extreme case in which the answer might be yes. Suppose A is ruled not by "its leaders" in any sense of the word, but instead by an outlaw band who recently has seized power. Suppose the band quite literally (the literalness is important) holds the citizens of A hostage or, even more accurately, uses them as shields. This is a desperate moral dilemma for the citizens of B and one to which there may be no morally "right" answer.[15]

However, let us not become too enthralled with this special case. Most dictatorships are not of this unusual sort. Indeed, they differ in ways quite important to the responsibility of their citizens for the actions of their governments and leaders. How?

1. Most dictatorships are ethnically and nationally *of* their own people. Furthermore, in some broad sense of "social institutions," most dictators acquire power through preexisting institutions, procedures, and traditions, even if not by democratic vote.

Stalin and all his successors have done that. Hitler and Mussolini did that, as did Pinochet and Marcos. Truly revolutionary dictators such as Lenin or Mao, perhaps by definition, did not.

2. The government almost certainly will make *claims to legitimacy*.

Whatever else political legitimacy means, it means in part that the government may act for and in the name of its people. In this sense the notion of agency taken from the law is more than analogous; it is morally homologous.

3. The citizens acquiesce in the claims their government makes to act for them.

No government can endure long without the passive acquiescence of most of its people. John Austin, the philosopher of law, calls this "a habit of obedience."[16] Most other philosophers of law agree that something like it is central to a government's ability to govern.[17] That acquiescence may come in part from political intimidation or even terror, but in the real world (as compared to antiutopian visions) it also must grow from a profound apathy on the part of many of its citizens and the positive support of a significant number. Surely Hitler's Germany or the Soviet Union today exemplify such a gradation from opposition through passive acquiescence to positive support.[18]

4. A government's claims of legitimacy must be given more credence *if the government has been in power for some long time*.

This point is closely connected to (3) in that duration increases both the reality of acquiescence and the perception of it on the part of third parties.

It is no accident that (1) through (4) are very close to the traditional criteria for the recognition of states and governments in international law.[19] That is the arena wherein governments act for and in the name of their people. Surely (1) through (4) do not exhaust the complex notion of legitimacy in international law, but they are just as relevant.

Understanding now the deep relationship between the concepts of agency and legitimacy, let us return to the law of agency as a guide to our moral intuitions. If a person claims to represent you for some period of time and it is within your knowledge that he does so and it is within your power to disclose to him and to third parties his lack of authority and you do not, then you will become liable for his actions within the reasonable scope in which he claims to be acting.[20] The primary reason for this is that others, knowing that you can object and do not, can reasonably conclude that he represents you.[21] In other words, you acquire an affirmative duty to prevent his further representations as your agent. But what can the citizens of a dictatorship do to prevent this putative "agent" (the government) from acting in their names?

First, citizens having any shred of political influence are responsible for exercising it against policies of aggressive war and attacks upon the homelands of others. For example, there exists a small but influential body of public opinion in the Soviet Union among the scientific and professional classes in the party apparatus, or so Soviet experts claim.[22] To the extent that peaceful means of political influence are open to such significant portions of the public, they are morally bound to exercise those means.

Second, a people can go into the streets. They can protest violently. They can organize rebellion. These are desperate options, but desperate moral issues call for desperate solutions. Surely we intuitively feel that Hitler represented the German people or that Gorbachev represents the Russian people in ways that Jaruzelski does not represent the Polish people nor Karmal the Afghan people nor Pinochet the Chilean people. These intuitions are morally justified, for the people of those dictatorships have given us *notice* in the most graphic way possible of their government's lack of legitimacy.

The central issue in modern Western political philosophy has been the rights and duties of states to citizens and citizens to states, what these rights are and how they are justified. Yet there is another equally important question: What duties do citizens have to third party states to control the actions of their state's government?

John Locke taught that when a government violated the natural rights of its citizens, they had a right, perhaps a duty, to rebel. The founding fathers of the United States agreed. Is there any less asked of citizens when their government threatens a massive assault upon the rights of *another* people? The general question of what these duties to control government specifically consist in or how they arise are topics that go beyond this chapter. But let us return to the war of A against B in order to discern answers to these questions as they specifically apply to noncombatant immunity.

Liability With Knowledge but Without Participation

Suppose that the dictatorship of A is of a rather unusual kind. Suppose that it has open and ample sources of information about the doings of its government; it merely excludes all but the elite from participation or control. (Whether such a system is practically possible or not is irrelevant.) Thus, the citizens of A *know* that their government intends to wage aggressive war on B without any justification for doing so. They even know that their government intends to attack B City with missiles and inflict many noncombatant casualties in the process. They just cannot "do anything about it" under their present system of government.

Are the citizens in this case more like the case of the child or the case of an apathetic citizen in a democratic A? The child, because of physical and mental limitations, is constrained by physical impossibility from doing anything about A's behavior. The apathetic citizen, on the other hand, *could* have participated in the decision. He was constrained only by the cost of participation, which in his preference scheme was too high. He preferred television game shows, and we found his preference morally wanting. It strikes me that the citizen of the dictatorship is far more like the apathetic citizen than the child. He or she can resist, as the citizens of Poland and Afghanistan have shown so nobly. To be sure, the cost of said resistance at the hands of the state security apparatus might be high indeed. But sometimes we are morally required to pay high costs to carry out our duties to third parties.

That this duty demands a great deal is manifest. But before we are tempted to say it demands too much, let us remember that the sanction for failure to discharge it is of a curious type. To fail to discharge my duty to third parties to try (very hard) to control my government *does not* entitle those third parties to kill me intentionally or punish me in any way. I lose one very special (and very strong) right I had against those third parties: my absolute immunity as a noncombatant not even to be put at risk. Although the defending country now can put me at risk and my immunity as a noncombatant is no longer absolute, it has

not disappeared. The attackers must do everything reasonably possible
not to kill me as they attack military targets in my vicinity.

Liability Without Knowledge or Participation

Let us change the example once again. The dictatorship of A is of a
more conventional kind. It controls the media, and the citizens of A
are more or less in the dark about the war plans of A's leadership. I
say "more or less" because outside of an Orwellian thought experiment,
the grapevine, reading between the lines of official publications and
announcements, direct or secondhand contacts from outside (BBC or
Voice of America in the Soviet Union) combine to give people a better
view of what is going on than we might think. This is especially true
if the citizen is willing to make the effort or take the risk to find out.

Are the citizens of A obligated to make that effort or take that risk?
I believe so. There is a doctrine in law and morals known as "culpable
ignorance." If you need to know something in order to do something
you should do, and reasonable people would know they needed to know,
then your ignorance is part of your culpability in not doing that thing.[23]
Thus, the mere lack of knowledge does not absolve the citizen of A of
the kind of moral liability he or she incurs by B's attempts to defend
itself.

In an era when weapons of mass destruction enable nation-states to
wreak havoc upon whole continents, citizens simply must be held
responsible for how their nations behave in regard to the use of those
weapons. Citizens are accountable to know and act upon that knowledge.
Any lesser standard rewards people who do not take responsibility for
their own political destiny and penalizes most cruelly those who do. It
penalizes them by obviating their right of self-defense at the hands of
immunized aggressive dictatorships.[24]

Conclusion

In the death of the typical German citizen killed collaterally when
the U.S. Eighth Air Force attacked the Schweinfurt ballbearing works,
for example, there seems to me to have been very little blood on the
Allies' hands. There seems a morally significant sense in which we could
have said to his shade, "Had you done something you should have done
and failed to do and had enough of your compatriots joined you in
doing what they should have done, the Eighth Air Force would not have
had to destroy the ballbearing plant and would not have inadvertently
killed you in the process. You could not control your compatriots, but
that does not matter. *Your* not doing what *you* should have done (regardless

of what your fellow citizens did or did not do) is what caused you to lose your immunity to risk by the Allied attack."

Similarly, when we consider the morality of nuclear deterrence today, the United States may morally threaten to destroy the Soviet Union's remaining strategic forces should they attack the United States first. (This does not mean that we can justify the present U.S. counterforce strategy with its much broader range of target types.) The United States may launch such narrow counterforce strikes knowing full well that such attacks would produce hundreds of thousands, perhaps millions, of collateral noncombatant casualties. For it is the duty of the Russian people to restrain their government from such a first strike. The Soviet dictatorship does not absolve the Russian people of that duty. If they fail to discharge it, they do not become the legitimate target of purposeful efforts to murder them in retributive countervalue attacks. But they do lose their right not to be put at risk, even grave risk, as the United States endeavors to defend itself and save the lives of millions of its own citizens from subsequent attacks. The same duties and loss of rights attend the U.S. population should it ever allow the U.S. government to launch a nuclear war.

Does this analysis show that we can conclude with aplomb that nuclear war waging is morally acceptable? No! Of course not. However, it does provide us with a better understanding of pertinent rights and duties as we endeavor to work out ways of avoiding nuclear war.

Notes

1. This issue has been discussed thoroughly in the literature in many places, including Gregory S. Kavka, "Some Paradoxes of Deterrence," *The Journal of Philosophy* 75, no. 6 (June 1978): 285–302, 505–525; "Third Draft of the Proposed National Pastoral Letter of the U.S. Bishops on War and Peace," *Origins* 12, no. 44 (April 14, 1983), pp. 707–714; Michael Walzer, *Just and Unjust Wars* (New York: Basic Books, 1977), pp. 269–274, 282.

2. There exists, of course, the simple (and I would say simpleminded) consequential argument that the purposive killing of civilians "breaks the will of the people," hastens an end to war, and thus on a cost-benefit analysis (following the rule of proportionality) is justified. This argument was central to the evolution of the doctrine of strategic bombardment. Generals Mitchell and Douhet both made it. See Lee Kenneth, *A History of Strategic Bombing* (New York: Scribners, 1982), Chap. 3. But that is of historical interest only. After World War II the air force sponsored *The United States Strategic Bombing Survey*, which showed that strategic bombardment actually *increased* the morale of the people subject to it.

I assert a near consensus against the purposive killing of civilians on the basis of a number of excellent articles published some time ago whose central thesis, to my knowledge, never has been questioned by members of the philosophic community. They are Elizabeth Anscombe, "War and Murder," reprinted in *War and Morality*, Richard Wasserstrom, ed. (Belmont, Calif.: Wadsworth, 1970), pp. 41–53; Robert Fullinwider, "War and Innocence," *Philosophy and Public Affairs* 4, no. 1 (1975); Jeffrie G. Murphy, "The Killing of the Innocent," *The Monist* 57, no. 4 (1973), reprinted in *War, Morality, and the Military Profession*, Malham M. Wakin, ed. (Boulder, Colo.: Westview, 1979), pp. 343–370; Thomas Nagel, "War and Massacre," *Philosophy and Public Affairs* 1, no. 2 (Winter, 1972), reprinted in Wakin, ibid., pp. 371–392.

3. The regnant position in rights theory is that immunities are special kinds of rights. Wesley Newcomb Hohfeld, *Fundamental Legal Conceptions* (New Haven, Conn.: Yale University Press, 1919), p. 65; Lawrence C. Becker, "Individual Rights," in *And Justice for All*, Tom Regan and Donald Van De Veer, eds. (Totowa, N.J.: Rowman and Allanheld, 1982); and Theodore M. Benditt, *Rights* (Totowa, N.J.: Rowman and Allanheld, 1982), p. 15.

4. Murphy, op. cit., pp. 347–351.

5. There is the single, apparently inexplicable exception wherein U.S. Eighth Air Force cooperated with RAF Bomber Command in the notorious area bombing of Dresden.

6. For fuller details of the history and strategy of the U.S. Eighth Air Force, see Thomas M. Coffey, *Decision Over Schweinfurt: The U.S. 8th Air Force Battle for Daylight Bombing* (New York: McKay, 1977); Kenneth, op. cit., Chaps. 7–10. For a moving testimony to the heroism and sacrifice such a strategy called for, see Elmer Bendiner's critically acclaimed memoir, *The Fall of Fortresses* (New York: Putnam, 1980). Bendiner was a B-17 navigator and holder of the Distinguished Flying Cross.

7. See Laurence Freedman, *The Evolution of Nuclear Strategy* (London: Macmillan, 1983), especially Chaps. 15 and 16; Albert Wohlstetter, "Bishops, Statesmen and Other Strategists on the Bombing of the Innocents," *Commentary* 75, no. 6 (June 1983), pp. 15–35; Caspar Weinberger, *Department of Defense Annual Report to Congress FY 1984* (Washington, D.C.: U.S. Government Printing Office, 1983), pp. 54–55.

8. Needless to say, morally justifying a doctrine of nuclear counterforce second strikes would be far more difficult than a similar doctrine regarding conventional weapons, precisely because of the awesome destructive power of those weapons and the consequent difficulty in discriminating between combatants and noncombatants.

9. Paul Ramsey, *The Just War* (New York: Scribners, 1968), Chap. 11, pp. 248–258, Chaps. 14 and 15.

10. Anscombe in Wakin, op. cit., pp. 294–296; Walzer, op. cit., pp. 278–283; Jonathan Bennett, "Morality and Consequences," *The Tanner Lectures on Human Values*, vol. 2 (Salt Lake City: University of Utah Press, 1981), pp. 95–105.

11. I see my theory as replacing double effect. However, in discussion James Sterba has argued that I am reintroducing double effect. He may well be correct. I do not find that a particularly objectionable interpretation, so long as it is

clear that in doing so I provide an *explication* and *justification* of double effect not heretofore offered by its defenders.

12. *Restatement of Agency*, 2nd edition (American Law Institute 1958), Section 1 (hereinafter *Restatement*); and Warren A. Seavey, *Agency* (St. Paul, Minn.: West Publishing, 1964), p. 204.

13. *Restatement*, Sections 7(c) and 35; Seavey, ibid., pp. 12–13.

14. This is not to say that it is not morally wrong for B to kill A's children. It is, and nothing can right it. However, A's behavior and B's right to defend its citizens might excuse such killing.

15. This is the problem of "innocent shield" posed but not solved by Robert Nozick in *Anarchy, State and Utopia* (New York: Basic Books, 1974), pp. 34–35.

16. John Austin, *The Province of Jurisprudence Determined* (New York: Noonday Press, 1954), Lectures 5 and 7.

17. Many disagree with Austin's formulation but agree that some such concept is necessary to the notion of a government based on rules. For a discussion see H.L.A. Hart, *The Concept of Law* (Oxford: Oxford University Press, 1961), pp. 50–60; Martin Golding, *The Philosophy of Law* (Englewood Cliffs, N.J.: Prentice-Hall, 1975), pp. 25–26; and Joseph Raz, *The Concept of a Legal System*, 2nd ed. (Oxford: Oxford University Press, 1980), pp. 5–7, 14–16, 93–95.

18. George Kennan, *The Nuclear Illusion* (New York: Pantheon, 1982), pp. 84–85, has noted "indifference" and a "curious sort of boredom and spiritlessness" as the primary feelings manifested by the Soviet people at their government's claims of legitimacy and its ideological justifications of its actions.

19. See Gerhard von Glahn, *Law Among Nations* (New York: Macmillan, 1981), pp. 90–116, especially pp. 98–99.

20. *Restatement*, Sections 8 and 27; Seavy, op. cit., p. 43.

21. Seavey, ibid.; and *Restatement*, Section 43.

22. Kennen, op. cit., pp. 83–84; and Seweryn Bailer, "Danger in Moscow," *New York Review of Books*, February 16, 1984, p. 9.

23. "Culpable ignorance" has been defined as "such ignorance as results from the failure to exercise ordinary care to acquire knowledge." 25 *Corpus Juris Secundum*, 29. A lucid and highly valuable philosophic treatment of the issue is Holly Smith, "Culpable Ignorance," *The Philosophical Review* 92, no. 4 (October 1983): 543–571.

24. Indeed, although I do not claim to have proven it, the consequences of my argument, if followed far enough, may well be that to allow a dictatorship to command a nation's actions and policies is by itself to fail a negligence-like moral standard. This in turn might well imply that a duty exists for any polity and the citizens thereof to rule themselves with a free and open democracy. Such a consequence would neither surprise nor trouble me.

Selected Bibliography

There are several good recent texts on war and morality. Two of the best and most topical are Michael Walzer, *Just and Unjust Wars* (New York: Basic

Books, 1977); and James Turner Johnson, *Can Modern War Be Just?* (New Haven, Conn.: Yale University Press, 1984).

Two standard anthologies, which between them contain most of the classic papers on noncombatant immunity cited in this chapter, are M. Cohen, T. Nagel, and T. Scanlon, eds., *War and Moral Responsibility* (Princeton, N.J.: Princeton University Press, 1974); and Richard Wasserstrom, ed., *War and Morality* (Belmont, Calif.: Wadsworth, 1970).

There is a plethora of new anthologies on nuclear deterrence. Two of the more interesting are Nigel Blake and Kay Pole, eds., *Objections to Nuclear Deterrence: Philosophers on Deterrence* (London: Routledge and Kegan Paul, 1984); and James P. Sterba, *The Ethics of War and Nuclear Deterrence* (Belmont, Calif.: Wadsworth, 1985).

4

The Ethics of
International Intervention

Jefferson McMahan

In recent years the U.S. government has persistently accused Nicaragua of unwarranted intervention in El Salvador, on the ground that Nicaragua has been supporting insurgents fighting against the Salvadoran government. Yet the United States has itself been providing extensive support for guerrillas fighting against the government of Nicaragua. U.S. officials also have complained of Cuban and Soviet intervention on behalf of the government of Nicaragua; yet in every respect in which Cuba and the Soviet Union are supposed to have intervened on behalf of the Nicaraguan government, the United States also has intervened, and usually to a greater extent, on behalf of the Salvadoran government. Thus, U.S. charges against Nicaragua, Cuba, and the Soviet Union have been echoed by Nicaraguan charges against the United States. At the formal level, the charges on each side are identical. Relatively few people believe that none of these interventions is justifiable, and even fewer believe that all are. But can one consistently support intervention by one side while objecting to intervention by the other?

Cases such as the U.S. interventions in El Salvador and Nicaragua and the alleged Nicaraguan intervention in El Salvador raise fundamental questions about the ethics of international intervention. What counts as intervention? What are the grounds for the common presumption that intervention always is unjustified? Can intervention ever be justified, and if so how and under what conditions? Can one give a plausible account of the ethics of intervention that is politically neutral? These are some of the questions this chapter will address.

The Concept of Intervention

Let us begin with the preliminary question of definition. Most accounts agree that intervention involves coercive external interference in the affairs of a population that is organized in the form of a state. But many accounts also insist that various restrictions should be imposed in order to narrow the scope of the definition. In most instances the aim of narrowing the definition seems to be not to provide an analysis of the concept that matches and explains ordinary use, but rather to accommodate the view that intervention is never morally justified. As we shall see, this view will be more plausible the more restrictive one's definition of intervention is. But in this case as in others, it seems a mistake to tailor our definition of an essentially nonnormative concept to fit our moral views—if only because the rights and wrongs of intervention are far too complicated for us to formulate a simple definition that counts as intervention all those forms of interference we think wrong while excluding those we regard as permissible.[1]

The various restrictions on the core definition that have been suggested seem not only incompatible with the way the term is ordinarily used but also entirely arbitrary. Three types of restriction have been proposed: restrictions on the mode of coercion, restrictions on either the agent or the target of the coercion, and restrictions on the aim of the coercion. In all three cases the restrictions have the effect of excluding paradigm cases of intervention.

Consider first some suggested restrictions on the mode of coercion. Many writers have assumed that intervention must involve the use of military force or at least the *threatened* use of military force.[2] Yet consider the U.S. intervention in Chile during the tenure of Salvador Allende— a paradigm case of intervention. There the U.S. intervention, which was aimed at (and successful in) bringing down the government, was based on a combination of nonmilitary means: economic pressure, assistance to the Chilean military, and acts of subversion such as covert interference with elections, bribing officials, and manipulating the mass media. It would not have mattered had other nonmilitary means been used instead; as long as the aim was coercive, the U.S. action would have been recognized as interventionary. Even arms sales, or other forms of support for military or police operations, can be interventionary if the aim and expectation are that the aid will be used for coercive purposes—either by the government against domestic rebels or by rebels against the government—within the beneficiary's own state.

Let us turn now to the second class of restrictions. Many proposed definitions of intervention have stipulated either that the coercive agent must be a state or that the target of coercion must be a state. Some definitions have insisted on both stipulations.[3] But both are again entirely arbitrary. What reason is there to exclude as possible agents of intervention such "nonstate actors" as multinational corporations, military or political organizations of national groups not represented by a state (the Palestine

Liberation Organization, for example), terrorist organizations, regional organizations, international organizations such as the United Nations, and so on? United Fruit Company played a key role in engineering the overthrow of the Arbenz government in Guatemala in 1954, while the U.S. government liked to pretend that the principal agent of intervention during the "rescue mission" in Grenada in October 1983 was the Organization of Eastern Caribbean States. It is hard to think of two more paradigmatic instances of intervention than these.

The requirement that the target or victim of intervention must also be a state is equally without justification. In order to explain why, let me first clarify what I mean by the term *state*. There is a sense in which states are transhistorical entities, in that they can survive and retain their identities through changes of government, population, and borders, and even through changes of institutional and constitutional structures. In this sense the United States now is the same state as the United States in 1800. In general when I use the term, however, I shall not be referring to states so conceived. For there is another sense of the term that is more relevant to the question of intervention, according to which a state consists of the union at a particular time of a population and a government, together with a formal or informal political constitution that shapes and determines the structure of the government and its relations with the people. Thus a single state in the first, historical sense can encompass a number of different states in this second sense. For example, while the state of Nicaragua was in the broad sense continuous through the 1970s and early 1980s, there is another sense in which one Nicaraguan state was destroyed and supplanted by another in 1979. It is with states in this second, narrower sense that I am primarily concerned.

Understood in this way, the state becomes closely identified with the government, the administrative structures, and with what might be called the state apparatus (that is, the military, the police, and so on). Thus, when a state is internally divided, without denying that the opposition is in some sense included within the state, we tend to identify the state with the government and its organs and supporters rather than with those fighting against the government. Intervention against the state therefore means intervention against the government, while intervention on behalf of the state means intervention on behalf of the government and against its domestic opponents. (The term *state* certainly attaches to and follows the government in this way in U.N. parlance.)

With that much said by way of clarification, I now can explain the requirement that the target of intervention must be a state. It is arbitrary because the requirement excludes the possibility of intervention *on behalf of* the state against the state's internal opposition. This requirement therefore would exclude numerous undeniable instances of intervention, including the U.S. intervention in South Vietnam (at least in its initial stages) and the present U.S. intervention in El Salvador (although in each case the United States has claimed, falsely, to be defending the state against external aggression).

Finally, let us consider the set of restrictions that limit the aims a course of action can have in order to qualify as an instance of intervention. One such restriction is that intervention must be directed at "the structure of political authority in the target society."[4] There is, however, no reason why an intervening agent's concern should be limited in this way; an intervening agent could just as reasonably be concerned with, for example, the mode of economic organization in some other country, or even some specific governmental policy (for example, a policy of torturing political dissidents). A second proposed restriction on an intervener's aims qualifies the first by insisting that the aim should be to *change* the structure of political authority in the target society.[5] This is obviously unacceptable, for, in addition to focusing exclusively on political structures, this restriction excludes an aim that historically has been an important motive for intervention: namely, to preserve the structure of political authority (or indeed the mode of economic organization) from the threat of endogenous change. A third, more generous restriction insists only that intervention must involve interference with the internal affairs of another country. But, insofar as this is not just a restatement of the requirement that the victims of coercion must be members of the state in which the intervention occurs, this final restriction is also arbitrary. An intervening agent might wish to influence not the target state's internal affairs, but its foreign policy, perhaps in particular the target country's policy toward the intervening agent itself.

Because none of the proposed restrictions on the core definition seems plausible, it would appear that this definition should stand unaltered. Intervention, then, is simply coercive external interference in the affairs of a population organized in the form of a state. This definition still leaves room for controversy—for example, what counts as coercion? (Is threatening to withhold a voluntary loan an instance of coercion?) But, even though this definition leaves room for dispute regarding marginal cases, it provides a sufficiently determinate account of what intervention is to allow us to proceed to the substantive part of this inquiry.

The Antipaternalist and Communal Autonomy Arguments

Most of the common arguments concerning the question of intervention are intended to show not that all intervention is wrong, but that intervention *against states* is wrong. This fact reflects the power of states in determining people's views. For it is natural to expect that states will support a principle ruling out intervention against states, while accepting that intervention on behalf of states is legitimate. (This is one reason for the common insistence that the target of intervention must be a state; this insistence, combined with the widespread assumption that intervention is morally wrong, implies that intervention against states is wrong but that external support for states contending with domestic opponents may be justified.)

Not surprisingly, the view that intervention against the state is wrong while intervention on behalf of the state is normally permissible is now enshrined in international law. The blanket prohibition on intervention against the state is emphatically stated in the Declaration on Principles of International Law Concerning Friendly Relations and Co-operation Among States in Accordance with the Charter of the United Nations, which was adopted by the U.N. General Assembly in 1970.

> No State or group of States has the right to intervene, directly or indirectly, for any reason whatever, in the internal or external affairs of any other State. Consequently, armed intervention and all other forms of interference or attempted threats against the personality of the State or against its political, economic and cultural elements, are in violation of international law.[6]

On the other hand, intervention *on behalf of* the state in order to assist it in combating domestic opponents is held by international law to be permissible—as long, that is, as the rebels or insurgents are not sufficiently strong, or in control of sufficient territory, that the conflict must be considered a civil war. In that case, the opposition acquires the rights of a belligerent, and intervention on behalf of the government also becomes impermissible.[7]

The position of international law is among the most stringently anti-interventionist of the major current views on the ethics of international intervention.[8] What is the moral foundation of this view? Its defenders commonly appeal to an argument known in the literature as the anti-paternalist argument. This argument draws on an analogy between persons and states. Just as persons are autonomous agents and are entitled to determine their own action free from interference as long as the exercise of their autonomy does not involve the transgression of certain moral constraints, so, it is claimed, states also are autonomous agents, whose autonomy is similarly deserving of respect. The implied right of states to freedom from coercion by other states (or by other external agents) is articulated in the doctrine of state sovereignty. According to that doctrine, the state alone has rightful jurisdiction over the conduct of its own affairs and may not be subject to external coercion as long as it avoids violating the rights and prerogatives of other states. In particular, respect for autonomy implies that states, like persons, may not be coerced in an effort to do them good. Thus all forms of intervention against the state, even what is known as humanitarian intervention, or other forms of intervention deemed to be in the interests of the state itself are ruled out.[9]

This argument has plausible implications in a great many cases. For example, it rightly condemns the attempt to impose democratic institutions on another country, for this is an objectionable form of paternalism that (paradoxical as it may seem) violates the self-determination of the people. The problem with the argument, however, is that it is not concerned with the autonomy or self-determination of *people*. Its emphasis is instead on the autonomy of the *state*. Moreover, the argument does not require that the autonomy of the state should be in any way derivative from or connected with the autonomy of the people, nor that respect for state autonomy should entail respect for the autonomy or self-determination of the people. Rather, the state's claim to sovereignty is based entirely on the analogy between persons and states. How valid is the analogy?

The analogy between persons and states holds in several important respects. States can be agents and can have ends. Like persons, they also can have interests. Just as persons can harm themselves, so states can harm themselves. Just as persons can harm or be harmed by other persons, so states can harm or be harmed by other states. But, unlike most persons, states are not always or even usually integrated agents with unified wills. They can be and often are divided, with the government engaged in the repression of the citizens and the citizens in revolt against the government. There is no serious analogue to the divided state in the case of an individual person. In this respect the analogy between persons and states breaks down.

When a state turns upon its own citizens, or some group of its citizens, intervention on behalf of the victims is not paternalism. This is especially clear in the case of requested intervention. The intervening agent is not pretending to be acting in the interests of the state; rather, the agent is acting to protect the interests of the state's victims. (Of course, intervention on behalf of the victims of state violence or repression ultimately may be in the best interests of the state as a whole, just as preventing a potential murderer from killing his intended victim may be in his or her own best interests.[10] But, as the latter example shows, not all instances of coercion that benefit the person coerced are paternalistic.) In the case in which a government turns upon its own citizens, as in all cases in which one person or group of persons causes unjustifiable harm to others or violates their rights, the government forfeits its claim to noninterference based on respect for autonomy. Neither personal nor state autonomy entails a right to disregard the rights or interests of others. Indeed, in cases in which the state authority abuses its autonomy by acting against its citizens, respect for autonomy may dictate intervention, for it is then the autonomy of the citizens rather than that of the state that may require defense.

One might attempt to rescue the antipaternalist argument by construing the case in which the state authority acts against its own citizens as simply a case of the state harming itself. After all, it might be argued, the state is composed of both government and citizens. On this view, intervention to protect the citizens from the government, even by request, would count as paternalistic intervention. This argument, however, presupposes a conception of the essential unity of the state similar to the view held by Hegel, according to which citizens lose their moral claims as individuals and simply disappear into the state—a view that is implausible at both the metaphysical and the moral levels.

This conception of the state contrasts with the more plausible view that states are mere constructions or artifacts that derive whatever moral status they have from their relation to the individuals of which they are composed. According to this latter view, if the state is to enjoy the rights of sovereignty, those rights must be granted to it by the people it represents.

This latter conception of the state underlies a further argument for nonintervention against the state that appeals directly to the value of human autonomy (rather than treating states as ends in themselves and basing the prohibition against intervention on respect for states per se, as the antipaternalist argument does). This argument begins with the claim that it is valuable for each distinct human community to be autonomous and self-determining (or, as some would prefer to say, that each human community has a right to autonomy or self-determination). Communities organized in the form of states are no exception. Indeed they are the paradigm case, for the citizens of a particular state normally share common interests and aims and are bound together by shared social, political, and cultural affinities and traditions. The more integrated and distinctive a community is, the more unjustifiable is any outside direction of its affairs by persons who neither fully share nor fully understand the values, aspirations, and traditions that bind the community together. Intervention against the state therefore may be presumed to involve an offense against the autonomy of the political community and to deprive the community, at least in certain respects, of its self-determining character. Correspondingly, the doctrine of state sovereignty, which implies a strong principle of nonintervention against the state, is justified on the ground that the inviolability of the state serves to protect the autonomy of the political community.[11]

This argument, which I shall refer to as the "communal autonomy argument," raises two groups of questions—the first about the meaning and value of self-determination and the second about the relation between communal autonomy and state sovereignty. What exactly is communal self-determination? Like intervention, the notion of self-determination has been defined variously. Perhaps the most common understanding is that a community is self-determining when it has established a state, so that a community's right to self-determination is simply its right to the establishment or maintenance of an independent state.[12] This is a perfectly acceptable use of the term, but it will not do for our purposes. Apart from the fact that groups too small to be eligible for statehood nevertheless can be said to be self-determining in the sense intended in the communal autonomy argument, the idea that self-determination involves statehood is incompatible with the argument's assumption that intervention can interfere with or undermine the self-determination of a political community without actually depriving the community of independent statehood. Czechoslovakia, for example, is an independent state, but it is subject to continual intervention that compromises its status as a self-determining entity in the sense intended by the communal autonomy argument.

Nor is it satisfactory, although some writers have thought that it is, to equate self-determination with self-government or democracy. Although it might be argued that self-government is a sufficient condition of self-determination, it is clearly not a necessary one. For the individuals of a community might be indifferent or even hostile to the idea of democratic self-government, while at the same time being evidently in command of their own collective destiny. This might be the case, for example, in the aftermath of a protracted and destructive popular revolution, when the people might want a powerful central authority (instead of political parties and elections) capable of acting immediately to restore order and economic stability, provide food and employment, organize relief work, and so on.

Communal self-determination has more to do with freedom from external coercion or domination than with the flourishing of democratic institutions, although, contrary to what some writers have claimed, a community cannot be said to be self-determining if its affairs are directed entirely by a domestic tyranny whose decisions take no account of the desires or interests of the larger community.[13] For a community to be self-determining, the people must be responsible at some level for the conduct and direction of their own collective affairs and the shaping of their collective future; there must be a sense in which decisions concerning the community's affairs are subject to the approval or, in some weak sense of the term, the consent of the community. That is vague, but it is perhaps as much as can be said; self-determination is not a precisely determinate phenomenon that must be recognizably present or absent. It is, rather, a matter of degree, and in some cases whether a community is self-determining may not be answerable in terms of a simple "yes" or "no." For this and other reasons, it is not always clear what respect for communal self-determination requires—a problem with important implications, to which I shall return.

Next we must ask why communal self-determination should be thought valuable. The short answer is simply that groups of people with a sense of collective identity actually do assign great value to the ability to act and function autonomously. Of course, although most moral theories (the most obvious example being preference utilitarianism) would allow that the fact that communal self-determination is valued provides a moral reason (although not a decisive one) for respecting it, it is nevertheless true that the mere fact that something is valued is not a sufficient condition of its being valuable. In the present case, however, there is more to be said than that self-determination is valued. For political (and other) communities rightly fear that surrendering control of important aspects of their collective lives to outsiders, even ones who are benevolently motivated, would mean that the community's affairs would then be determined by persons with less than complete understanding of and sympathy for the community's values, aims, and traditions and thus that the community's interests would be likely to suffer.

But the worry about the efficiency or impartiality of outsiders is not all that lies behind the resistance of communities to external control. Just as individuals are loath to relinquish control of major decisions in their lives even if they would fare better by so doing, so individuals in groups feel a fundamental need for the group itself to exercise control of its own destiny, even if the group might fare better by submitting to external direction. To some extent the desire for communal autonomy is an extension of the need of individuals to control their own lives. It can also be partially explained in terms of the fact that people desire that the conduct and development of their community should be an authentic expression of the community's identity and the values that inform it. But the deep-seated desire of persons, both individually and as members of communities, to control their own affairs is itself a fact of fundamental importance that must be reflected in our morality.

As noted earlier, the communal autonomy argument raises important questions about the relation between communal autonomy or self-determination and state sovereignty. We can introduce these questions by first noting that there is a problem of determining which groups or types of group are the ones whose self-determination international actors are required to respect. As it is normally stated, of course, the communal autonomy argument assumes that states encompass or constitute single political communities and thus that the boundaries around the relevant groups are already drawn and, figuratively speaking, coincide with the boundaries of states. But, as our earlier discussion of divided states shows, this assumption often is false. A state may be divided in various ways—some or all of the political communities within the state's boundaries may be unrepresented by the state and may fail to identify themselves with it. In cases in which the state is not representative of *any* major community, the state itself is an obstacle to communal self-determination. Hence intervention against the state may not be inimical to communal self-determination, but may on the contrary promote it. In cases in which there are two or more political communities, some but not all of which are represented by the state, it may be exceedingly unclear what respect for self-determination requires. For the efforts at self-determination by different communities may be incompatible and may bring the communities into conflict. Intervention against the state therefore may inhibit or be detrimental to the self-determination of the community or communities represented by the state, while promoting the self-determination of the rival community or communities. By the same token, nonintervention (or, alternatively, intervention on behalf of the state), may respect the self-determination of the community or communities represented by the state, but may be inimical to the self-determination of the community or communities that reject the state's authority.

Because there are cases—for example, of colonial rule, revolution, and secession—in which respect for state sovereignty does not necessarily coincide with respect for communal self-determination, the principle of nonintervention implied by the communal autonomy argument will be more limited in scope than that derived from the antipaternalist argument. To see just how strong a principle of nonintervention the argument is capable of yielding, we need to examine more closely the relation between state sovereignty and communal self-determination.

It is often claimed that the rights of state sovereignty, including the right of nonintervention, are a corollary of a state's *legitimacy*—that is, its right to rule and to be obeyed—and hence that only legitimate states have a right against intervention.[14] The ground for this assertion is normally that states can have rights only insofar as those rights are voluntarily transferred to them by the people. Hence the state can have the right to govern only if it is granted that right by the consent of the people. If the state is granted the right to govern, then it follows that the state also has a right of nonintervention. The state's right to govern implies a duty on the part of others not to interfere coercively with its exercise of that right. The right against intervention is thus a corollary of the state's domestic legitimacy.

This is a "rational reconstruction" of an argument that is not uncommon in the literature on intervention. If valid, this argument shows that the domestic legitimacy of a state is a sufficient condition for the state to have a right of nonintervention. This conclusion suggests further that domestic legitimacy is also a necessary condition of the right of nonintervention, for the right of nonintervention, as possessed by states, would seem to be nothing more than a corollary of the right to govern. If a state lacked domestic legitimacy—that is, if it had no right to govern—what reason could there be to protect the state (as distinct from the people) from external coercion?

The problem with this argument is that in terms of the criterion it proposes there are no legitimate states and hence no states that possess the rights of sovereignty. There are no states that enjoy the consent of their citizens, if consent is understood as the intentional and voluntary transfer of rights and the acceptance of corresponding obligations.[15] However, one can derive substantially the same conclusion (viz, that only legitimate states have a right of nonintervention) by first appealing to the communal autonomy claim that the right of nonintervention is justified in terms of the protection of communal self-determination and by then demonstrating that the same facts that would show a state is a vehicle for and an expression of communal self-determination also would show that the state is legitimate. Of course, our criteria of legitimacy must be weaker than those proposed by the consent theorist. Without going too deeply into the matter at this point, we can say that a state enjoys domestic legitimacy if, first, it is representative of (that is, works for and on behalf of) the political community or communities within its territorial boundaries and, second, if it operates with the general approval and acceptance of those communities.[16] Any state that is legitimate by these criteria also will be an instrument of communal self-determination, while any state that is illegitimate by these criteria will not. Thus, if the importance of positing a right of nonintervention is to protect communal self-determination, then the only states that will possess the right will be those that are instruments or expressions of communal self-determination—that is, those that are legitimate.

With this as background, I am now in a position to present a more exact restatement of the communal autonomy argument. As before, the argument begins with the claim that it is valuable for political communities to be autonomous and self-determining. Next, we note, not that states *do,* but that they *can* serve as vehicles or expressions of communal self-determination. States do so when they are representative, impartially working for and serving the interests of their citizens, and when they enjoy the citizens' acceptance and approval—in short, when they are legitimate. Since a legitimate state is thus one that in general promotes and expresses communal self-determination, intervention against it normally will be detrimental to the community's efforts at self-determination. Respect for communal self-determination therefore requires that there should be a strong presumption against the justifiability of intervention against states that enjoy domestic legitimacy.

As noted earlier, the conclusion of this version of the communal autonomy argument is considerably weaker and more limited than that of the antipaternalist argument. Although this version implies a presumption, based on respect for self-determination, against intervening in the affairs of legitimate states, it also implies that there is no such presumption (that is, one based on respect for self-determination) in the case of illegitimate states. Hence in order to apply the argument to actual cases, we must be able to distinguish in practice between legitimate and illegitimate states.

State Legitimacy

Roughly speaking, a state is legitimate if it is representative of and enjoys the approval of the mass of its citizens and if it correspondingly protects and promotes their communal self-determination. In practice, however, it may be difficult to determine when a state satisfies these criteria. Is there some simplified test for legitimacy—a shortcut to determining when a state protects and promotes the self-determination of the community or communities it encompasses and thus has a presumptive right of nonintervention?

Before addressing that question, let me be a bit more explicit about what I mean when I speak of a state as "illegitimate." Recall that I am using the term *state* in such a way that the state is identified closely with the government and the particular political and constitutional structures that give the government shape and determine its relations with the citizens. I distinguished this sense of the term from a broader sense in which the state is to a certain extent distinct even from particular institutional and constitutional structures. Thus, when I speak of a state being illegitimate, I do not mean to imply that the state in this broader sense is illegitimate, and in particular I do not mean to imply that there should be no state at all, or that the people have no right to independent statehood. Rather, I mean only that the particular governmental, institutional, and constitutional structures of the state (in the broader sense) are illegitimate and hence that the state in the narrower sense—that is, the government, its organs, and the constitution in terms of which it operates—lacks the domestic and international rights and privileges it claims for itself as a state.

Let us return now to the question of how legitimacy is to be determined. Various tests have been suggested. Michael Walzer, in his influential book *Just and Unjust Wars,* has proposed two. His first suggestion consists of the familiar claim that legitimacy depends on consent, although the type of "consent" he has in mind is "of a special sort." For Walzer, the "contract" through which consent is expressed "is a metaphor for a process of association and mutuality," of "shared experiences and cooperative activity of many different kinds," through which a community "shape[s] a common life."[17]

The problem with this suggestion, however, is that it describes certain relations among people but tells us nothing of their relation to the government; hence this suggestion does not describe anything that could reasonably by construed as consenting to the state.[18] If consent, even of a special sort, is what confers legitimacy on the state, then the relations among people that Walzer describes cannot be the basis of state legitimacy. Indeed, it is not difficult to imagine a country in which the people share the relations Walzer describes, but in which the state is clearly illegitimate. Nicaragua in the years preceding the overthrow of the Somoza dictatorship presumably was such a country.

Walzer's second proposal is that a state can be seen to enjoy popular support, and hence be legitimate, if it passes what he calls the test of "self-help." "A legitimate government is one that can fight its own internal wars."[19] (Governmental legitimacy is not always a sufficient condition of state legitimacy, but we may ignore the exceptions here.)

The capacity for self-help is, however, an extremely fallible and unreliable indicator of popular support. At best self-help provides a reliable indication of a state's military strength, which, for obvious reasons, is not necessarily correlated with popular support. For a government can build up a formidable military machine without the support or approval of the mass of its citizens. It can do so through the assistance of foreign governments. The fact that the government's military strength would not be of its own creation would not compromise its status as a government capable of *self*-help. If the capacity for self-help meant the capacity to maintain power against opponents without external assistance, where external assistance includes weapons and training acquired at some time or other without payment or on specially favorable terms from external sources, then there would be very few governments capable of self-help. (In cases in which arms sales and military assistance constitute a form of intervention—that is, when they are intended to enable a government to defeat its internal opponents—then they compromise the recipient's status as a government capable of self-help. But military sales and assistance are not always interventionary. More often they are used as bribes, payments, or simply as a means of cultivating influence.)

Walzer rejects this objection. He contends that "armies and police forces are social institutions; soldiers and policemen came from families, villages, neighborhoods, classes. They will not fight cohesively, with discipline, or at length unless the regime for which they are fighting has some degree of social support." Hence, he concludes, even if its military hardware has come from external sources, a government that passes the self-help test will be shown thereby to enjoy popular support.[20]

This reply is inadequate. States that lack legitimacy often are characterized by the fact that the government, the military, and the police are controlled by a wealthy elite, whose interests they serve, while the mass of the population lives in terrible poverty. In these conditions, when people are desperate for employment and the military can offer stable jobs with comfortable wages, it is not difficult for the oligarchs to put together a viable "security" apparatus. This is the case, for example, in El Salvador today, where the rank and file of the army consist primarily of illiterate and demoralized teenage peasants who have joined the army in order to escape starvation.

Hiring some of the victims of state oppression to fight the others is only one way in which illegitimate governments can maintain themselves in power without external assistance. Some are able to survive even without the direct assistance of their victims. Consider the case of South Africa. There the white minority is sufficiently large, disciplined, and cohesive, as well as sufficiently wealthy and technologically advanced, to be able to maintain its patently illegitimate rule over the black majority without substantial external support of any kind. South Africa, indeed, is a clear case of an illegitimate state whose government is perfectly capable of fighting its own internal wars.

In spite of these problems, the self-help test is not irrelevant to the question of a state's legitimacy. Given the enormous advantages that states by their very nature have over their internal opponents (such as the ability to raise taxes to pay for arms, the ability to expand their armies by conscription, and so on), it would be surprising if there were a state that enjoyed popular support, and hence was legitimate, which nevertheless required outside intervention in order to avoid defeat at the hands of its domestic opponents. In short, failure to meet the self-help test is a fairly reliable indicator of a state's illegitimacy. But it does not follow that the ability to pass the self-help test is an indication of legitimacy.

The failure of Walzer's two proposals suggests that the search for a simplified test for legitimacy is vain. Whether a state is legitimate depends on whether it is representative, whether it commands popular support, and whether it protects and promotes the self-determination of the people it claims to represent. Whether and to what extent a state satisfies these criteria is something that it may not always be possible to determine. There are clear cases of states that do enjoy popular support and that are clearly legitimate (contemporary Sweden), and clear cases of states that do not have popular support and that are clearly illegitimate (Nicaragua under Somoza); but there also are cases of states that are sufficiently divided that it cannot be said that they enjoy popular support or that they lack it. If popular support is the criterion of legitimacy, then the question whether the states in this category are legitimate may not have a "yes" or "no" answer. We will consider the implications of these facts for the question of intervention nearer the end of the chapter. First we must complete our review of the arguments against intervention.

The Arguments of Mill and Walzer

The next two arguments we shall consider are intended to show that even in the case of divided states a strong principle of nonintervention can be supported by appealing to the value of self-determination. In effect, these arguments attempt to buttress the communal autonomy argument in cases in which that argument appears to fail.

The first of these arguments was put forward by John Stuart Mill and has been developed and defended more recently by Michael Walzer.[21] According to this argument, the requirement of respect for self-determination rules out intervention against the state even if the state is illegitimate and even if the aim of the intervention would be to promote the self-determination of the state's internal opponents. Mill supports this paradoxical claim by arguing that "it is during an arduous struggle to become free by their own efforts" that people have the best chance of becoming genuinely free and self-determining: "The liberty which is bestowed on them by other hands than their own will have nothing real, nothing permanent."[22] Because intervention, even on behalf of those struggling against an illegitimate state, thus denies people the opportunity to exercise and develop their own capacities, it ultimately is inimical to the development and flourishing of self-determination.

There is certainly something to this argument, but, as Walzer's critics have suggested, it may set the value of self-determination too high relative to other values.[23] The benefit that people might be deprived of by intervention—namely, the benefit of developing a more robust capacity for self-determination—must be weighed against the harms they might be spared by intervention. For example, intervention could make the difference between a quick and relatively bloodless campaign against an illegitimate state authority and a protracted struggle involving an enormous number of casualties not only among the combatants on both sides, but also among the civilian population. It is far from obvious that the loss of these lives is an acceptable price to pay for the enhanced capacity for self-determination that the survivors would enjoy.

It is the internal opponents of the illegitimate state whose capacity for self-determination supposedly would be impaired by the receipt of external assistance in their struggle. They would suffer more at the hands of the state in the absence of intervention. Why should *they* not be allowed to choose whether to accept or reject external assistance? To refuse them this choice is to fail to respect their autonomy. It is indeed an objectionable form of paternalism to refuse people assistance, not on the ground that helping them would itself be paternalistic but on the ground that facing adversity by themselves will be good for them. This insistence on what Walzer calls a "stern doctrine of self-help" is seldom the right position to take toward individuals who are in trouble; it is even less likely to be appropriate when a nation-state comes under *external* attack.[24] And few (not even Walzer) seem to think it an appropriate position to adopt toward governments facing domestic rebellion. If the reason for denying external assistance to the domestic opponents of a doubtfully legitimate or even obviously illegitimate state is that to do so might impair their capacity for self-determination, then the same reasoning should apply in the three other types of case just cited. The fact that this reasoning is seldom decisive in these other types of case suggests that it cannot be very powerful in the present case either.

The second argument designed to buttress the communal autonomy argument also has been put forward by Walzer. Walzer distinguishes between the domestic and the international legitimacy of a state and claims that at the international level a state is always presumptively legitimate. The reason for drawing this distinction is essentially epistemological. According to Walzer, people are always sufficiently distanced from a state not their own that they cannot know all that they would need to know in order to make a reliable assessment of its legitimacy.

> They don't know enough about its history, and they have no direct experience, and can form no concrete judgments, of the conflicts and harmonies, the historical choices and cultural affinities, the loyalties and resentments that underlie it. Hence their conduct, in the first instance at least, cannot be determined by either knowledge or judgment. It is, or it ought to be, determined instead by a morally necessary presumption: that there exists a certain "fit" between the community and its government and that the state is "legitimate."[25]

Like Mill's argument, this argument overstates a valid point. Insofar as Walzer's point can be interpreted as a counsel of caution based on the recognition of the fallibility of an external observer's judgment, then it is valid. Some presumption against intervention remains even in the case of doubtfully legitimate states or of states that seem to outsiders to be clearly illegitimate. (Given that even those immersed in the culture and traditions of a particular state may be unable to determine whether or not the state is legitimate, a similar counsel of caution could be usefully addressed to domestic insurgents as well.) But Walzer intends for the argument to establish more than this. He sees it as a decisive objection to all but a very limited number of types of intervention. However, the argument cannot establish that much. At best it shows that all states enjoy a presumptive legitimacy at the international level, but presumptive legitimacy does not translate automatically into a virtually nonoverridable right of nonintervention. Even a state that is clearly legitimate may overstep its mandate, in which case it may be permissible to bring some pressure to bear on the state in order to coerce it into honoring its obligations.[26] Consider, for example, a case in which a government that enjoys broad popular support nevertheless persistently persecutes a particular minority group. Here the imperative to defend this minority might override the moral reason foreigners would have to respect the autonomy of the larger community. Here, moreover, there would be no epistemological problems. Even if they lacked familiarity with the history, traditions, and culture of the society, foreigners would be unlikely to be so misled by the society's alien character as to misinterpret as the systematic violation of a minority's internationally recognized human rights what was in reality some innocent and domestically acceptable practice.

Walzer's claims about the fallibility of external judgments are quite exaggerated. What reason is there for supposing that foreigners are necessarily lacking in historical knowledge or knowledge about what is occurring within another country? There are many cases in which external observers can know *more* about what is happening within a country than its inhabitants, if the government is particularly efficient at controlling the information that reaches its citizens. There are other cases in which the illegitimacy of a state must be obvious to anyone; even foreigners are entitled to conclude that the near universal revolt of a population against its government and state institutions (as occurred in Nicaragua in 1979) is unlikely to be an alien society's unusual way of expressing consent.

The Stability Arguments

The final two arguments against intervention that I shall consider apply, like the earlier ones, primarily to intervention against states (as opposed to intervention on behalf of states) and, unlike the earlier arguments, apply almost exclusively to *military* intervention. Both arguments, which I shall refer to as the first and second stability arguments, have been summarized succinctly by Stanley Hoffman, who writes that even "a state based on morally wrong foundations nevertheless has not only legal rights but moral rights because . . . if its legal rights are not upheld, international society will collapse into a state of war or universal tyranny."[27] The first stability argument maintains that intervention in general is wrong because of its tendency to lead to counterintervention, escalation, and wider war. The second maintains that intervention is wrong because it threatens the stability of the system of world order based on the existence of a plurality of sovereign states (and hence threatens to lead to "universal tyranny").

Let us consider the first argument. It usually is articulated by saying that because a permissive principle of nonintervention would be a threat to peace and stability, a highly restricted principle must be adopted instead. This claim can be interpreted in either of two ways. According to one interpretation, the problem is that a permissive principle is more open to abuse or more likely to be exploited as a cover for intervention motivated entirely by considerations of self-interest. There are two replies to this claim, so interpreted. First, the fact that a principle is likely to be abused, and thus is likely to have bad consequences, is not an objection to the principle's *validity,* but only to its *adoption.* It is perfectly possible that the morally correct principle of nonintervention is one that, for consequentialist reasons, we ought not in practice to espouse and adopt. Here, however, our concern is to discover the correct principle or principles and not (if there is a divergence) the principle or principles it would be expedient to adopt.

Second, states are unlikely to be influenced significantly by adoption of one principle of nonintervention rather than another. It is implausible to suppose that adoption of a permissive principle of intervention would tempt states to intervene when otherwise they would not or that if they were tempted to intervene by reasons of self-interest, they might be deterred by the general adoption of a more restrictive principle. In short, this interpretation of the argument overestimates the extent to which states are influenced by considerations of principle.

The second interpretation is that any but the most restrictive principle of nonintervention will sanction interventions that carry too high a risk of escalation and war. However, there is no reason why this should be thought true. The principle can be suitably qualified to take account of the risk of escalation and yet remain permissive in cases in which this risk is minimal or in which it seems to be outweighed by other considerations. The suggested alternative—viz, a highly and indiscriminately restrictive principle of nonintervention—would serve to sanction the violence of the status quo, which in many cases might be greater than the probable violence resulting from intervention.

Let us now turn to the second stability argument, according to which the practice of intervention threatens the stability of the world order based on the existence of separate and sovereign states and, by doing so, calls "into question the dominant values of [international] society: the survival and independence of the separate political communities."[28] As this quotation from Walzer suggests, the breakdown of the system of sovereign states is to be feared primarily because it would mean the end of political pluralism: "There will be no place left for political refuge and no examples left of political alternatives."[29]

It is not clear, however, why it should be thought that the practice of intervention will have these consequences. States have intervened regularly in one another's affairs since the doctrine of state sovereignty was first enunciated, yet the system of sovereign states has yet to show any signs of strain. Moreover, even if the practice of intervention were to threaten the system of sovereign states, the breakdown of that system would not necessarily lead to "universal tyranny" and the stifling of pluralism. The breakdown of the system instead could occur through a process whereby states would surrender sovereignty to a world government. Just as the surrender of sovereignty by individuals to states need not involve the elimination of individuality or the variety of human types within political communities, so the surrender of sovereignty by states to an international authority should be compatible with the maintenance by distinct human communities of political independence and cultural diversity.

Were it to occur in this way, the breakdown of the system of sovereign states in fact would be highly desirable. The doctrine of state sovereignty serves to sanction and reinforce notions of nationalism, state chauvinism, and the priority of the national interest, all of which, in an era in which states jealously guard their sovereign prerogatives by threatening "aggressors" with nuclear annihilation, are not only barbarous but profoundly dangerous. If the acceptance of a more permissive principle of nonintervention, by challenging the doctrine of state sovereignty, would facilitate the erosion of support for that doctrine and for the cult of state worship, then there would be an important consequentialist reason for adopting such a principle.

Outlines of a General Theory of Intervention

That completes my review of the major arguments against intervention. I shall now conclude by briefly sketching a proposed account of the ethics of intervention that draws on the results of the previous survey of the arguments.

This account begins by acknowledging the relevance of the question of state legitimacy, where legitimacy indicates that the state is both an instrument and an expression of the self-determination of the community or communities the state encompasses. Thus the legitimacy of a state entails a presumption against outside intervention against it. This presumption is grounded in a requirement of respect for communal self-determination. In some cases the presumption is decisive. In general this will be the case where intervention would challenge or destroy those features of the state that contribute to its legitimacy. But, like all presumptions, this one can be overridden, and there are cases in which intervention against a legitimate state might be permissible. One such case might be that of a state that enjoyed popular support but whose foreign policy was extremely aggressive and threatening to other states. We have considered already another such case—namely, that in which a state that enjoys broad popular support nevertheless persistently persecutes some minority group. Even here, of course, whether or not intervention on behalf of the persecuted minority could be justified will depend in part on the mode of intervention. In general, intervention can be justified only at the lowest effective level—for example, using military means where economic pressures would suffice is nearly always wrong, for military intervention normally has broader coercive effects, has greater costs for both sides, is more likely to seduce the intervening agent to exploit its advantage over the target state for self-interested ends, and carries a greater risk of counterintervention, escalation, and wider war. (This is not to deny that in some instances economic pressures may result in greater harm to the citizens of the target state than military intervention would and hence would be a less defensible mode of intervention, other things being equal.)

As noted earlier, all the arguments against intervention that we have considered are either primarily or exclusively concerned with intervention against states. Most writers seem to take it for granted that intervention on behalf of states in general is morally permissible. But it actually may be the case that intervention on behalf of the state is in general less likely to be justified than intervention against the state. The reason for this stems from a point made earlier—although not all states that pass the self-help test are legitimate, those that are legitimate generally can pass the test. Thus if a state *requires* intervention on its behalf in order to defeat its domestic opponents, and there has been no significant intervention on the other side, then the state requiring intervention to ensure its survival is unlikely to be legitimate. In short, cases in which intervention is needed by a legitimate state will be extremely rare, and cases in which intervention on behalf of an illegitimate state can be justified will be rarer still.

In the case of an illegitimate state, there is no presumption, based on respect for state autonomy, against intervention against the state, except perhaps a weak presumption based on doubts about the veracity of external perceptions of the state's legitimacy. However, there still may be a reason to refrain from intervening based on respect for the self-determination of the people, either because they may not welcome external interference (and indeed might resist it) or, less plausibly, because of the considerations advanced by Mill. Another consideration that would militate against intervention even against an illegitimate state is that the potential costs of certain forms of intervention might outweigh the potential benefits—for example, if there were a significant probability of escalation or a significant probability that the intervention would be ineffective or even counterproductive.

On the other hand, where these countervailing reasons are absent, or only very weak, intervention may be justified. If the moral reasons favoring intervention are very strong, then intervention may even by morally *required*. (This suggestion of course raises questions about how much external agents may be required to do or how much they may be required to sacrifice. This is an important question, but I must pass over it here.) Cases in which there may be a requirement of intervention include instances of attempted secession, cases of requested intervention on behalf of a population struggling to free itself from colonial rule, cases of requested intervention on behalf of revolutionaries or insurgents fighting against an illegitimate government that is unjust and oppressive, and cases in which intervention seems the only effective way to stop the persecution or repression of a group or community by their government. In cases where, because intervention is not desired by the intended beneficiaries, or would be too costly, it is *not* justifiable to intervene on behalf of the opponents of an illegitimate state, it also would be unjustifiable to intervene on behalf of the state against its opponents.

Indeed, in these circumstances, intervention on behalf of the state would be wrong even if it were in response to previous and unjustified intervention on behalf of the state's opponents. This may seem paradoxical, for *unjustified* intervention on one side is normally thought to make counterintervention on the other side permissible. There are two reasons for this, each connected with the ground for thinking the initial intervention unjustified. One is that the initial intervention may give the advantage to one side in the conflict that does not deserve assistance. The counterintervention then is justified because it deprives the undeserving side of its advantage. In the case we are considering, however, it is not true that the initial intervention is unjustified because it gives the advantage to the undeserving side. On the contrary, the opponents of the state may merit assistance. The reason assistance would be unjustified is that it would be unwelcome or that its costs would outweigh its benefits. Another reason counterintervention might be thought justified is that it would serve to restore the initial balance, so that the outcome of the conflict would reflect and be determined by the *internal* balance of forces. However, this assumes that the balance of forces within a country reflects the popular strengths of the contenders. And as we saw earlier, this often is false. In the case we are considering, the state is by hypothesis illegitimate and hence is known to lack popular support (even if it has considerable force at its disposal), so that an outcome determined solely by the internal balance of forces might be undesirable.

Michael Walzer, again following Mill, argues that counterintervention is always just.[30] But it is hard to see how this could be so, unless *all* initial interventions are wrong. For if, as Walzer concedes, some initial interventions are justified, this would seem to suggest that it is desirable in these cases if the initial balance of forces is shifted. How, then, could it be right to shift the balance back to its original, undesirable position? Walzer replies that the rule of counterintervention must be neutral; for, as with the rules of war, if these rules were not neutral, "there could be no rules at all but only permissions addressed to the Forces of Good entitling them to do whatever is necessary (though only what is *necessary*) to overcome their enemies."[31] But this reply seems beside the point, for to deny that counterintervention is always just is not to increase anyone's license to act, but is instead to impose further *restrictions* on what may be done.

Having now considered the ethics of intervention where legitimate and illegitimate states are concerned, I turn, finally, to the case of states whose status as legitimate or illegitimate cannot be decisively determined. In these cases, the state will be divided, and the society may be torn. One must attempt to respect the wishes and the self-determination of the people, but where the people are divided, both their wishes and their efforts at self-determination will be in conflict. Thus there is no formula for dealing with these cases, nor is a neutral approach acceptable. We must consult our own values. Would intervention advance the cause of social justice in the target country? Would it increase or decrease the overall level of violence? These and many other questions must be answered before the question of intervention can be settled.

Cases of divided states are therefore the most difficult. They also may be the most common cases in which the question of intervention arises. Although there may be cases of this sort in which it is fairly obvious that some form of intervention would be right, in general it will be best to treat these cases conservatively and with caution. This is so for a number of reasons, many of which derive from arguments that I have criticized but that nevertheless retain a measure of validity. For example, external assessments of the legitimacy of potential target states, as Walzer notes, are not infallible and are prone to bias and distortion. Moreover, states always are inclined to exploit any occasion for intervention in order to serve their own ends, even if their initial motivation is not self-interested. Hence there is a general presumption that even if intervention perhaps *could* advance the self-determination of people in the target state, it probably would not do so and would more likely be inimical to self-determination. Finally, there is always a chance of escalation and wider war, and the risks war involves are steadily increasing. So even in cases in which the legitimacy of a potential target state is uncertain, there still will be a strong presumption against intervention.

Because it will have to take account of the distinction between legitimate and illegitimate states, as well as the many other relevant considerations discussed earlier, the correct principle of intervention will be a principle of considerable complexity, hedged about by numerous qualifications. As noted earlier, however, the correct moral principle is not always the one that ought to be adopted for declaratory purposes. In the present case, the correct principle of intervention will be too complex to have any chance of actually being accepted and respected as a standard of international conduct. Despite my earlier expressions of skepticism about the role of moral principles in guiding the conduct of states, principles are not entirely without influence, and it therefore is important that we should have a principle closely approximating the correct principle of intervention and that is sufficiently simple to be held up as a standard to guide states. Because in the world as it is the dangers of intervention are generally greater than the dangers of nonintervention, this latter principle presumably will be more restrictive than the position for which I have argued.

The position I have defended has definite implications for the cases of El Salvador and Nicaragua to which I referred at the beginning of the chapter. What is most clear is that the U.S. interventions in those countries cannot conceivably be justified. In both countries the forces the United States is backing represent the interests and concerns of tiny elites who have sought to maintain their privileged positions at the expense of the mass of people by means of the most bestial and vicious forms of repression. In El Salvador the United States has maintained in power a very doubtfully legitimate state that has ruled by terror and intimidation.[32] Insofar as Nicaragua has intervened by supplying arms to the domestic opponents of that state, it has been engaged in a morally defensible form of counterintervention. In Nicaragua the United States has been sponsoring the despised remnants of the illegitimate Somoza regime in their attempts to bring down the Sandinista government. The evidence, which I have reviewed elsewhere,[33] suggests that the present Nicaraguan state is legitimate. The minimal forms of assistance Cuba and the Soviet Union have provided to help the present regime defend itself against U.S.-sponsored aggression, when viewed dispassionately, are difficult to criticize. In both El Salvador and Nicaragua, the U.S. interventions have been inimical to social justice, have increased the flow of blood, and have violated the will of the people.

Notes

An earlier version of this chapter has been published in *Ethics and International Relations,* ed. Anthony Ellis (Manchester: Manchester University Press, 1986). Reprinted by kind permission of the Manchester University Press, the Fulbright Commission, and Anthony Ellis. This earlier version was read at the 1984 Fulbright Anglo-American Colloquium on Ethics and International Affairs at the University of St. Andrews, Scotland, and at a meeting of the Moral Sciences Club at Cambridge University. In preparing the present version I have benefited from the discussion on both of these occasions. I also have profited from discussions with Noam Chomsky and Raymond Geuss and from comments by Virginia Held on the earlier version.

1. See Charles R. Beitz, *Political Theory and International Relations* (Princeton, N.J.: Princeton University Press, 1979), p. 74.

2. See, for example, Percy H. Winfield, "Intervention," *Encyclopedia of the Social Sciences,* vol. 8 (New York: Macmillan, 1932), p. 236; and R. J. Vincent, *Nonintervention and International Order* (Princeton, N.J.: Princeton University Press, 1974), p. 8.

3. See, for example, Winfield, "Intervention," p. 236; Hersch Lauterpacht, *International Law and Human Rights* (London: Steven, 1950), p. 167; Ann Van Wynen Thomas and A. J. Thomas, Jr., *Non-Intervention: The Law and Its Impact in the Americas* (Dallas: Southern Methodist University Press, 1956), pp. 67–69, 72; and Mark R. Wicclair, "Human Rights and Intervention," in *Human Rights and Foreign Policy,* ed. Peter G. Brown and Douglas MacLean (Lexington, Mass.: Lexington Books, 1979), pp. 142–144.

4. James N. Rosenau, "Intervention as a Scientific Concept," *Journal of Conflict Resolution* 13 (1969):161.

5. See Beitz, *Political Theory,* p. 72. This restriction contends that the target of intervention must be a state.

6. Quoted in Thomas Buergenthal, "Domestic Jurisdiction, Intervention, and Human Rights: The International Law Perspective," in Brown and MacLean, *Human Rights,* pp. 112–113.

7. See Richard J. Barnet, *Intervention and Revolution: The United States in the Third World* (New York: New American Library, 1972), p. 67; and Michael

Walzer, *Just and Unjust Wars: A Moral Argument with Historical Illustrations* (Harmondsworth: Penguin, 1977), p. 96.

8. This is not to suggest that those who believe that the principle enunciated by the United Nations is the appropriate principle for international law also must believe that it is the correct *moral* position on the question of intervention. One could believe consistently that although some other principle is the correct moral principle, the adoption of that principle as an international legal norm would have worse consequences, perhaps even in the principle's own terms, than the adoption of the U.N. principle. Nevertheless there are a great many people who do believe that the U.N. principle *is* the correct moral principle.

9. Versions of the antipaternalist argument have been put forward by S. I. Benn and R. S. Peters, *Social Principles and the Democratic State* (London: Allen and Unwin, 1959), pp. 361–363; Vincent, *Nonintervention,* p. 345; Walzer, *Just and Unjust Wars,* pp. 58, 89; and Gerard Elfstrom, "On Dilemmas of Intervention," *Ethics* 93 (1983):712 ff. The argument has been criticized by Beitz, *Political Theory,* pp. 75–81; Wicclair, "Human Rights and Intervention," pp. 145–146; and Alan H. Goldman, "The Moral Significance of National Boundaries," in *Midwest Studies in Philosophy VII: Social and Political Philosophy,* ed. Peter A. French et al. (Minneapolis: University of Minnesota Press, 1982), p. 438 ff.

10. Here and elsewhere in this chapter the words "he" and "his," where not used to refer to specific individuals, should be understood to mean "he or she" and "his or her." 234/99

11. Variants of this argument are presented and discussed by Benn and Peters, *Social Principles,* pp. 361–363; Walzer, *Just and Unjust Wars,* pp. 87–90; Beitz, *Political Theory,* pp. 77–91; Wicclair, "Human Rights and Intervention," pp. 146–147; and Goldman, "Moral Significance," p. 438 ff.

12. The term is used in this way by, for example, Beitz, *Political Theory,* pp. 92–93; and by Stanley French and Andres Gutman, "The Principle of National Self-determination," in *Philosophy, Morality, and International Relations,* ed. Virginia Held, Sidney Morgenbesser, and Thomas Nagel (New York: Oxford University Press, 1974), p. 138.

13. That self-determination is compatible with domestic tyranny is defended by Walzer, *Just and Unjust Wars,* p. 87. Walzer here follows John Stuart Mill, "A Few Words on Non-Intervention," in *Dissertations and Discussions: Political, Philosophical, and Historical,* vol. 3 (London, 1875), pp. 153–178.

14. See David Luban, "Just War and Human Rights," *Philosophy and Public Affairs* 9, no. 2 (Winter 1980): 160–181; and compare Gerald Doppelt, "Walzer's Theory of Morality in International Relations," *Philosophy and Public Affairs* 8, no. 1 (Fall 1978): 3–26. As both Doppelt and Luban point out, to deny that the *state* has a right against intervention is not to deny that the *people* might.

15. On the consent theory of political obligation and state legitimacy, see A. John Simmons, *Moral Principles and Political Obligations* (Princeton, N.J.: Princeton University Press, 1979), Chaps. 3 and 4.

16. When this chapter was presented to Cambridge University's Moral Sciences Club, Edward Craig suggested to me that a state's legitimacy may depend not only on the level of popular support it enjoys but also on how its popular

support arises. In support of this suggestion, Craig cited a hypothetical case in which a state achieves popular support by simply expelling dissenters. Another case that supports Craig's contention is a state that achieves and maintains popular support through the devious but skillful manipulation and indoctrination of its citizens. These deviant modes of achieving popular support within a state's territorial boundaries pose quite a general problem for anyone who thinks that popular support, consent, the will of the people, or other related notions are relevant to the determination of a state's or a government's legitimacy.

17. Walzer, *Just and Unjust Wars*, p. 54.

18. Compare Luban, "Just War and Human Rights," p. 169.

19. Walzer, *Just and Unjust Wars*, pp. 98, 101.

20. Michael Walzer, "The Moral Standing of States: A Response to Four Critics," *Philosophy and Public Affairs* 9, no. 3 (Spring 1980):221.

21. Mill; and Walzer, *Just and Unjust Wars*, pp. 87–88.

22. Mill, pp. 258–260.

23. See David Luban, "The Romance of the Nation-State," *Philosophy and Public Affairs* 9, no. 4 (Summer 1980):396; and Gerald Doppelt, "Statism Without Foundations," *Philosophy and Public Affairs* 9, no. 4 (Summer 1980): 402–403.

24. Compare Stanley Hoffman, *Duties Beyond Borders: On the Limits and Possibilities of Ethical International Politics* (Syracuse, N.Y.: Syracuse University Press, 1981), p. 66.

25. Walzer, "The Moral Standing of States," p. 212.

26. In fairness to Walzer it should be mentioned that he generally tends to conceive of intervention in terms of *military* intervention, and it may seem that his point becomes more persuasive when the term is restricted in this way. I am inclined to think, however, that it does not. His argument against intervention is based on a claim about the importance of self-determination and as such should apply equally to all forms of intervention because all forms of intervention interfere with self-determination. Hence we might agree with Walzer that military intervention can be justified only in the limited range of cases he describes (namely, in support of an attempted secession, in response to a previous intervention, or to prevent the wholesale massacre or enslavement of a people), but our reason for restricting permissible military interventions in this way would focus on the undesirability of resorting to military force rather than on the undesirability of intervention per se.

27. Hoffman, *Duties Beyond Borders*, p. 58. It is a mistake to derive a *right* against intervention from considerations of international stability. To attribute a right against intervention to an illegitimate state is to imply that intervention would be wrong because of the *wrong* it would do to the *state*, whereas the clear thrust of the stability arguments is to condemn intervention because of the *consequences* it would have for *people* everywhere.

28. Walzer, *Just and Unjust Wars*, p. 61.

29. Walzer, "The Moral Standing of States," p. 228.

30. Walzer, *Just and Unjust Wars*, pp. 96–101.

31. Walzer, "The Moral Standing of States," p. 217.

32. The U.S. intervention in El Salvador and the character of the regimes the United States has supported are discussed at length in my *Reagan and the World: Imperial Policy in the New Cold War* (New York: Monthly Review Press, 1985), Chap. 5.

33. Ibid., Chap. 6.

Selected Bibliography

Beitz, Charles R. "Nonintervention and Communal Integrity." *Philosophy and Public Affairs* 9, no. 4 (Summer 1980):385–391.

————. *Political Theory and International Relations.* Princeton, N.J.: Princeton University Press, 1979.

Bull, Hedley, ed. *Intervention in World Politics.* Oxford: Oxford University Press, 1984.

Doppelt, Gerald. "Statism Without Foundations." *Philosophy and Public Affairs* 9, no. 4 (Summer 1980):398–403.

————. "Walzer's Theory of Morality in International Relations." *Philosophy and Public Affairs* 8, no. 1 (Fall 1978):3–26.

Goldman, Alan H. "The Moral Significance of National Boundaries." *Midwest Studies in Philosophy,* vol. 7. Ed. Peter A. French, Theodore E. Uehling, Jr., and Howard K. Wettstein. Minneapolis: University of Minnesota Press, 1982, pp. 437–453.

Hoffman, Stanley. *Duties Beyond Borders: On the Limits and Possibilities of Ethical International Politics.* Syracuse, N.Y.: Syracuse University Press, 1981.

Luban, David. "Just War and Human Rights." *Philosophy and Public Affairs* 9, no. 2 (Winter 1980):160–181.

————. "The Romance of the Nation-State." *Philosophy and Public Affairs* 9, no. 4 (Summer 1980):392–397.

Walzer, Michael. *Just and Unjust Wars: A Moral Argument with Historical Illustrations.* Harmondsworth: Penguin, 1977.

————. "The Moral Standing of States: A Response to Four Critics." *Philosophy and Public Affairs* 9, no. 3 (Spring 1980):209–229.

Wicclair, Mark R. "Human Rights and Intervention." *Human Rights and U.S. Foreign Policy.* Ed. Peter G. Brown and Douglas MacLean. Lexington, Mass.: Lexington Books, 1979, pp. 141–157.

Williams, William Appleman et al. "Special Issue: Intervention." *The Nation* 228, no. 22 (June 9, 1979).

PART TWO

The Ethics of
Nuclear Deterrence

Introduction to Part Two

Kenneth Kipnis

Controversy about nuclear weaponry is as old as the atomic bomb itself. Since Hiroshima and Nagasaki we have been troubled by the new and awesome responsibilities assumed in possessing the means to obliterate humanity. Perhaps no other technological advance has so altered the politics of our world, changing, as this one has, the essential character of superpower conflict. War—the venerable practice of nation-states—never before has posed such risk. Since the 1950s, it has been generally agreed that a full-scale nuclear war cannot be won. The most widely advanced justification for the stockpiling of such weapons has been that they serve to deter the other side from using them. Nations possess them so that they will not be used.

It is helpful to tease apart at least four ethical issues that are intertwined with deterrence. In the first place, there is the question of whether it is justifiable to possess nuclear weaponry. Those who urge total nuclear disarmament often hold that it is not.

In the second place, assuming the possession of some nuclear weaponry to be legitimate, there are questions of type, amount, and deployment. What size warheads can nations possess? Where may they be kept? How should one balance accuracy and survivability? Should warheads be aimed at military targets, at control centers, or at cities comparable to ones that might be lost?

In the third place, assuming it is legitimate to possess the nuclear weapons at hand, there still are questions about the content of public statements concerning when these would be used. Although it is logically possible to possess weapons without considering this, national policies also can be formulated and announced. What should the publicly stated policies be? It is within this context that problems arise concerning specific threats to use nuclear weapons.

In the fourth place, there is the question of the actual conditions under which nuclear weapons can justifiably be used, apart from any announced policy. Because it is possible to bluff—for example, by publicly expressing an intention to use nuclear weapons under certain conditions while at the same time firmly intending not to use them under those same conditions—the answer to question three is not necessarily the same as the answer to question four. Given that it may be legitimate to lie about intentions concerning the use of weaponry, publicly expressed policies therefore may be quite different from actual policies. We may believe, as some do, that although the use of such weaponry is impermissible, it may be legitimate falsely to threaten their use.

The chapters in Part 2 all are centrally concerned with this constellation of questions. In "The Ethic of Nuclear Deterrence," Philip Bobbitt despairs that the traditional utilitarian and deontological approaches to ethical issues can resolve questions about the legitimacy of U.S. nuclear policy. Part of the problem involves the institutional constraints upon those who occupy decisionmaking roles; these actors are bound to further the national interest rather than what is good for humanity in general. Although there may be a place for "common-room moralizing"—applying universal principles to the behavior of nations—Bobbitt urges that it is more productive to look at the specific context within which deterrence is supposed to protect national values and then to consider whether deterrence actually would work and whether nuclear weaponry is an essential element of it. It is clear to Bobbitt that the state has a right to defend its territories and ecological security. There appear to be plausible scenarios within which attacks might occur but for the presence of a nuclear deterrent. Because it is legitimate for nations to provide for their self-defense and because, in the light of Bobbitt's scenarios, situations can exist in which a nuclear deterrent would be necessary for national self-defense, it follows that the possession of a nuclear deterrent is legitimate. In concluding, Bobbitt suggests that philosophical analyses that reject nuclear deterrence, if implemented, would make nuclear war more likely.

James Sterba's contribution, "Between MAD and Counterforce," follows Bobbitt's in accepting that there are "some circumstances in which a limited use of nuclear weapons would be morally justified." But Sterba's main concern is with the third question, the morality of the threat to use nuclear weapons as opposed to some actual decision to use them. As with a shotgun mounted in plain sight over a fireplace, so a survivable nuclear force can achieve a measure of deterrence if it is understood that the national interest supports the threat to retaliate and use such weapons if necessary and proper. Note that although Sterba supports "the moral legitimacy of threatening or bluffing nuclear retaliation under certain conditions," he is very specific that nations may not threaten such retaliation unless those conditions obtain. The weaponry and policy surely will provide some foreseeable deterrence value, but they also serve as insurance in the event that circumstances someday arise in which it is legitimate to threaten or bluff nuclear retaliation. Sterba concludes by sketching three moral constraints on nuclear defense policy: that only a limited nuclear retaliation can foreseeably be justified, that neither bluffs nor threats are permissible under present circumstances, and that bluffs and threats are only permissible to avoid a first strike.

Steven Lee, in "How to Achieve Deterrence," takes issue with Sterba's claim that nuclear deterrence can be achieved without threats. Distinguishing between making and posing threats, Lee notes that implicit threats surely can be posed in the absence of an expressed statement of policy. If part of the U.S. purpose in maintaining a nuclear force is to deter the Soviet Union, then the United States intends to pose a threat to the Soviets whether or not it says that is what it is doing. Policies may be read accurately from the practices of possession. Moreover U.S. "anticommunist hysteria" suggests that the United States has had in mind the Soviet Union in constructing the U.S. nuclear arsenal, not some other possible nuclear adversary rearing its head in the dimly perceived future. Lee protests that the distinction between threats and bluffs will not bear the weight that Sterba places on it. What is wrong with deterrence is not the mere intention that is present in a threat but absent in bluffing—it is the overall policy of hostage holding.

In their dialogue, "Nuclear Deterrence as Bluff," John Hare and J. Ralph Lindgren take a closer look at the bluff/threat distinction. Can it serve to mark part of the line between justifiable and unjustifiable nuclear policy? Hare notes that it often is unclear to the actor at the time whether the threat/bluff will be carried out, whether, in other words, it is a threat or a bluff. Politicians seldom have "firm conditional intentions." Taking issue with Sterba's shotgun analogy, Lindgren observes that nuclear weaponry involves command structures layered with personnel. Although the commander in chief may be able to delay the formation of intention, the lieutenants in the missile silos surely do not have that luxury. Must these officers be prepared to execute impermissible threats if ordered to do so? Hare and Lindgren, in focusing on the cost, conclude by considering what nations may give up in creating a nuclear deterrent and whether other means might exist for achieving its purpose.

Leslie Pickering Francis pursues further the matter of costs and benefits. In "Nuclear Threats and the Imposition of Risks," she considers whether the strategy of nuclear deterrence is more likely than others "to prevent some markedly greater evil," such as Stalinist world domination. Noting that the choice of strategy involves uncertainty rather than quantifiable risk, Francis suggests that when probabilities are "shadowy," one should avoid courses of action that pose risks of more widespread and more basic harms. Given that Stalinist world domination appears to be a lesser evil than nuclear devastation, one should choose a strategy that minimizes the likelihood of the latter. The choice between unilateral disarmament and continued nuclear posturing must be made on that basis.

Richard Werner's chapter, "The Morality of Nuclear Deterrence," is an effort to refute the view that nuclear war is such a horrible catastrophe that we are justified in doing anything—including threatening to engage in such a war—that will make it less likely. Werner argues that in targeting civilian populations, deterrence violates the Kantian principle of respect for persons. Because of command and control problems expected in the course of a nuclear war, bluffing is not a realistic option either. When a nation is under attack, submarine commanders and bomber captains may find themselves on their own. Even though it may be national policy not to retaliate (and having such a policy carries its own risks), a nation's weapons may be used. In thus holding hostage another nation's civilian population, deterrence inescapably violates the moral prohibition against using other persons merely as means.

Werner is equally dubious about consequentialist justifications of nuclear deterrence. Although there is much speculation about the possible outcomes of deterrence and their probabilities, far too little is known to make responsible assertions about either. There is no science of foreign affairs that can assign probabilities and values to possible outcomes of alternative courses of action. Thus one cannot justify the creation of a nuclear deterrent on the ground that doing so is the best means of averting nuclear war. Far from preventing catastrophe, one may be inflating the balloon to its breaking point. Werner concludes by urging, as a first step toward eventual bilateral disarmament, the unilateral elimination of all except submarine-based nuclear weaponry.

5

The Ethic of
Nuclear Deterrence

Philip Chase Bobbitt

Roughly speaking, two approaches are taken to the question of whether or not the strategy of nuclear deterrence can be morally justified. These are, on the one hand, utilitarian and consequentialist—for example, does the strategy succeed in reducing the likelihood of war and the lethality of war if it comes?—and, on the other hand, Kantian or deontological—for example, is it *just* to hold innocent millions hostage as a necessary element in a politico-military strategy if we hold, as a first principle, that some human beings may not be used as a means by others? Considering the focus of these approaches on the individual, calculating conscience, I do not see how either is capable of determining whether the U.S. policy of nuclear deterrence is ethically legitimate, nor do I think that either approach can resolve the more general question of which approach to choose between the two. In the following pages, I will not try to persuade the reader of this conviction but merely attempt to reflect the views that are its consequences.

Nuclear strategies are national strategies. Ethical systems that treat all nations alike and permit no political preferences ignore the very objective of strategy—namely, to preserve, protect, and often to promote certain *cultural* values rather than individual preferences. This shortcoming applies to both utilitarian and deontological approaches. In conflict, who can say whether the strategies that serve X to defeat Y are morally justified without making some assessment about national interests beyond the individual. For example, renouncing a particular national nuclear strategy by the United States might sacrifice millions of innocent Americans and Europeans. Can this possibly be the plausible outcome of a morality that holds the United States may not threaten innocent persons in pursuit of its objectives and thus must not risk innocent Russian lives? Could such a choice really be made by a U.S. president by simply counting up the total number of lives risked, regardless of whose lives they may be?

Preferences perhaps are nonproblematical when we are discussing individual acts, at least in the abstract, that is, outside the roles they may play in society. We may infer a ranking of individual preferences simply from the existence of individual choices and the postulates of rationality. But once we move to the question of national interests, we no longer can assume such a ranking. The individual making a crucial decision (for example, the U.S. president) cannot act merely on the basis of his individual preferences for he is an agent, empowered to act only insofar as he does so in the nation's interest. If we wish to make normative recommendations about rational behavior, we must introduce factual assumptions about the utility function of nations, their strategic options, the information available to them, and so on. This undercuts the axiomatic validity of the theoretical role of individualism and rationality. For we no longer can rely on the unquestioned ontological status of the individual; the individual is not consulting his or her own interests. Nor can we say of his decisions that, so long as they are internally consistent, they reflect the preferences of his society as a whole.

Nuclear weapons and nuclear strategies are deployed by *nations* for the pursuit of policies that are the temporary culmination of loyalties, histories, and customs that have their character precisely because they are not universal. To apply a universal rule to national policy is very sensible in the common room, and perhaps this is all morality today means: "what moralists talk about." The deontologist, like other moralists, surely wishes it to mean more. He or she wishes to have a standard that could be applied universally by moral politicians, and this is precisely what I doubt to be available in the context of international relations between two ideologically and culturally antagonistic nations. We live within the moral conventions of a particular society; there is nowhere else to live. One cannot say that whatever the facts or developments a particular moral rule must be obeyed and, at the same time, concede that the character and nature of obedience are conditioned by the facts and development of a particular political ideology. Yet if we are deciding on the basis of what it is right for a nation-state to do, this is the first concession we must make.

*   *   *

Consider a celebrated strategic problem that is nonnuclear: the calculated withholding of information by the British government that the city of Coventry was about to be bombed by the Nazis, on the ground that because this information was gained by the secret possession of a

German cryptographic cipher, its disclosure would alert the enemy, who would change its codes.

F. W. Winterbotham has given us this account:[1]

> In November, since the London raids didn't seem to be having the desired effect, Goering decided to start on some of the other big cities. Sometimes we would get warning of such a raid but the exact target was hidden by a code name which, of course, we did not know.
>
> However, at about 3 P.M. on November the fourteenth someone must have made a slip-up and instead of a city with a code name, Coventry was spelt out. This was something we had not met before. Churchill was at a meeting so I spoke direct to his personal secretary and told him what had happened. These were, perhaps, four or five hours before the attack would arrive. It was a longish flight north and the enemy aircraft would not cross the coast before dark. I asked the personal secretary if he would be good enough to ring me back when the decision had been taken, because if Churchill decided to evacuate Coventry, the press, indeed everybody, would know we had pre-knowledge of the raid and some counter measure might be necessary to protect the source which would obviously become suspect. . . . In the event, it was decided only to alert all the services, the fire, the ambulance, the police, the wardens, and to get everything ready to light the decoy fires.

At about the same time Sir William Stephenson, British liaison between the prime minister and President Roosevelt, was relaying this information to the U.S. president. Stephenson reports that Roosevelt observed, "War is forcing us more and more to play God. . . . I don't know what I should have done."

It is in this godlike mode that such questions are usually addressed. Is it good or bad for the British government to conceal from its own citizens knowledge that doubtless would have saved their lives and spared much of their suffering? A cruel and crude antiphonal set of replies might be: It is a good thing because by doing so the secret of the cryptographic penetration was preserved, and, in time, many lives were saved through the assistance this provided Allied military planning, and ultimately the war won; *or,* it is a bad thing because by doing so the British government willingly sacrificed its own noncombatants by deceiving them as to the knowledge of Nazi bombing plans.

One does not see how the conscientious political leader who was persuaded that the morality of the individual should guide his or her decision could choose among these alternatives—utilitarian or deontological—without reference to the ordinary, personal intuitions that derive from the idiosyncratic and cultural histories that such theories attempt to overcome. It is instructive that the realm of morality—once reserved for faith—has become the last refuge of philosophical systems whose claim to universalism has been discredited in so many other areas.

As Stuart Hampshire recently has written:[2]

> We ought not to plan for a final reconciliation of conflicting moralities in a perfect social order; we ought not even to expect that conflicts between moralities, which prescribe different priorities, will gradually disappear, as rational methods in the sciences and in law are diffused. We know virtually nothing about the factors determining the ebb and flow of moral beliefs, conventions and commitments; and we know very little about the conditions under which an intense and exclusive attachment to a particular way of life develops, as opposed to a more selective and critical attitude to the moral conventions that prevail in the environment. We are still in the dark about the dominant phenomenon in contemporary politics: nationalism.

I find it disquieting, therefore, that so many critics appear to ignore the politico-strategic basis for conflict. They treat nuclear deterrence, ironically, in the same contextless way that game theorists have been criticized for doing.

I recognize that we want to say that there are some means that it is wrong for a state to employ in pursuit of its political survival. It may be that, for example, some feel that the coercion of a slave army or the use of biological weapons is one such means, and this may depend, for other persons, on the objectives sought by such means. I submit that this question, posed in this way, is incoherent and cannot be answered. It is the result of one's desire to go through the world labeling various actions "moral" or "immoral," "ethical" or "unethical" and as such is akin to the ostensive fallacies of earlier philosophical systems and arises from a desire for a godlike perspective.

*   *   *

If we wish to determine the ethical legitimacy of current U.S. nuclear strategy, we must ask two separate questions: (1) does the policy of deterrence purport to protect national values in the customary way that the society of nations has assigned to the national security apparatus; and (2) is nuclear deterrence an essential element in that strategy? Such a determination ought to be done, I think, by concrete reference to the specific contexts in which the strategy is supposed to operate. It is tempting to say that such questions, because they must be resolved by individuals, amount to no more than saying, Is an individual justified in taking a particular action—that is, by threatening the lives of countless innocent persons?

Individuals do not have nuclear strategies; nations do. Whether it is right for an individual to execute a particular strategy will be a different question than whether a state may devise and implement such a strategy, and it is scarcely obvious that the former question is anterior to the latter. I am not claiming that nations, because they do not have an individual conscience or self-consciousness, are beyond morality, can have no moral sense, cannot have moral standards applied to them. I simply mean that the *analysis must be different*; nations must fit within some community of values to which they bear a relation similar to that borne by the individual to his or her community.

If we may take the United Nations Charter as a guide to those rules to which nations have concurred regarding their behavior as states, then there is ample support for a rational strategy of self-defense, and collective defense, by the threat of reprisal. Article 51 of the charter expressly reserves the use of force to the context of self-defense. From this reservation alone the legitimacy of the threat of force might be concluded because the article itself, providing as it does a means to assemble a U.N. force, is an example of political arrangements made in the service of deterring attack on the territories of nations. The charter, unlike other treaties, has the status in international law of a customary norm, in light of the comprehensive range of the signatories. Virtually every state has agreed to its provisions.

Although it might be possible for a state to abdicate its right of self-defense to some organization of states and thereafter to be restricted in the reassumption of this responsibility, this—despite the hopes of some of the charter drafters—has not come to pass. If we posit the legitimacy of the nation-state as a political entity, then it is difficult to doubt its right to defend its territories and ecological security because the political apparatus of the nation must be enclosed by a sort of cellular stability. A nation-state must be more than a state of mind. I take the considerable body of collective defense treaties to be evidence of the acceptance by nations of the legitimacy of the objective of self-defense.

Are there politico-military requirements of deterrence such that the United States requires a *nuclear* strategy? That is, if the deterrence of attack is a legitimate goal of national policy, are there some attacks that can be deterred only by nuclear strategies? I shall list four such sorts of attacks, and I shall try to specify plausible political contexts within which these might occur. These speculative scenarios are provided simply to show that there exist realistic political contexts within which the Soviet Union rationally might attack the United States or other nations but would otherwise be deterred from so doing by U.S. nuclear capabilities and doctrines. There is no need to postulate an especially aggressive Soviet Union in this exercise.

1. A limited Soviet nuclear attack (or the threat of such) on North Atlantic Treaty Organization (NATO) forces in Europe, perhaps as a precedent to a conventional Warsaw Pact Organization (WPO) invasion.

Hypothetical A: Political turbulence in Belgrade has led to the dissolution of the Supreme Executive Council and the declaration of secession by Vojvidina, Slovenia, and Croatia. Despite profession of neutrality from the truncated central government and the secessionist regions, Russian airborne troops have landed at numerous sites, and mobilized Russian armor has crossed the Hungarian and Bulgarian borders into Yugoslavia. Yugoslav and Rumanian representatives have appealed to the U.N. Security Council where action is stalemated by a Soviet veto. Fierce fighting is underway in Slovenia, with large numbers of refugees fleeing across the Austrian border.

In this context, Austria has appealed for NATO membership and has been admitted. Russian reaction has been intense and hostile. To avoid provocation, no Allied troops have assumed forward defense positions in Austria, but fearing the eventual deployment of such troops the Soviet Union is preparing an invasion force to reoccupy central and western Austria. This will secure the postwar settlement and consolidate the Warsaw Pact. But without theater nuclear strikes, consolidation probably cannot be accomplished in the face of resistance and a counteroffensive. With such strikes, it hardly can fail.

Hypothetical B: Demonstrations in Poland culminate in bloody confrontations between the Polish Army and marchers in several Polish cities. Mobs attack Soviet installations and are fired upon. General Jaruzelski resigns, and Polish officers refuse to leave their barracks in a one-day general strike. An anti-Soviet political committee seizes power in Warsaw with the apparent assistance of the Polish armed forces. Appeals are made to the West for arms; these are rebuffed. The Russian Army invades Poland, stripping East Germany and Czechoslovakia of their Russian divisions. NATO goes on alert and orders a partial mobilization. Rioting breaks out in East Berlin. The Soviet Union fears that NATO will take this moment to demand compliance with the Yalta guarantees. Volunteer regiments are being raised in West Germany.

A Russian nuclear attack, or its threat, against NATO military assets only relieves the pressure from the West while solidifying WPO cohesion because any NATO nonnuclear retaliation would fall on the most exposed WPO members.

Hypothetical C: New, nonnuclear weapons of remarkable accuracy are about to be deployed by NATO to replace obsolete systems. Arms control talks have foundered because the Soviet Union insists that such systems threaten the Soviet homeland directly and thus circumvent the limitations negotiated on strategic arms. The U.S. proposal to postpone the new deployments in exchange for a withdrawal of Soviet weapons threatening West Europe has been rejected. The first deployments have begun in a remote portion of a largely uninhabited island off Sicily. The Soviets have confidence that a nuclear strike can obliterate the weapons before they become operational and will serve as a wholesome antidote to future deployments.

    2. A preemptive attack on a third nation's nuclear forces.

    Hypothetical A: Following the adoption of a House-Senate Joint Resolution calling for the withdrawal of U.S. troops from Germany, the Federal Republic of Germany (FRG) announced that in conjunction with Britain and France it would seek to develop a nuclear capability under the control of a European Defense Community. The German Democratic Republic (DDR) has objected strongly and terminated all border contacts; the Soviet Union has made equally strong protests. It refuses to guarantee the security of the German state on the grounds that the division of Germany is temporary, reunification having been thwarted by the FRG conclusion of an anti-Soviet treaty. The USSR has offered a mutual nonaggression treaty, although it is not expected that this would result in a diminution of Soviet nuclear and conventional capabilities against West Germany. In this context the assembly of nuclear warheads has begun at several clandestine sites in the FRG. The Soviet Union has concluded that even a successful conventional assault might not preempt the acquisition of a German nuclear capability and that, in any event, a nuclear attack might well be needed to ensure conventional success. Now it has been proposed that a nuclear strike be used against a probable assembly site on the ground that even if this proves incorrect as to the site, the *in terrorem* effect will halt further government production and perhaps collapse the current regime.

    Hypothetical B: Israeli attacks on Syrian positions have destroyed a Soviet command position assigned the task of controlling air defense. It is widely thought that the Israelis have managed a technological breakthrough that allows them to penetrate Russian manned surface-to-air missiles (SAM) and fighter-assisted air defenses at will. Moreover, the Israelis have issued a statement to the effect that further Soviet resupply will be prevented "by whatever means necessary." This has been interpreted in Moscow as a veiled nuclear threat. Soviet resupply has been delayed pending a reassessment in Moscow. In these circumstances, Israel has decided to launch a combined air/land drive on Damascus. The Soviet Union has threatened retaliation if an immediate cease-fire is not agreed; the United States has joined in a U.N. appeal for a halt to hostilities. Israel has retorted only with reference to its own deterrent capability. The Soviet Union is considering these options: immediate airlift of war supplies to Syria, plus advisers; doing nothing;

or punitive raids on Israeli territory. In light of the obvious shortcomings of each of these courses of action, some serious attention is being given to a proposal to preempt Israeli nuclear capability because it has been learned that Israel's small arsenal is deployed on bombers without the range to hit the Soviet Union. This course would permit an effective Soviet ultimatum, even in the event it was not wholly successful tactically, and other courses of action that at present are unpromising.

Hypothetical C: The National Security Agency reports that the People's Republic of China has mobilized a multidivision force in its southern provinces, opposite Vietnam. A marked slowdown in aircraft operations in the southern military district in the past forty-eight hours has been reported. Finally a Soviet note to Beijing has been intercepted that threatens retaliation—"at a place of our own choosing"—if China invades Vietnam. No response has been forthcoming, but satellites have observed the Chinese arming their liquid-fueled medium-range ballistic missiles (MRBMs), perhaps to prevent preemption by enabling them to be launched in retaliation during an attack. The Soviets have twenty hours in which to decide whether to preempt the Chinese nuclear arsenal. If they succeed, then they can expect in this crisis and in the future a more pliant neighbor so long as no other nuclear power guarantees Chinese independence.

3. An attack on U.S. continental-based forces.

Hypothetical A: At the annual celebration of the Cuban revolution, Premier Fidel Castro announced to an enthusiastic crowd that more than five hundred cruise missiles had been shipped to Cuba and currently were deployed in a variety of seaborne and airborne modes. He did not specify whether these were nuclear or conventionally armed. The United States responded to this announcement with the demand that these weapons be removed; a naval quarantine was imposed. A Soviet oil tanker and an accompanying destroyer attempted to run the blockade and were boarded successfully by U.S. forces. A joint statement was issued subsequently by Cuba and the Soviet Union announcing that each country would regard an attack upon the personnel or vessels of the other as an assault on its vital interests and would respond with all available forces. The United States readied an invasion force in Florida.

In this context U.S. intelligence discovered and confirmed that the cruise missiles were nuclear armed but had not yet been deployed and that it would take two weeks at least to make the missiles fully operational. Pressure for a U.S. invasion mounted in Washington; Soviet leaders concluded that only a nuclear attack could possibly tip a balance so geographically favorable to the United States conventionally. Their military analysts proposed to strike at the invasion force itself, with simultaneous blows at U.S. strategic air force bases only, to prevent retaliation against the Soviet Union and to deflect U.S. reprisals toward Cuba and away from the Soviet Union.

Hypothetical B: After an intense debate in the nation and in the Congress, the U.S. president signed legislation authorizing the procurement and deployment of a ballistic missile defense. The entire system relies on the coordination of satellite sensors, space-based, nonnuclear attack vehicles, and low altitude intercept missiles. Government analysts consider it to be 90 percent+ effective for point defense, although not practicable for area defense. Despite the president's announced intention not to deploy these systems if negotiations can lead to the removal of Soviet intercontinental ballistic missiles (ICBMs) capable of destroying U.S. forces and command and control centers (which otherwise are slated for missile defense), no agreement is forthcoming. The Soviets are understandably reluctant to tear down systems that also are needed to deter attacks from third nations. Moreover, the Soviet reliance on land-based ICBMs, a plausible result of their geographic position, now forces the Soviets to largely abandon their countercity force if limits on ICBMs are negotiated; this is impossible for domestic political reasons. Accordingly, the president renounces the Anti-Ballistic Missile Treaty of 1971 and orders the commencement of ballistic missile defense (BMD) deployment, including antisatellite systems. The Soviet Union has only a week to decide whether to acquiesce in this development or to attempt preventing it. One faction in Moscow is arguing for an ICBM attack against U.S. offensive forces (the forces that BMD systems would protect). Such an attack, according to this faction, would moot the BMD deployment threat and, in its way, amount to a sort of forced mutual disarmament with the result that socialist forces, committed to peace, would hold the monopoly on postattack weapons.

4. An attack on U.S. cities in an effort to terminate a conventional conflict.

Hypothetical A: The Iran-Iraq war continued with some significant Iranian advances. The Soviet Union sent air defense missiles to Iraq. For ten weeks, sizable Soviet military exercises were underway in the provinces opposite Iran. At least four and possibly five divisions were involved, including one airborne division, plus supporting air and air defense forces. A special operational headquarters was activated near Moscow for the command of these forces; this unit had last been activated to control Soviet forces in the invasion of Afghanistan.

This intelligence information was relayed by Washington to Teheran. Subsequently, the assassination of Ayatollah Khomeini took place by agents, it is presumed, of a radical peace faction of the *majlis*. The speaker of the majlis, the Ayatollah Rafsanjani, denounced this group. Street fighting broke out in Teheran. The Revolutionary Council for

Peace broadcast appeals for Soviet help from Tabriz, where a provisional government was set up. Regular Iranian forces moved north to take possession of the city and erect a defensive position along the Iranian/ USSR border.

The Iranian government appealed for international aid; a multinational force, ferried by the U.S. Sixth Fleet, landed in the Persian Gulf almost simultaneously with Soviet air attacks on Teheran. After a brief hiatus in the fighting while diplomatic options were pursued, Soviet armor and mobilized divisions crossed the frontier into Azerbaijan. The United States mobilized one and one-half divisions and sent them by air-assisted sealift to Iran. Contact between the two forces occurred; U.S. forces held Teheran while Soviet armor consolidated its position in the areas north of the city.

Although the United States was prepared for nuclear and chemical attacks on its soldiers in Iran, the U.S. president might not have been as publicly defiant of Soviet demands for withdrawal had he known that Moscow was considering a countercity attack on U.S. targets. Division in the United States, a series of antiadministration statements in Congress, and a substantial movement for impeachment based on the president's refusal to enforce the War Powers Resolution convinced the most astute Soviet analysts of U.S. behavior that countercity strikes would bring the U.S. intervention to an immediate end. These attacks—one or two at most would be necessary—would collapse U.S. political support for the war while avoiding the ecological contamination of the Persian peninsula and local religious hostility that would result from theater strikes. Theater strikes would be difficult to manage in the Teheran area in any case without civilian casualties at least equal to those from a countercity strike in the United States; and there was some support in Moscow for the conclusion that the United States would not be so prone to worldwide intervention if it once actually had the costs of war brought home. The two cities proposed were Los Angeles and Houston, each with incidental research and military value.

Hypothetical B: North Korean raids across the 38th parallel occurred with increasing frequency and seriousness for about fifteen months. South Korean forces managed to repel these raids, which had the effect, in retrospect, of dulling U.S. intelligence sensitivity to the signals that preceded the North Korean invasion. This complete tactical surprise was achieved by the North Korean Army, operating with Soviet advisers and Soviet air support.

The South Korean government has withdrawn to Taejon; U.S. forces have been surrounded on three sides. South Korea has protested to the United Nations, where it is supported by the United States and China. No action has been taken owing to the Soviet veto.

China entered the conflict with air attacks on North Korean bases near the Manchurian border. SAM sites have been constructed by the Soviet Union in North Korea, and these are manned by Soviet personnel. It is expected that some Russian casualties have resulted.

A joint U.S.-Chinese declaration demanded the withdrawal of North Korean troops to the 38th parallel. Chinese troops are being supplied by U.S. C-5As operating out of Japan, with the hope that a Chinese invasion of the North Korean rear will relieve pressure on U.S. forces in the South.

At this point, two nuclear threats have passed. The USSR informed Beijing that the Chinese invasion force will be met with theater strikes on Chinese bases in North China and possibly tactical strikes along the Yalu. Nothing is ruled out, including attacks on Chinese cities. China, in turn, replied that any nuclear use against Chinese personnel would be promptly met by a Chinese nuclear attack on one hundred Russian cities.

Moscow now turns to Washington. Soviet analysts believe that a U.S. cease-fire—or withdrawal—would collapse South Korean resistance regardless of Chinese support. The United States, however, has become intransigent as its forces now have engaged the North Koreans and appear to be holding their own. The first Chinese troops have crossed into Korean territory by barge under Soviet air attack.

In this context the Soviet Union considers a nuclear strike against U.S. cities. If no action is taken, a Soviet communications brigade will be overrun in a matter of days and the North Korean offensive will itself be encircled with far-reaching strategic implications for eastern Russia. Tactical strikes against U.S. forces are impossible because the two sides are intermingled and the North Korean successes have carried them beyond a well-defined perimeter. The Chinese reply has had its effect; a nuclear strike against their forces is not considered realistic. Conventional invasion is out of the question: The necessary numbers could be achieved, if at all, only by stripping Eastern Europe and the Western Military District of their troops, a highly risky enterprise. Border incidents launched from Mongolia will help, but these are far too minor to affect matters. The U.S. position seems promising to the Soviets, but the United States also has much to lose by a failure to stand its ground; Washington officials believe that the effects on Japan of a U.S. pullout would be devastating. How might the Soviets coerce such an abrupt surrender? Limited counterforce strikes against the United States are considered but are likely to be ineffectual; the U.S. war effort is sufficiently well supported so that many dozens of attacks would have to be made before a withdrawal could be forced. The enthusiasm for a countercity blow increases. This would lead to an immediate cease-fire and, in the long run, might even save lives.

*   *   *

In each of the foregoing examples, the reader should ask whether the use of the nuclear option is made more or less likely by the existence of a U.S. nuclear strategic arsenal and whether a policy of deterrence, in these contexts, can be managed by the United States without nuclear elements. I have avoided the most likely scenario—the threat of attack on European cities following an intense political crisis—to confine the hypotheticals to examples that would seem both plausible but not obvious, for political circumstances are unpredictable. What makes nuclear war likely is the intersection of various strategic conditions with certain political conflicts. I conclude that if it is legitimate for nations to provide for their self-defense, then the United States is justified in devising a nuclear strategy because there are some situations in which U.S. self-defense cannot be maintained without a nuclear deterrent.

*   *   *

If a philosophical analysis yields a conclusion whose implementation makes nuclear war much more likely and much more devastating when it comes, then I have little hesitation in believing that it is the analysis that is flawed rather than the will of politicians who reject that analysis. To conclude that

> when I say that the deterrent is morally evil, I do not mean that we ought to dismantle it if and when world amity is established. I mean that we ought to dismantle the deterrent immediately, regardless of consequences. The end simply does not justify the means.[3]

is to condemn morality itself. The adoption of such a view is, it seems to me, a recipe for the slaughter of innocents, not for the preservation of their morals. Yet I would not look for guidance to those who say that the calculation of expected numbers lost from the choice of various strategies reveals that the conflict is not a prisoner's dilemma; that, in the light of this ordering of preferences, unilateral disarmament makes good sense and leads to the best of all superpower worlds; and that the first preference of each side is to disarm no matter what the other side does.

We want to recognize that because nation-states differ in the political objectives they pursue and the geostrategic positions they occupy, the appropriateness of their nuclear strategies also will differ. We should not be indifferent to the proliferation of nuclear weapons to states that would use them in pursuit of the conquest of others or render the U.S. strategy of deterrence impossible. For the United States, there is no political objective that would possibly justify nuclear war save its ultimate deterrence. This conviction is the central idea in the ethic of deterrence.

In this chapter I have argued that conventional moral systems usually grouped as deontological and utilitarian are not helpful in resolving the issue of what nuclear strategies are ethically legitimate for a particular nation-state. I have given some examples of political crises within which U.S. nuclear plans have an important role, but I emphatically do not mean that geopolitics ought to replace moral discourse. Rather, morality must address national problems with a focus on institutional roles and a sensitivity to the interplay of those roles.

Notes

1. F. W. Winterbotham, *The Ultra Secret* (New York: Harper & Row, 1974), pp. 60–61.

2. Stuart Hampshire, *Morality and Conflict* (Cambridge, Mass.: Harvard University Press, 1983), p. 160.

3. Germain Grisez, "Toward a Consistent Natural-Law Ethics of Killing," *American Journal of Jurisprudence* 15 (1970):64–96, at 93.

6

Between MAD and Counterforce

James P. Sterba

Current U.S. nuclear defense policy seeks to combine and compromise the competing strategies of mutual assured destruction (MAD) and Counterforce.[1] MAD recommends the deployment of nuclear weapons capable of inflicting unacceptable damage on an adversary's industrial and population centers. Counterforce recommends the deployment of nuclear weapons capable of delivering a limited and precise strike on an adversary's tactical and strategic forces. MAD has the advantage of favoring just the type of nuclear retaliation that the United States is most capable of delivering, for until recently, the U.S. submarine force, which is the most survivable component of the U.S. arsenal, lacked the capacity to carry out anything like limited and precise retaliation.[2] Other advantages of MAD are that it is relatively cheap to maintain and it promises such a horrendous response to nuclear attack that it surely seems capable of deterring a massive first strike on industrial and population centers. MAD's basic disadvantage is that it is not sufficiently credible in cases of limited attack. It is difficult to imagine the United States responding to a limited attack on its tactical and strategic forces with a massive attack on the industrial and population centers of its adversary when that would invite a comparable attack on its own industrial and population centers. It is this disadvantage of MAD that Counterforce seeks to remedy.

Counterforce recommends responding to nuclear attack in a manner that is proportionate to the severity of the attack. Accordingly, although an adversary might reasonably doubt U.S. commitment under MAD to respond to a limited attack with massive retaliation, an adversary could not similarly doubt U.S. commitment under Counterforce to respond to a limited attack with limited retaliation. In this way, Counterforce promises a more credible response to a limited attack.

But this advantage of Counterforce over MAD is closely linked with the strategy's basic disadvantage. For in attempting to control the destructive consequences of a limited attack, Counterforce tends to make such an attack less risky and hence more likely. Obviously, there are serious strategic disadvantages to both MAD and Counterforce.

Thus, current U.S. nuclear defense policy seeks to combine and compromise both these strategies. Current U.S. nuclear defense policy endorses Counterforce for a limited attack and MAD for a massive attack, thereby attempting to secure the credibility of Counterforce to deter a limited attack and the credibility of MAD to deter a massive attack.[3] Unfortunately, this combined strategy retains the same basic strategic disadvantage of Counterforce: It tends to make limited nuclear war less risky and hence more likely. In addition, this strategy is subject to the very same moral objection that applies to its component strategies: Its implementation could involve the killing of large numbers of innocent people. Consequently, in order to determine whether it is possible to combine MAD and Counterforce into a morally and strategically sound nuclear defense policy, I propose to consider, first of all, what moral constraints apply to the use of nuclear weapons; second, what related moral constraints apply to threatening the use of such weapons; and third, whether the moral constraints proposed for these contexts can be strategically justified.

Moral Constraints on the Use of Nuclear Weapons

Problems in morally justifying the use of nuclear weapons begin with the realization that a massive use of nuclear weapons either against military and strategic targets or against industrial and population centers would be prima facie immoral because such use would involve the killing of large numbers of innocent people. That killing innocent people is prima facie immoral is certainly a bedrock moral principle. Nevertheless, such killing may yet be morally justified, all things considered, either to prevent a greater evil or to secure a greater good. Yet the evil to be prevented or the good to be secured must be sufficiently greater than the foreseen evil consequence or the intended evil means (possibly many times greater depending on the context) before the pursuit of such goals would be morally justified. To see that this is the case, we need only utilize a social contract decision procedure and evaluate our actions from the standpoint of persons who have discounted the knowledge of whether they personally would benefit or be harmed by those actions. Using this decision procedure, it seems clear that the evil to be prevented or the good to be secured would have to be significantly greater before we would favor the pursuit of such goals at the cost of innocent lives.[4]

Not surprisingly, therefore, we cannot employ the foregoing sorts of justification to legitimate a massive use of nuclear weapons against either tactical and strategic forces or industrial and population centers because the killing of large numbers of innocent people is so morally abhorrent that it cannot be justified on the grounds of preventing a greater evil or securing a greater good.[5] There simply is no greater evil or greater good that could outweigh the killing of large numbers of innocent people in the massive use of nuclear weapons.

Consider the massive use of nuclear weapons by the United States or the Soviet Union against industrial and population centers. Such a strike, involving three to five thousand warheads, could destroy between 70 and 80 percent of each nation's industry and result in the immediate death of as many as 165 million Americans and 100 million Russians, respectively, in addition to running a considerable risk of a retaliatory nuclear strike by the opposing superpower.[6] Carl Sagan and others have estimated that such a strike is very likely to generate firestorms that would cover much of the earth with sooty smoke for months, thus creating a "nuclear winter" that would threaten the very survival of the human species.[7] Now there simply is no foreseeable end that could justify such morally horrendous consequences.

The same holds true for a massive use of nuclear weapons against tactical and strategic targets. Such a strike, involving two to three thousand warheads, directed against only intercontinental ballistic missiles (ICBMs) and submarine and bomber bases could wipe out as many as 20 million Americans and 28 million Russians, respectively, in addition to running a considerable risk of a retaliatory nuclear strike by the opposing superpower.[8] Here, too, there is a considerable risk of a "nuclear winter" occurring. This being the case, what greater evil might foreseeably be prevented by such a use of nuclear weapons?

Of course, it should be pointed out that this argument does not rule out a limited use of nuclear weapons against tactical and strategic targets. Such a use is still possible. Yet practically it would be quite difficult for either superpower to distinguish between a limited and a massive use of nuclear weapons, especially if a full-scale conventional war were raging. In such circumstances, any use of nuclear weapons is likely to be viewed as part of a massive use of such weapons, thus increasing the risk of a massive nuclear retaliatory strike.[9] Henry Kissinger once proposed that in a limited nuclear war a nation might announce that it would not use nuclear weapons of more than 500 kilotons explosive power unless an adversary used them first. Unfortunately, however, neither the United States nor the Soviet Union has a system of instantaneous damage assessment to determine whether such a limit was being observed. In addition, war games have shown that if enough tactical nuclear weapons are employed over time in a limited area, such as Germany, the effect on noncombatants in that area would be much the same as in a massive nuclear attack.[10] As Bundy, Kennan, McNamara, and Smith put the point in their recent endorsement of a doctrine of no first use of nuclear weapons: "Any use of nuclear weapons in Europe, by the Alliance or against it, carries with it a high and inescapable risk of escalation into the general nuclear war which would bring ruin to all and victory to none."[11] For these reasons, even a limited use of nuclear weapons generally would not be morally justified, all things considered.

Nevertheless, there are some circumstances in which a limited use of nuclear weapons would be morally justified. For example, suppose that a nation was attacked with a massive nuclear counterforce strike and it was likely that if the nation did not retaliate with a limited nuclear strike, a massive attack on industrial and population centers would follow. Under such circumstances, a limited nuclear retaliatory strike would be morally justified. Of course, the justification for such a strike would depend on what effect the strike would have had on innocent lives and how likely it was that the strike would have succeeded in deterring a massive attack on the nation's industrial and population centers. But assuming a limited nuclear retaliatory strike was the best way of avoiding a significantly greater evil, it would be morally justified, all things considered.

Moral Constraints on Threatening the Use of Nuclear Weapons

Once the foregoing moral constraints on the use of nuclear weapons are recognized, comparable constraints on threatening the use of such weapons would seem to obtain in accord with the *wrongful threatening principle*: If an act is wrong, then threatening to perform that act also is wrong. According to this principle, threatening nuclear destruction would be morally justified only if carrying out such threats would be morally justified.

This principle, however, has been challenged by Gregory Kavka, who argues that it fails to apply when threats are adopted solely to prevent the occurrence of the circumstances in which the threats would have to be carried out.[12] For Kavka, a policy of threatening massive nuclear retaliation is justified provided that a nation threatens to retaliate with a massive use of nuclear weapons only to prevent the occurrence of those circumstances in which it would so retaliate. Unfortunately, this line of argument also would serve to justify the threats standardly employed by armed robbers! Robbers, in threatening "Hand over your money or I'll shoot," usually hope to avoid just those circumstances where their victims do not hand over the money and they do shoot.

Obviously, Kavka is primarily concerned with situations where people threaten *in order to prevent an unjust offense*, and certainly such motivation typically would be lacking in cases of armed robbery.[13] Nevertheless, when Kavka comments upon what is distinctive about those situations where he thinks such threatening is justified, he refers only to the effects the threats have that are independent of their actually being carried out— that is, to their "autonomous effects." But threats by armed robbers have just the same autonomous effects. Consequently, if a policy of threatening massive nuclear retaliation is not to be condemned on the basis of the wrongful threatening principle, it must be for reasons other than those Kavka provides.

Now others, such as Michael Walzer, have recognized the wrongful threatening principle as a moral constraint on legitimate threats, but then have argued that where national defense is at issue the principle can be overridden for the sake of deterrence.[14] According to Walzer, "We threaten in order not to do it, and the doing of it would be so terrible that the threat seems in comparison to be morally defensible."[15]

So, presumably, Walzer would say that what distinguishes a nation's legitimate threatening from a robber's illegitimate threatening is not the presence of autonomous effects; such effects are found in both cases. Rather, the cases can be distinguished on the grounds that the beneficial autonomous effects that flow from legitimate threatening by a nation are not matched, even proportionately, by the beneficial autonomous effects that flow from the threats standardly employed by armed robbers.

Yet Walzer fails to recognize that what he is attempting to justify is not threatening at all. There is another applicable principle that makes threatening impossible in this case. That principle, which turns on the fact that threatening involves an intention to carry out the threat if the desired response is not forthcoming, is the *impossible threat principle*: X cannot threaten to do w if Y does z, if X expects that if Y does z, X still will not do w.

Now many of the purported threats employed by nations to deter their adversaries, such as the one Walzer would justify, fail to satisfy this principle. For example, it is frequently claimed that a massive nuclear attack on industrial and population centers would be so grossly immoral that neither U.S. leaders nor Soviet leaders could conceive of themselves as carrying out such a strike, even in retaliation. Yet many of those, like Walzer, who think that this is the case, still believe that it is possible for the leaders to threaten each other with such an attack. But according to the impossible threat principle this cannot be done. A nation's leaders simply cannot threaten nuclear retaliation if an adversary strikes first and yet expect that even if that adversary were to strike first, they would still not retaliate.

Needless to say, others also have thought that there was a logical flaw involved in this talk about threats, but they have failed to state correctly what the flaw is. Jonathan Schell, for example, claims that there is a contradiction at the heart of the doctrine of deterrence employed by the superpowers.[16] The contradiction is that "we cannot both threaten ourselves with something and hope to avoid that same thing by making the threat."[17]

But the contradiction Schell claims to have discovered is not a contradiction at all but rather a commonplace. As noted previously, even robbers threaten harmful consequences while hoping never to have to carry out those threats. What would be contradictory is not a threat coupled with a hope that the threat never would have to be carried out, but rather a threat coupled with the expectation that one never would carry out the threat no matter what others did.

It follows that the only way a nation's leaders can threaten to use nuclear weapons is if they can envision themselves using those weapons under certain circumstances. This means that for the leaders who recognize the moral constraints on the use of nuclear weapons, the possibility of threatening nuclear destruction would be circumscribed drastically. Unless these leaders commit themselves to acting immorally, they can threaten only a form of limited nuclear retaliation, and even then there would have to be a justification for actually threatening such retaliation.

In order to see why a justification for threatening is required, let us consider three possible stances a nation's leaders might take with respect to nuclear weapons.

1. A nation's leaders might be willing to carry out a nuclear first strike against an adversary only if they expected that a negligible loss to their own nation would result.
2. A nation's leaders might be willing to carry out a nuclear first strike against an adversary only if they expected that an acceptable loss to their own nation would result.
3. A nation's leaders might be willing to carry out a nuclear first strike against an adversary even though they expected that an unacceptable loss to their own nation would result.

Now it should be clear that threats of nuclear retaliation would be totally ineffective against a nation whose leaders adopted stance (3) and were willing to carry out a nuclear first strike against an adversary even though they expected that an unacceptable loss to their own nation would result. Yet what about a nation whose leaders adopted stance (1) and were willing to carry out a nuclear first strike against an adversary only if they expected a negligible loss to their own nation would result?

Might not a threat of nuclear retaliation be effective against such a nation? This clearly is not the case if the nation's leaders were either unimpressed by the capabilities of their adversary's nuclear retaliatory force or greatly impressed by the effectiveness of their own nuclear defense system. But suppose that the nation's leaders were impressed greatly by the capabilities of their adversary's nuclear retaliatory force and unimpressed by the effectiveness of their own nuclear defense system. When then? Would a threat of nuclear retaliation further deter those leaders from attacking their adversary? Possibly it would, but such additional deterrence would seem to be needed only in the unlikely event that even when a nation's leaders are faced with the impressive capabilities of their adversary's nuclear retaliatory force and the unimpressive effectiveness of their own nuclear defense system, their expectations as to whether they would suffer a negligible loss from launching a nuclear first strike still would depend upon whether their adversary actually had threatened nuclear retaliation! Only then would the threat of nuclear retaliation have a very important deterrent role to play.

Similarly, a threat of nuclear retaliation would be of little use against a nation whose leaders adopted stance (2) and were unimpressed by the capabilities of their adversary's nuclear retaliatory force for inflicting an unacceptable loss on their nation when countered by their own nuclear defense system. However, if a nation's leaders in fact were impressed by the capabilities of their adversary's nuclear retaliatory force for inflicting an unacceptable loss on their nation even when countered by their own nuclear defense system, then the threat of nuclear retaliation may provide some additional deterrence. Nevertheless, such additional deterrence would seem to be needed only in the unlikely event that even when a nation's leaders are faced with the impressive capabilities of their adversary's nuclear retaliatory force for inflicting an unacceptable loss on their nation, their expectations as to whether they would suffer an unacceptable loss still would depend upon whether their adversary actually had threatened nuclear retaliation.

Now one might conclude that threatening or appearing to threaten nuclear retaliation adds so little deterrent value to the possession of an adequate nuclear retaliatory force simply because the possession of such a force already involves an implicit threat to use it. However, this need not be the case because possession of nuclear weapons need not involve even an implicit threat to use such weapons. To see how this is possible, let us begin by considering the following examples.

Suppose you live in a city known for its high crime rate and you decide to purchase a gun for your personal protection. Suppose that after purchasing a gun and becoming skilled in its use, you post the following notice at all the entrances of your home: INTRUDERS BE-

WARE! THIS HOUSE IS PROTECTED BY AN ARMED OCCUPANT. In so doing, you would be deterring potential intruders from breaking into your home by threatening undesirable consequences, and given the high crime rate in your city, presumably your threatening would be legitimate.

Suppose, however, that you are concerned only mildly about the high crime rate, yet you are an avid hunter, and, for that reason, you own several guns, which you keep in your home. To those would-be intruders who know of your avocation, the presence of these guns surely would tend to deter them from breaking into your home, even though you have not threatened to use the guns against them. Accordingly, this is a case where deterrence would be achieved without threatening harmful consequences. Why then could not a nation do something comparable?

Suppose that a nation were to maintain a survivable nuclear force yet refuse to threaten its use in retaliation on the ground that under present conditions such threats would not be morally justified. Would this be a case of achieving nuclear deterrence without threatening nuclear destruction? Not as the case has been so far characterized. For in the previous example the guns you purchased can have a legitimate and independent use. But what would be the legitimate and independent use for a nation to maintain a survivable nuclear force? The only use for such a force would seem to be that of presently threatening nuclear retaliation. Of course, as I have constructed the case, the nation would not threaten explicitly to use its nuclear force in retaliation. However, the nation would be deploying these weapons, and if such weapons cannot be viewed as having any other use than to presently threaten nuclear destruction, then deploying them would have to involve at least an implicit threat of nuclear destruction. Needless to say, it may serve to reduce tensions and promote better relations for a nation to threaten nuclear retaliation implicitly rather than explicitly, yet either way the nation would be threatening nuclear retaliation.[18]

Accordingly, if a nation is to avoid threatening altogether, while possessing a survivable force of nuclear weapons, there must be some legitimate and independent use for those weapons. For example, suppose a nation possesses a survivable nuclear force capable of inflicting unacceptable damage upon its adversary, yet possession of such a force alone would not suffice to deter an adversary from carrying out a nuclear first strike unless that possession were combined with a threat of limited nuclear retaliation or a bluff of massive nuclear retaliation. With respect to massive nuclear retaliation, bluffing would be required because leaders who recognize and respect the previously cited moral constraints on the use of nuclear weapons in fact could not threaten such retaliation. Under these circumstances, I think the required threat or bluff would be morally justified. But I also think that there is ample evidence today to indicate that neither the leadership of the United States nor of the Soviet Union is that committed to carrying out a nuclear first strike.[19] Consequently, under present conditions, such threats or bluffs would not be morally justified. Nevertheless, under present conditions, a nation could legitimately maintain a survivable force so that it could quickly threaten or bluff nuclear retaliation should conditions change for the worse. For as long as nations remain armed with nuclear weapons, such a change could occur simply with a change of leadership that brought to power leaders who could be deterred only by a threat or bluff of nuclear retaliation. Consequently, it would be a legitimate and independent use of nuclear weapons to maintain a survivable nuclear force at the present moment in order to deal effectively with such a possibility in the future. Happily, such a use of nuclear weapons also would serve to deter other nuclear powers from presently launching a nuclear first strike, and it would do so without even implicitly threatening or bluffing nuclear destruction.

Now a nuclear force deployed for this purpose should be capable of surviving a first strike and then inflicting either limited or massive nuclear retaliation on an aggressor. During the Kennedy-Johnson years, Robert McNamara estimated that massive nuclear retaliation required a nuclear force capable of destroying one-half of a nation's industrial capacity along with one-quarter of its population, and comparable figures have been suggested by others. Clearly, ensuring a loss of this magnitude should constitute unacceptable damage from the perspective of any would-be aggressor.

Notice, however, that in order for a nation to maintain a nuclear force capable of inflicting such damage, it is not necessary that components of its land-, air- and sea-based strategic forces all be survivable. Accordingly, even if all the land-based ICBMs in the United States were destroyed totally in a first strike, surviving elements of the U.S. air and submarine force easily could inflict the required degree of damage and more. In fact, any one of the 41 nuclear submarines maintained by the United States, each with up to 160 warheads, almost single-handedly could inflict the required degree of damage. Consequently, the U.S. submarine force alone should suffice as a force capable of massive nuclear retaliation.

But what about a nuclear force capable of limited nuclear retaliation? At least with respect to U.S. nuclear forces, it would seem that as Trident I missiles replace less accurate Poseidon missiles, and especially when Trident II missiles come on line in the next few years, the U.S. submarine force will have the capacity for both limited and massive nuclear retaliation. However, until this modernization is complete, the United States still will have to rely in part on surviving elements of its air- and land-based strategic forces for its capacity to inflict limited nuclear retaliation. It would seem that the Soviet Union also is in a comparable situation.[20]

Now a nation that currently refuses to threaten nuclear retaliation still should inform its adversaries that it recognizes that threatening retaliation is in its national interest. The situation is analogous to that of a person who recognizes that it is in his or her self-interest to do a particular action but rejects that possibility because of its morally unacceptable effects on others. Moreover, given the novelty of such a unilateral acceptance of moral constraints in the international arena, it is imperative that a nation in accepting such constraints convince its adversaries that its leaders are not muddle-headed, but are as capable as anyone else of appreciating what is in the national interest. By making such an announcement, while maintaining a survivable nuclear force, a nation should be able to deter any adversary from testing whether in response to nuclear attack the nation actually would follow its moral principles rather than its national interest.

Finally, by refusing to threaten nuclear retaliation while maintaining a survivable nuclear force and announcing that it is in the national interest to threaten such retaliation, a nation achieves two purposes. First and foremost, such a refusal enables a nation to preserve the moral integrity of its citizens, for its citizens are not being asked to maintain a threat or bluff of nuclear retaliation when doing so cannot be morally justified. Second, by affirming a commitment to moral principles over national interest, a nation makes an important contribution toward motivating a political resolution of the arms race. Of course, for a nation to pursue nuclear deterrence in this fashion would involve sacrificing the additional degree of deterrence that would result from combining the possession of a survivable nuclear force with the threat to use it. Yet only by making this sacrifice can a nation preserve the moral integrity of its citizens and hope to motivate a political resolution of the arms race.

So far I have argued that under present conditions what is morally justified is (1) the maintenance of a survivable nuclear force by a nation; (2) the announcement by the nation that it is in its national interest to threaten nuclear retaliation; and (3) the refusal by the nation to even threaten such retaliation on the ground that under present conditions the use of such means cannot be morally justified. By following this approach under present conditions, a nation would be led to achieve nuclear deterrence without threatening nuclear destruction. Thus, although the approach does recognize the moral legitimacy of threatening or bluffing nuclear retaliation under certain conditions, the approach still places significant moral constraints on threatening nuclear destruction.

Moral Constraints and Strategic Requirements

It is now appropriate to consider whether the moral constraints I have proposed can be strategically justified. To some degree this strategic question already has been addressed. Any discussion of moral constraints must presuppose one of the most fundamental principles of morality, namely, the "ought" implies "can" principle. According to this principle, people are not morally required to do what they lack the power to do or what would involve so great a sacrifice that it would be unreasonable to ask them to perform such an action. Thus morality never can impose such severe constraints on those who would defend themselves against aggression that it would be unreasonable to ask them to accept those constraints.

A problem arises, however, when it appears as though the most effective means for defending oneself or one's nation involves killing or threatening to kill innocent people. Of course, one might deny that this ever happens on the ground that the failure to observe moral constraints leads others to do the same and thus that everyone is worse off than she or he otherwise would be. But at least sometimes it does appear that strategic and moral requirements do diverge so that those who follow moral requirements can turn out to be losers. Accordingly, it would be too much to ask of defensible moral constraints that they never depart from what best serves the interests of oneself or one's nation. Therefore, to ask whether the proposed moral constraints can be strategically justified is not to ask whether such constraints ever demand us to sacrifice these interests at least to some degree—obviously these constraints do. Rather the relevant question is whether the proposed constraints sufficiently respect strategic considerations so as not to impose unreasonable sacrifices on those who would adhere to them. Or, put another way, what is at issue is whether the proposed moral constraints are strategically sound enough to be morally justified.

Now there are at least three areas where the proposed moral constraints might be thought to conflict significantly with strategic requirements: (1) the required limit on the size of nuclear forces; (2) the recourse to bluffing to achieve nuclear deterrence; and (3) the acceptance of a form of limited nuclear retaliation. Let us examine each of these areas in turn.

First, concerning the size of nuclear forces, it has been proposed that once the U.S. submarine force has been rendered more accurate, reliance on that force alone would be morally required. Now it might be objected that this proposal is strategically unsound because it abandons the greater security that comes from the existing triad of nuclear forces. However, even if we disregard the fact that the existing triad of nuclear forces had its birth in interservice rivalries rather than strategic considerations, it is obvious that the strategic considerations that favored the triad have been seriously undercut in recent years by the increasing vulnerability of land- and air-based strategic forces. In addition, strategic forces that cannot survive a first strike only seem capable of delivering a first strike themselves. Of course, if the U.S. submarine force ever became vulnerable to a first strike, there would be a need to shift to some other mode of basing nuclear weapons, and obviously, in the absence of a resolution of political difference, research and development should continue into more survivable modes of basing nuclear weapons. But at the moment there are no weighty strategic considerations against eventually relying on the U.S. submarine force alone.

Second, a policy of resorting to bluffing massive nuclear retaliation when there is no other way to prevent a first strike might be challenged on the grounds that if an adversary ever found out that a nation was bluffing, it could strike with relative impunity. But if bluffing includes deploying a survivable nuclear force and preparing that force for possible use in such a way that leaders who are bluffing massive nuclear retaliation need outwardly distinguish themselves from those who are threatening such retaliation only in their strong moral condemnation of this use of nuclear weapons, then it is difficult to see how an adversary ever could be reasonably confident that a nation's leaders were only bluffing in this context.

Furthermore, bluffing massive nuclear retaliation is advocated only when there is good reason to think that neither a policy of not threatening nuclear retaliation nor one of threatening only a limited form of nuclear retaliation would prove sufficient to deter an adversary from a first strike. Thus, bluffing in this context provides the kind of deterrence MAD was designed to provide but does so in a morally less objectionable manner because there is no actual commitment to massive nuclear retaliation. Of course, it might be objected that even greater deterrence could be achieved in this context if a nation's leaders were either immoral or amoral agents who were willing to commit themselves to massive nuclear retaliation and, hence, actually were capable of threatening such retaliation.[21] But strategically this increment of deterrence hardly seems to be needed, and morally, leaders who have committed themselves to acting in a morally horrendous manner in one context might easily be willing to do the same in other contexts, sometimes with disastrous consequences.

Third, it might be argued that by accepting a form of limited nuclear retaliation the proposed moral constraints make limited nuclear war more likely by making it morally acceptable. But in fact acceptance of these moral constraints would render nuclear war less likely than either MAD or Counterforce. For, as noted previously, MAD lacks a credible response to limited nuclear attacks and thus makes such attacks relatively attractive options for an adversary to take. In this regard, Counterforce is surely the correct response to MAD, and the proposed constraints, by justifying a form of limited nuclear retaliation, retain this advantage of Counterforce. But these constraints also render limited nuclear war less likely than Counterforce. For in addition to deterring would-be aggressors, as Counterforce would, these constraints also would render limited nuclear war less likely because of the commitment of those who adhere to them to avoid a wide range of counterforce strikes. Although those who accept these constraints recognize that nuclear retaliation is morally justified under certain foreseeable conditions, they also recognize that it is extremely unlikely for those conditions to ever be satisfied.

Summing up, I have argued for the following moral constraints on nuclear defense policy:

1. Only a form of limited nuclear retaliation can foreseeably be morally justified.
2. Under present conditions, nuclear deterrence must be achieved without the threat or bluff of nuclear retaliation.
3. Only when it is necessary to avoid a first strike would either threatening limited nuclear retaliation or bluffing massive nuclear retaliation be morally justified.

I have further argued that these constraints retain MAD's advantage of being able to deter a massive nuclear first strike and Counterforce's advantage of being able to deter limited nuclear strikes while incorporating additional moral and strategic advantages. On the basis of these arguments, I conclude that accepting the proposed constraints is the first step toward combining MAD and Counterforce into a morally and strategically sound nuclear defense policy.

Notes

1. See Lawrence Freedman, *The Evolution of Nuclear Strategy* (New York, 1981) especially Section 8; Peter Pringle and William Arkin, *S.I.O.P.* (New York, 1983); Solly Zuckerman, *Nuclear Illusion and Reality* (New York, 1983) especially Chapter 4; and Freeman Dyson, *Weapons and Hope* (New York, 1984) Part 4.

2. Freedman, ibid., pp. 352–354; Union of Concerned Scientists, "The New Arms Race," *Briefing Paper*, no. 4 (1983); Mark Hatfield, "The Age of Anxiety" *AEI Foreign Policy and Defense Review* (1980):13–14. Les Aspin, "Judge Not by Numbers Alone," *The Bulletin of Atomic Scientists* (1980):81–83.

3. Casper W. Weinberger, "Why We Must Have a Nuclear Deterrent," *Defense* (1983):2–5; and *Annual Report to the Congress*, (Washington, D.C., 1984), p. 31ff.

4. For further discussion of such a decision procedure, see my book, *The Demands of Justice* (Notre Dame, 1980), Chaps. 2 and 3. Also see John Rawls, *A Theory of Justice* (Cambridge, 1971). A consequence of this line of reasoning is that the principle that the end does not justify the means, although generally valid, is not universally so, all things considered.

5. For the most part, I propose to limit discussion to the bilateral use of nuclear weapons and nuclear deterrence by the United States and the Soviet Union. If a moral assessment can be worked out in this case, it is to be hoped that it can be extended to cases involving other nuclear powers.

6. Office of Technology Assessment, *The Effects of Nuclear War* (Washington, D.C., 1979), pp. 94, 100; Nigel Calder, *Nuclear Nightmare* (New York, 1979), p. 150; and Sidney Lens, *The Day Before Doomsday* (Boston, 1977), p. 102.

7. Carl Sagan, "Nuclear War and Climate Catastrophe: Some Policy Implications," *Foreign Affairs* (1983):257–292.

8. Office of Technology Assessment, *The Effects of Nuclear War*, pp. 83, 91; Jerome Kahan, *Security in the Nuclear Age* (Washington, D.C., 1975), p. 202; and Lens, *The Day Before Doomsday*, pp. 98–99, 102.

9. Lens, ibid., pp. 78–79; Spurgeon Keeny and Wolfgang Panofsky, "MAD Verse NUTS" *Foreign Affairs* (1981-2):297–298; and Ian Clark, *Limited Nuclear War* (Princeton, N.J., 1982), p. 242.

10. Lens, ibid., p. 73.

11. McGeorge Bundy, George F. Kennan, Robert S. McNamara, and Gerald Smith, "Nuclear Weapons and the Atlantic Alliance," *Foreign Affairs* (1982):757. It should be noted that Bundy, Kennan, McNamara, and Smith believe that their endorsement of a doctrine of no first use of nuclear weapons *may* involve increased spending for conventional forces in Europe. Others, however, have found NATO's existing conventional strength adequate to meet a Soviet attack. See David Barash and Judith Lipton, *Stop Nuclear War* (New York, 1982), pp. 138–140; and Harold Brown, *Department of Defense Annual Report* (Washington, D.C., 1981).

12. Gregory Kavka, "Nuclear Deterrence: Some Moral Perplexities" in *The Ethics of War and Nuclear Deterrence*, edited by James P. Sterba (Belmont, Calif., 1984), pp. 285–302.

13. Gregory Kavka, "Some Paradoxes of Deterrence" *The Journal of Philosophy* (1978).

14. Michael Walzer, "Nuclear Deterrence" in *Morality in Practice*, edited by James P. Sterba (Belmont, Calif., 1983), pp. 315–323.

15. Ibid., p. 318.

16. Jonathan Schell, "The Contradiction of Nuclear Deterrence" in Sterba, *Morality in Practice*, pp. 324–330.

17. Ibid., p. 325.

18. For a related discussion, see Thomas Schelling, *Arms and Influence* (New Haven, 1966), pp. 49–50, 154.

19. Much of this evidence is reviewed in my paper "How to Achieve Nuclear Deterrence Without Threatening Nuclear Destruction," in Sterba, *The Ethics of War and Nuclear Deterrence*.

20. U.S. Department of Defense, *Soviet Military Power* (Washington, D.C., 1983); David Holoway, *The Soviety Union and the Arms Race* (New Haven, 1983); and Andrew Cockburn, *The Threat* (New York, 1983), Chap. 12.

21. Kavka has argued in favor of this option. See his "Paradoxes of Deterrence."

Selected Bibliography

Bundy, McGeorge et al. "Nuclear Weapons and the Atlantic Alliance." *Foreign Affairs* (1982):756–768.

Cockburn, Andrew. *The Threat: Inside the Soviet Military Machine.* New York: Random House, 1983.

Cohen, Arnes, and Lee, Steven. *Nuclear Weapons and the Future of Humanity.* Totowa, N.J.: Rowman & Allanheld, 1985.

Fosberg, Randall. "A Bilateral Nuclear-Weapon Freeze." *Scientific American* 247 (1982):52–61.

Ground Zero. *Nuclear War: What's in It for You?* New York: Pocket Books, 1982.

Harvard Study Group. *Living with Nuclear Weapons.* New York: Bantam Books, 1983.

Kahan, Jerome. *Security in the Nuclear Age.* Washington, D.C.: Brookings Institution, 1975.

Kennan, George. *Nuclear Delusion.* New York: Pantheon, 1983.

National Conference of Catholic Bishops. *The Challenge of Peace.* Washington, D.C.: U.S. Catholic Conference, 1983.

Nitze, Paul. "Strategy in the Decade of the 1980s." *Foreign Affairs* (1980):82–101.

Powers, Thomas. "What Is It About?" *The Atlantic Monthly* (1984):35–55.

Schell, Jonathan. *The Fate of the Earth.* New York: Knopf, 1982.

Stein, Walter. *Nuclear Weapons and the Christian Conscience.* London: Merlin Press, 1961.

Union of Concerned Scientists. *Beyond the Freeze.* Boston: Beacon Press, 1982.

U.S. Office of Technology. *The Effects of Nuclear War.* Washington, D.C.: U.S. Government Printing Office, 1979.

7

How to Achieve Deterrence

Steven Lee

The present direction of U.S. nuclear weapons policy toward a greater emphasis on counterforce targeting has caused great concern among members of the public and among many strategic theorists. Although U.S. policy has been moving in this direction for many years, the speed of the movement has increased greatly, with talk of flexible response giving way to that of escalation dominance and nuclear war fighting. The public concern this has raised has led the philosophical community belatedly to begin considering issues such as the morality of nuclear deterrence. But most of the philosophical examinations of this issue have focused on the moral status of nuclear deterrence in general and thus on the choice between nuclear deterrence and unilateral nuclear disarmament. This misses much of the contemporary debate on nuclear weapons policy, which is concerned mainly with the choice between present policy and some form of minimum deterrence.

James Sterba's chapter, "Between MAD and Counterforce," has the virtue of taking as the subject of its moral examination present nuclear deterrence policy rather than nuclear deterrence in general. Sterba sees present policy as a combination of mutually assured destruction and counterforce strategies, and he asks at the beginning whether this combination policy, instead of joining the advantages of its component strategies, has joined their liabilities, both strategic and moral. This is surely the right question with which to begin. Sterba concludes, in accord with many participants in the contemporary debate, that the United States should adopt, at least as a first step, a form of minimum deterrence. I will argue, however, that there are serious problems with the arguments by which Sterba arrives at this conclusion.

The question in all of this is, How should we achieve deterrence? Strategic objections to present policy are that present policy does not achieve deterrence as well as a form of minimum deterrence would, in that present policy is more likely to lead to nuclear war. In the eyes of its critics, this is present policy's strategic liability. Sterba is more concerned with the moral liability of present policy, but he argues that a policy that avoids the moral liability also would avoid this strategic liability. The moral liability, as Sterba sees it, is that present policy involves the *threat* to use nuclear weapons in a way that would kill a large number of innocent persons. Sterba's answer to the question of how we should achieve deterrence is that we should do so without the threats. Later I shall examine his argument that it is morally important to avoid making threats and show that it has serious problems. But first I shall argue that he is mistaken in holding that nuclear deterrence can be achieved without threats.

Sterba argues that the United States can achieve nuclear deterrence without threats by possessing a nuclear retaliatory capacity and announcing to the Soviets that although it is in the national interest of the United States to make a threat of retaliation, for moral reasons it will not do so. He acknowledges that a mere verbal disclaimer is not sufficient to constitute an absence of threat. What is necessary in addition is that there be some legitimate and independent role for these weapons other than to threaten retaliation. Such a role exists, Sterba claims—it is to have the capacity to make a nuclear threat in the future should a Soviet leader come to power who would require threats to be deterred. Sterba's view seems to be that the fact that the U.S. nuclear arsenal could plausibly play such a role, when coupled with the claim not to be making a threat with the weapons, would constitute the absence of making such a threat. The policy then would avoid what Sterba regards as the chief moral liability of present policy.

But if the issue of threats puts so much morally at stake, we need to be more careful in our analysis of what it is to make a threat. As Sterba recognizes, making threats can be implicit and explicit. (*Making* a threat must be distinguished from *posing* a threat because one can pose a threat without making one. Making threats, which I am discussing here, is of moral relevance for Sterba.) Presumably, explicit threats are primarily verbal, and implicit threats are nonverbal. Because there are implicit as well as verbal threats, the mere claim not to be making a threat does not constitute the absence of making a threat. What explicit and implicit threats have in common is what constitutes making a threat, and it seems to be this: A's making a threat against B is A's engaging in behavior (verbal or not) that exhibits an intention to instill a belief in B that infliction of harm by A on B would follow the performance of certain actions by B. If A behaves in a way that is intended to instill such a belief, whatever else A is intending that behavior to do as well, then A is making a threat.

Given this understanding of what it is to make a threat, can the United States achieve nuclear deterrence without threats? The answer is clearly no. If the purpose is to deter, the United States ipso facto has an intention to instill in the Soviets a belief that retaliation would be consequent upon their aggression, and the United States must behave in a way that communicates that intention. Sterba clearly frames his proposed policy so that it achieves deterrence in the present, for he regards it as a crucial point in favor of his policy that it can achieve deterrence without (explicit) threats. His policy has a deterrent intention and so involves the making of threats.

What about the independent role for A's weapons under Sterba's policy—that is, the possibility that the weapons could be used later to back up a future (explicit) threat should such become necessary to deter the aggressiveness of some new Soviet leadership? Of course, the mere fact that the weapons could play this other role does not show that A intends them to play this role. But even if A intends them to play this role, this does not show that A does not intend them also to deter present Soviet leadership; and if the policy has the latter intention, then it involves making threats. In fact, public policies usually have more than one intention or purpose.

Sterba might respond to this by distinguishing between intended and merely foreseen consequences, arguing that the achievement of deterrence in the present under his policy would be a merely foreseen consequence of possessing the weapons and so the policy would have no intention to deter. But concerning the two ends of his policy, present deterrence and the capacity for future deterrence, it is simply more intelligible to regard both as intended rather than one as intended and the other as merely foreseen. Even if one of these ends is merely foreseen, on what basis could it be argued that the achievement of deterrence in the present is the end that is merely foreseen, especially given the great importance the United States places on the achievement of deterrence in the present? The only conditions under which a nuclear weapons policy would not involve an intention to deter would be if it achieved deterrence *accidently*, but one cannot set out to achieve deterrence accidently. Thus, the independent role for A's weapons cannot show that the policy involves no intention to deter and so cannot show that a threat is not being made.

In response to this line of criticism, Sterba has in discussion suggested the following argument. U.S. policy would not involve making even implicit threats if U.S. leaders believed that there is no need to threaten the Soviet Union. To deter a nation is to cause that nation not to perform some aggression it otherwise would have performed. If the United States were to believe that the Soviet Union's military intentions were inherently and purely defensive, so that the USSR would not be aggressive even in the absence of U.S. military power, it follows that the United States would not believe that its military posture is deterring the USSR. Hence, given this assumption, Sterba's policy of retaining nuclear weapons as a deterrent force for future contingencies regarding changes in Soviet leadership would not be a policy involving even implicit threats in the present. But this response is not adequate to meet the criticism. Whether or not it is true that Soviet military intentions are inherently defensive is not the issue; rather this issue is whether it is reasonable to expect the United States to come to this belief. Only if the United States were to believe this would U.S. intentions be such that its nuclear weapons policy would not constitute the making of threats. But it is hardly reasonable to expect such a belief, given the anticommunist hysteria to which the U.S. public and leadership are prone.

There is, moreover, another serious objection. Sterba's response may not, in fact, even be relevant to a defense of his proposed policy. For a belief that Soviet military intentions are defensive in practice is unlikely to be compatible with the belief that there may be a real need for a deterrent force to restrain the USSR in the future, a belief that is essential to the rationale for Sterba's policy. If the United States were to be convinced that the basic intentions of the Soviet Union toward the United States were so benign that deterrence is unnecessary in the present, the United States would see this benign attitude as deeply embedded in the Russian national character and would not take seriously the prospect of leadership suddenly coming into power in the Soviet Union that would pose an aggressive threat. Under such a belief in Soviet benignity, there would be no more strategic or moral justification for U.S. possession of nuclear weapons other than that provided by a fear that in the future Britain or France might suddenly acquire leaders who would engage in aggression against the United States.

But in any case, an analytic examination of what constitutes the making of a threat is of special interest only if the making of threats has the kind of moral relevance Sterba claims for it. Before sketching an alternative account of what is of moral relevance in these matters, I would like to make some comments on Sterba's argument that nations should not make nuclear threats. One possible source of confusion in his argument is that he initially uses the term *threat* in a nonstandard way, to exclude bluff. Thus he is able to relabel Gregory Kavka's wrongful intentions principle as the wrongful threatening principle. Because of Sterba's moral opposition to nuclear threats, one might expect that he would regard this principle as showing nuclear deterrence to be morally unacceptable. But he seems to accept that Kavka and Michael Walzer have shown that the principle is morally overridden by the consequences of deterrence. As a result, Sterba introduces the impossible threat principle, which holds that one (logically) cannot make a threat that one does not expect to carry out should it fail to deter. (This principle also requires a definition of threat that excludes bluff.)

But what prescriptive consequences does the argument now yield? If one accepted the wrongful threatening principle as showing that nuclear deterrence is morally unacceptable, contra Kavka and Walzer, then the prescriptive consequence would be complete unilateral nuclear disarmament. But Sterba does not prescribe complete unilateral nuclear disarmament, nor does he regard the wrongful threatening principle as showing that nuclear deterrence is morally unacceptable. Instead he introduces the impossible threat principle and his own policy prescription of deterrence without threats, apparently meaning to argue that the former implies the latter. But there is no such implication, for this principle yields no policy prescription. The principle does not require that practitioners of present policy do anything differently, such as verbally disclaiming the making of threats. Instead, the principle, being a merely logical principle, requires, if anything, only that what they are doing be redescribed as bluffing rather than sincerely threatening.

In fact, Sterba may be committing the fallacy of equivocation. He assumes in the impossible threat principle that threats are not bluffs, for only under such an assumption is the principle true. But for the principle to have the policy prescription he desires, he must tacitly presuppose the standard usage of threats as including bluffs, for otherwise the principle would not disallow bluffing and so would not require the verbal disclaimer that threats were being made. Sterba does allow that a bluff of massive retaliation would be morally permissible if Soviet leadership in the future were to become more aggressive, but he believes that his argument shows that bluffing is morally excluded under present conditions. But to the extent that his argument rests on the impossible threat principle, it does not show this.

Let me now sketch an account somewhat different than Sterba's of the deontological wrongness of nuclear deterrence. For Sterba it is the threat or intention to retaliate that is morally wrong with nuclear deterrence. The moral wrong, however, is not the mere intention itself, but the entire policy that involves that intention, a policy of hostage holding. People often speak of nuclear deterrence as a policy of hostage holding, but the moral implications of this idea need to be worked out. Hostages are innocent persons put at risk of harm without their consent, and hostage holding in general and nuclear deterrence in particular are morally wrong because innocent persons are put at such a risk of harm. Although the intention to retaliate is usually part of what creates this risk, a nation that has a nuclear retaliatory capacity for the sake of deterrence creates such a risk for innocent persons even if it is bluffing about retaliation or it issues a disclaimer about making a retaliatory threat, for the weapons might be used deliberately in any case or might go off accidently. Thus, getting rid of the intention to retaliate may not remove the moral wrong, if one still has the weapons.

Further, if a nation with a nuclear retaliatory capacity decided to eschew the intention to retaliate, the risk to the policy's hostages might even be increased. For example, nation A, with a nuclear deterrence policy that issues a disclaimer about making a threat, might destabilize the international political situation to the point that the use of nuclear weapons by the other side becomes more likely. Because A might retaliate despite its intention not to, if an attack by the other side becomes more likely, it may be more likely that A's policy will result in harm to its hostages. If this were the case, the risk to innocent persons would be greater under a policy in which a retaliatory intention is lacking than it would be under a similar policy that included a retaliatory intention. So the moral wrongness of the policy, far from disappearing when the intention is eschewed, as Sterba's assumption implies, would remain and might even be intensified.

This account of the deontological wrongness of nuclear deterrence policy has important implications for Sterba's argument. Even if it were possible to achieve nuclear deterrence without threats, such a policy would not avoid the moral wrong because the risk of harm to innocents would remain. If one's concern is to avoid this wrong, no halfway measures will do; the policy prescription is complete unilateral nuclear disarmament. One must face in the present the moral question Sterba thinks we can avoid for the present: Is the deontological wrongness of the policy overridden by the value of the policy's consequences? It is only through facing this question squarely that the moral case for minimum deterrence can be made.

I will conclude with two brief remarks on the strategic advantages or disadvantages of Sterba's proposed policy. As I mentioned earlier, Sterba claims that the implementation of his policy would be a form of minimum deterrence (many fewer warheads carried primarily or exclusively on invulnerable submarine missiles) and that this policy avoids not only the moral liabilities of present policy, but the strategic liabilities as well. Contrary to many visions of minimum deterrence, Sterba's has a counterforce component, one small enough, he argues, to secure a strategic advantage of present policy—the deterrence of a Soviet limited nuclear attack—and to avoid a strategic liability of present policy—an increased risk of nuclear war. My first remark concerns this component. Sterba has not shown that any counterforce component is needed to deter such an attack; nor has he shown, assuming that such a component is needed, that one can achieve this deterrence while avoiding the greater risk of war. If a counterforce component is needed to deter a limited attack, it may be the case that the size of the required component is large enough to create an increased risk of war (due to Soviet first-strike fears, for example) that would more than cancel out the advantage from the lessened risk of limited attack. In either case, of course, minimum deterrence policy should have no counterforce component.

My second point concerns the question raised earlier: How should the United States achieve deterrence? Sterba agrees with many others that the answer is some form of minimum deterrence. Such a policy, according to this view, poses less of a risk of war than present policy. But it should be recognized that many proponents of present policy would understand this question in a broader way. For them the important issue is, What does one seek to deter? They are supporters of extended deterrence, the view that nuclear weapons should be used to deter more than an attack with nuclear weapons. A policy is to be judged, in their view, not merely on its effectiveness in avoiding nuclear war, but also on its effectiveness in achieving the goals of extended deterrence. Proponents of present policy would see the ineffectiveness of minimum deterrence in achieving the goals of extended deterrence as a severe strategic liability. If moral philosophers are going to enter the contemporary debate by considering not just nuclear deterrence in general but present policy in particular, this is an aspect of the problem that must be taken up. The case for minimum deterrence requires a critique of extended deterrence.

8

Nuclear Deterrence as Bluff:
A Dialogue on the Moral Costs

John E. Hare
J. Ralph Lindgren

R: After reading Jim Sterba's chapter and Steven Lee's response there are some questions I find myself asking. I've been thinking about nuclear deterrence and the moral position it puts us in. It seems to me that wars, if they can be justified at all, have to be justified on the basis of some value that is under threat. They are not just about real estate. This value has to be pretty fundamental if it is to justify the sort of destruction that wars characteristically bring about. In the nuclear age we seem to be in a situation where in order to protect fundamental values we have to be ready to destroy them. (One thinks of what was said in Vietnam: "We have to destroy the village in order to save it.") How can we justify possessing an arsenal of these weapons of indiscriminate mass destruction in the name of human dignity or any other value?

I know you will say that the point of possessing these weapons is just to prevent their use. This is the conventional justification. But if to use the weapons is wrong, intending to use the weapons is wrong. The conventional justification neglects what Jim Sterba calls the wrongful threatening principle, which states that "if an act is wrong, then threatening to perform that act also is wrong." The mere fact that we are not currently using the weapons does not make all that much moral difference.

J: I don't have the answer to this. I don't think anyone does completely. The conventional justification of deterrence is shaky at exactly this point. I remember Bryan Hehir, who was involved intimately with drafting the Catholic Bishops' Pastoral Letter, saying that it was possible to write "A" papers on both extremes of this question—either get rid of all nuclear weapons or be prepared to use them all—but between these extremes, where most people are, a "B+" paper is the best we can get. There is more to be said, however. Your concern about the morality of deterrence depends on a connection between intention and possession that can be questioned. For it is possible to agree that the intention to use the weapons is immoral and still justify possessing them.

It is true that we possess nuclear weapons as an implicit threat, to deter our opponents from some kinds of action. Here I think Steven Lee's critique of Sterba's position is correct. There is some kind of threat as long as there is an intention on the part of one person to instill a belief in another person that an infliction of harm by the first would follow the performance of certain actions by the second. But having said that, I think we have to distinguish between three kinds of threat. The first kind is accompanied by the intention to carry out the threat; the second is accompanied by the intention not to carry it out; and the third is not accompanied by an intention one way or the other. All three exhibit intentions, but the third involves only the intention to instill a belief of a certain kind in the person threatened.

We are familiar with this distinction in ordinary life. If my child continually spills the milk, I may threaten punishment. When I threaten, I may intend to carry it out, I may intend not to carry it out, or I may not have decided one way or the other. If a threat of either the second or the third kind can be called a bluff, then the objection you raised about intentions will have been met. Even if the intention to use the weapons is wrong, the possession of them, and the implicit threat to use them, may not require the presence of an intent to use them.

Jim Sterba would deny that these two kinds of bluff are threats at all. But this is probably a purely verbal disagreement. For he, too, thinks there is a moral advance from the threat plus the commitment to carry out massive retaliation to a bluff minus such commitment.

R: But it doesn't seem possible that our nuclear deterrent policy is a bluff in either of the two senses you distinguished—that is, in the sense that we have formed an intention not to use the weapons or in the sense that we haven't formed an intention one way or another on the use of the weapons.

It seems to me that this amendment of the conventional justification is flawed in two ways—it's unrealistic and it's incoherent. It's unrealistic because there isn't enough time, once the other side has fired its weapons, to make a decision if that decision has to be made from scratch. Leaders already must have decided, albeit conditionally, how to use these weapons, when they come into the office of commander in chief.

J: Actually I think this bluff account gives a realistic picture. I would support that in three ways. First there is the historical record. The presidential papers that are now public show that none of the presidents in the nuclear age decided in advance under what conditions to authorize massive retaliation, even though they were under pressure to do so. That is apparently also true of President Carter, who steadfastly resisted pressure from his national security adviser to make this decision. My observation after two years working on congressional staff gives me my second reason. Politicians prefer not to make up their minds in advance. They very seldom form firm conditional intentions. One reason for this is to preserve flexibility; they want to be able to decide at the last minute because the nature of the choice changes with the changing political context. If the issue is new, and especially if it is new and momentous, they will leave the decision until the last possible minute. Finally, the official doctrine of both superpowers is not to launch on warning. This suggests, although it doesn't entail, that neither side has formed even a conditional intention to authorize the use of the weapons. Each side knows that the decisions may look different when they actually arise than they did in any of the previously thought-through "scenarios."

R: Okay, that meets the "unrealistic" objection. Still, there is my second objection that the bluff account is incoherent. If deterrence is to work, the threat must be credible. Credibility cannot be maintained without a conspicuous intention to use the weapon under specified conditions. If the commander in chief has formed no intention, however conditional, to use these weapons, then surely their mere possession will not be seen by the opponent as a threat at all.

J: I don't see that a bluff is incoherent. Of course the leaders of both sides have to pretend to have the relevant conditional intentions, but we have to distinguish between rhetoric that is a necessary part of deterrence and actual intention. Credibility can be analyzed as dependent on two variables: the size of the stake at issue between the parties and the availability of the threatened force. A threat will be credible if the other side can form the judgment that the force threatened might be used for the stake at issue. This makes sense of the difference between the Cuban missile crisis and the Hungarian crisis, for example. The United States felt free to make nuclear threats in the first case, not in the second; this was possible because of the difference in the stakes at issue for the United States. The Cuban and the Hungarian crises threatened the inner ring of defenses of the United States and the Soviet Union, respectively. Moreover, the conventional forces available to the United States in the first case and the Soviet Union in the second were significantly superior. But the main point here is that neither the size of the stake nor the availability of the force is dependent upon the existence of a conditional intention to use the weapons.

R: Your bluff amendment may be solid as a description of our nuclear deterrence practices, but the question still remains as to whether it blunts the moral objection raised to the conventional account. The objection I raised to the standard account was that if it's wrong to use weapons of indiscriminate mass destruction, then it's also wrong to possess them. One way to construe this objection is that if it's wrong to use them, it's wrong to intend to use them; and if it's wrong to intend to use them, it's wrong to threaten to use them; and if it's wrong to threaten to use them, it's wrong to possess them. Now your bluff amendment holds that if the commander in chief has not formed an intention to use the weapons, then the mere possession of them is not wrong. You are trying to break the chain of inferences from wrongness of use to wrongness of possession.

The bluff argument, however, derives its plausibility in part from a misleading analogy. It treats "possessing" nuclear weapons as basically the same as "possessing" a shotgun. Jim Sterba explicitly relies on that example. But, the former, unlike the latter, involves a lot more than owning certain exotic hardware. In addition, the possession of nuclear weapons involves command structures as well as support, communications, and maintenance systems. Each of these includes large numbers of trained personnel. In order to see that the possession of nuclear weapons, even if it works by bluff, imposes significant moral costs, we need to look at the situation of the people who operate these systems.

You've shown me that it's possible that commanders in chief have not formed an intention to use these nuclear weapons, but what about all the other people involved in these weapons systems—the rank and file? Think, for example, of the air force lieutenant in a missile silo in North Dakota. Even if his commander in chief has formed no intention to use the weapon under his control, the lieutenant has. He has formed the intention to fire the weapon if commanded to do so. Now if intending to use these weapons is wrong, then it also is wrong to intend using them on command. Hence, our nuclear deterrence strategy, even when described as a bluff, sacrifices the moral integrity of all the people who operate these weapons.

You recognize, of course, that there is more than a handful of people who are in the position of the lieutenant. Although the number of people in the position of the lieutenant is quite modest at any one time, those people have backups, and both teams of people turnover at a significant rate. As a result, the number of people involved is multiplied several times during each year.

Now you may say that members of our armed forces are required to evaluate their orders morally before carrying them out. However, the whole system of military training is designed to prevent that. Practice alerts are designed, among other things, to get our lieutenant used to turning the switch on command.

J: Yes, I can see that your "rank and file objection" is valid against the amended account. I also agree with you on the whole system of training, even though the instruction to evaluate orders morally is in the manuals of the services. Still, two things can be said in mitigation. First, the centralization of command and control mechanisms is developing fast. We may get to the point where either turning the key may not fire the missile without some subsequent coded radio approval from the commander in chief or the commander in chief actually may be able to fire the missile directly. In either case it will not be the lieutenant himself who fires it. Second, if neither of these is possible, at least it can be said that there are sufficiently few whose integrity is sacrificed in this way so that nuclear deterrence is worth it.

R: I think you jump too quickly to the conclusion that a very few people are involved here. Look at the situation where the missile is not fired after turning the key because no subsequent radio approval was received. Here the lieutenant, in turning the key, is purposefully facilitating the commander in chief's firing the weapon by providing essential aid in its launch.

If that's a valid point, then even in the present state of technology the number of people implicated in the moral action is not limited to a few. Think of the millions of people who supply essential aid in the form of materials, services, and taxes. They are in the same position as the lieutenant in your example.

J: That's an interesting line of argument, but we need to make another distinction. There are two different cases here. In the first case the lieutenant shares the actual purpose of using the weapon, and in the second case he doesn't. In the second case he merely purposes to do something, namely, turning the key, under the description "providing aid to the commander in chief," even though he is hoping against hope that this is just an exercise and that the radio approval, or whatever, will not be given. In the first case he purposes to aid the commander in chief in launching the missile under that description. Perhaps he is a rabid anticommunist and simply can't wait, so to speak, to bomb the Soviets back into the Stone Age. In the second case he is not morally an accomplice. For to be an accomplice, a person has to have the purpose of promoting or facilitating the commission of the wrongful act. There is an analogy then with all the members of the rank and file who are providing essential aid, but not taking the last and irreversible step. As long as they do not have the purpose of helping in the use of the weapons (supposing the use is morally wrong), but merely of maintaining deterrence, they can carry on in good conscience. This is a response also to those people who withhold taxes on the grounds that they do not want to be accomplices to murder. For they are not in the position to know that they are taking the last and irreversible step toward nuclear war. They can pay their taxes in good conscience, if they are proponents of deterrence, but not of nuclear use.

I want to reassert that the number of people whose integrity is being sacrificed is pretty small.

R: Your restriction on moral accomplices to those whose actual purpose is to cooperate in the performance of a wrongful act has a parallel in the criminal law. There it is justified by pragmatic considerations about overwhelming the criminal justice system. I doubt that such a restriction is justified, however, where the concern is the assignment of moral responsibility.

You admitted earlier that the lieutenant, who intends to turn the key that fires the missile if commanded to do so, is morally responsible for intending to fire the missile. Now either the actual purpose limitation applies to the lieutenant or it does not. If it does, then the lieutenant will not be morally responsible for intending a wrongful act if he intends to turn the key "under the description 'providing aid to the commander in chief.' " One of the main points of the lieutenant's training is to motivate his action under precisely that description. However, an endorsement of that restriction would encourage moral myopia and self-deception on the part of all agents, and that is surely not a result a moral theorist would want to promote. If, on the other hand, the actual purpose limitation does not apply to the situation of agents, but only to that of purported accomplices, another problem arises. Why should that be so? Is that not simply an arbitrary limitation on the moral responsibility of accomplices? If one is morally responsible for the negligent and even the inadvertent acts one performs as a primary agent, why should the same not be the case for acts of secondary agents as well? Absent a principled justification of this difference, I find unpersuasive your limitation on the number of people whose moral integrity is sacrificed because they provide essential aid to the commander in chief in posing a nuclear bluff.

J: I agree that the actual purpose restriction on the moral responsibility of accomplices is too narrow. I also agree that it is not clear why we should remove this restriction for principal agents. But if we do not accept the actual purpose limitation, there seems to be no nonarbitrary way to draw the line between those who are and those who are not moral accomplices in preparing for the use of nuclear weapons. As a result, we are not now able to estimate accurately the full extent of moral casualties that result from possessing these weapons.

R: Even on the most conservative estimate, however, the moral costs of possessing nuclear weapons are not nearly as insignificant as your bluff argument suggested. At present our deterrence strategy sacrifices the moral integrity of at least those members of the armed forces who know that they may be in a position to take the last and irreversible step toward firing these weapons. Given that moral integrity or something like it was the value we were supposed to be protecting, that takes us back to the point where I began. How can we justify possessing an arsenal of weapons of indiscriminate mass destruction in the name of human dignity or any other value? The sacrifice of the moral integrity of those members of the rank and file who operate the deterrent is a very significant cost of the deterrence strategy, even one that works by bluff. If that is added to the other costs of the practice, the case against nuclear deterrence is very substantial.

J: I have to agree about those costs. There are other direct costs of deterrence, whether it works by bluff or not. The most apparent is the financial cost of more than $12 billion annually just for procurement. There is the constant possibility that the nuclear threat may be carried out by miscalculation or accident or madness. Possession makes use more likely with or without the (conditional) intention to use. There is the gradual dulling of conscience in nations that possess nuclear weapons. There is the declining will to move effectively toward arms control and disarmament, and with that the increasing threat of proliferation. Also, the arms race itself produces new weapons that destabilize deterrence, thereby making the use of the weapons more likely. All these are direct costs even on the bluff theory, and this list is certainly not exhaustive.

R: In addition to the direct costs of deterrence, there are also the opportunity costs. These include all the projects that would have been undertaken had the resources not been devoted to the deployment of nuclear weapons. Of course, it's incredibly difficult to identify what those projects might have been, but surely we might speculate that they include projects in the areas of health, education, and welfare.

J: The moral cost of possessing nuclear weapons indeed is substantial. However, when all these costs are added up, direct and indirect, they have to be weighed against the benefits that deterrence yields, the benefits of preserving the world and preserving those values we have been talking about. The costs also must be weighed against the costs of any alternative ways of providing those benefits. The alternatives are the other ways we could conduct the struggle with our opponents, granting that this is likely to continue for the foreseeable future. I can think of four. We might do so by using only nonnuclear weapons, by using economic leverage, by internationalizing force under world law, or by nonviolent civilian resistance. These are all ways to conduct the struggle without nuclear weapons. We weigh the costs of nuclear deterrence against those of the alternatives in promoting those same benefits.

R: It is not an easy choice, but this discussion of the cost of deterrence points up two observations. One is that the marginal benefit of a deterrence strategy over one of nuclear war is not as great as many people have supposed. Look at all the different kinds of costs that we've listed for deterrence. The second is that we are under moral obligation to make that choice. In normal life when the costs of furthering a valued result burgeon, prudence dictates that we seriously and actively search out alternatives. Our record on that has been rather spotty to say the least.

J: I agree about the spotty record. We certainly do need to be more concerned about genuine research into alternative means of conducting international conflict. However, we also need to decide what to do in the interim.

R: Up until now we've been discussing the moral justification of nuclear deterrence on something like a model of criminal responsibility. Our focus has been on intention. We've assumed that unless the possession of nuclear weapons of mass destruction is linked to their use by way of an intention, moral responsibility is not at stake. But tort law suggests an alternative model of responsibility. Nuclear weapons, like dynamite, are, as the legal saying goes "ultrahazardous substances." In torts, people are held strictly liable for any harm that might result from the discharge of such substances. Responsibility there does not require demonstrating intention or even negligence. The mere possession of such substances, should they discharge, is sufficient to establish responsibility. The analogy between dynamite and strategic nuclear weapons suggests that moral responsibility for nuclear deterrence need not be dependent upon intentions.

J: That's an interesting point. I'm not sure what to say about it. But there is a disanalogy here, too. The dynamite case misses the deterrent aspect of nuclear weapons. Nuclear weapons are held for the purpose of threatening; dynamite ordinarily is not.

There are analogies, however, where threatening is involved. In civil assault cases one can be convicted on the basis of threatening with an unloaded gun, even though the gun is known to be unloaded by the one who threatens. The absence of a conditional intention to fire the weapon is irrelevant in that context. Similarly, extortion cases are actionable even if the extortioner lacks the power to impose the threatened sanction.

It may well be that criminal law is the wrong model for a discussion of the moral cost of nuclear bluff. It seems to be an open question whether the presence or absence of intention is of much significance for moral responsibility in that context.

Selected Bibliography

Hare, John E. "Credibility and Bluff." In *Nuclear Weapons and the Future of Humanity,* Avner Cohen and Stephen Lee (eds.). Totowa, N.J.: Rowman and Allanheld, 1985.

————. "The Intention to Use Nuclear Weapons." In *Evangelicals and the Bishops' Pastoral Letter.* Grand Rapids, Mich.: Eerdmans, 1984.

Hoekema, David. "Intentions, Threats and Nuclear Deterrence." In *The Applied Turn in Contemporary Philosophy.* Bowling Green State University, Ohio: Applied Philosophy Program, 1983.

Joynt, Carey B. "The Anatomy of Crises." In *The Year Book of World Affairs* 28 (1974):15–22.

Joynt, Carey B., and John E. Hare. *Ethics and International Affairs.* New York: Macmillan, 1981.

Paskins, Barrie, and Michael Dockrill. *The Ethics of War.* Minneapolis: University of Minnesota, 1979.

Sharp, Gene. *The Politics of Non-Violent Action.* Boston: Beacon Press, 1973.

9

Nuclear Threats and the Imposition of Risks

Leslie Pickering Francis

A wide variety of recent discussions of nuclear deterrence, by both consequentialists and deontologists, agree that the strategy can be justified only if it is more likely than other available strategies to prevent some markedly greater evil. All agree that nuclear devastation is one of the most horrible outcomes imaginable. If nuclear threats (it is convenient to call threatening with nuclear weapons "deterrence," but misleading to do so when we do not know whether nuclear threats actually will succeed in discouraging the use of nuclear weapons) were undeniably the best method available to ward off nuclear destruction, the case for it would be correspondingly clear. Some writers, however, also include preventing the serious evil of Soviet world domination as a goal of nuclear threats (Gauthier 1984; Hardin 1983; and Kavka 1983). This addition is a significant moral step, and I shall try to show that it cannot be justified.

Let me begin with some significant features of the choice situation in which nuclear threats are adopted as policy. First, consider members of the set of outcomes. Among the outcomes considered by strategists are nuclear devastation; limited nuclear war; Soviet world domination, partial or complete; U.S. world domination; and nuclear proliferation. Strategists seem to agree that any of these is at least a possible outcome of any of the nuclear weapons policies presently under discussion—development of first-strike capacity, MAD or Counterforce, mutual disarmament, or unilateral disarmament. Even the most optimistic policy analyst must admit that if the West tries nuclear threats but "loses the arms race," Soviet hegemony is a possible outcome of the deterrence strategy. Similarly, even unilateral disarmament poses some risk of full-scale nuclear war. Rather, the differences among the policies lie in the relative probabilities assigned the various outcomes under the policy.

Second are the probabilities. Choice of a nuclear strategy most closely resembles decisionmaking under uncertainty, yet the choice often is presented as if it were decisionmaking under risk. We do not know what the probabilities are of various outcomes given particular nuclear strategies. We do not even have a prior series of clinical trials from which to extrapolate results. (To be sure, we have tried nuclear threats to date, with more or less constancy, and nuclear war has not yet resulted. But one partial history is by no means a controlled trial.) At best, we can make some rough guesses about the relative probabilities of particular outcomes given particular strategies. Thus Hardin (1983) and Kavka (1983) agree that unilateral disarmament increases the likelihood of Soviet domination and perhaps also of limited Soviet use of nuclear weapons to bully less powerful adversaries. Lackey (1982; 1983) believes that escalating nuclear threats increase the probability of global nuclear war; Gauthier (1984) appears to believe that nuclear threats are the very best chance we have to avoid Hobbesian nuclear war. These rough guesses enable us to structure the choice of nuclear policy as decisionmaking under risk. But the structuring is tenuous. If we do grant that some probabilities can be assigned, we must bear in mind that they are at best rough, little substantiated estimates.

Third, there are the actors. The nuclear situation involves choices made by leaders, for others who have not themselves participated in the choices except perhaps in that they have voted. Many of those affected—both within and beyond the country adopting a nuclear weapons strategy—will not even have participated in this attenuated sense. In this, nuclear strategy is not like the choice situation of an individual who trades off the pleasures of a risky activity against the increased chances, however unknown, of a shorter life. It is not even like the choice of an individual who asserts that he would rather be Red than dead or, for that matter, rather be dead than Red. Instead, the nuclear choice situation involves the leaders choosing for others amid relatively unknown probabilities. Game-theoretic matrices that rank strategies (cf. Hardin 1983) mask this complexity.

A simplified version of the nuclear choice situation is this. Leaders choose between one strategy—nuclear threats—that has an unknown greater probability of preventing Soviet domination but an unknown greater risk of nuclear devastation, and a second strategy—unilateral disarmament—that has an unknown greater probability of avoiding nuclear devastation but an unknown greater risk of Soviet domination. How, morally, should the leaders decide? One kind of answer is that their choice should be a function of their citizens' preferences among available outcomes. Another kind of answer is that the leaders morally ought not to jeopardize the innocent.

A third kind of answer also is possible in terms of a theory about what kinds of risks it is permissible to impose on others. As a start, I would suggest that when probabilities are shadowy, we should analyze as best we can the levels and distribution of harms that will occur under each outcome. If there is an outcome with more widespread and more basic harms, we should rank it below outcomes with less basic and widespread harms. We then should choose the strategy that has the best chance (for all we know) of avoiding the lower ranked outcome. As yet this theoretical sketch says nothing about what we should do when one outcome includes more basic harms but another includes harms that are more widespread. But it is all we need to argue that prevention of Soviet domination should not be decisive to the case for nuclear threats.

Neither nuclear devastation nor Soviet domination is a singular harm. Each is a cluster of horrors. In the worst-case scenario, nuclear devastation involves at least these horrors: Everyone now alive will die, some quickly and others in prolonged and painful ways; there will be no one left to procreate the human species; most other animals and plants also will die; and the earth will become incapable of supporting the kinds of life it now supports. There will be no human future, and the past will lose all significance. In scenarios of more limited nuclear devastation, the earth will remain capable of supporting life, at far more rudimentary levels than now. Some species will survive, including perhaps human beings. Many will die; possibly more of these deaths will be prolonged and painful than if the devastation were more complete. Reproduction is likely to be difficult and accompanied by increases in birth defects, infant mortality, and early deaths from diseases such as leukemia.

If we take Stalinist Russia as the worst-case prototype, Soviet world domination involves some of the same evils. People will die, some after prolonged and painful torture. These deaths may be concentrated among those who held economic or political power in the newly dominant countries, among certain ethnic groups, or among groups in the dominant regime as it consumes its own. Those who remain alive in dominated areas will face reduced life prospects: limited incomes, recurrent shortages of basic needs such as food, assigned jobs, and the terror of recurring purges. These persons will lack political and intellectual freedom and will live in constant fear that the price of an independent or rebellious thought is death. They may face legal restrictions on marriage, procreation, or child-raising. These evils will persist as long as domination does, but there is no way of knowing how long this will be.

There are some simple ways to compare these conjunctions of evils. Nuclear devastation involves more deaths and probably more physical pain. Under Soviet domination, death will be less equally distributed, occurring more frequently among the U.S. wealthy and the powerful.

The worst nuclear devastation wipes out the future and the past entirely and with them any possibility for human flourishing, whereas Stalinism may crumble. Lesser devastation may produce circumstances of life as reduced as Soviet domination, with one exception. Under Stalinism, a significant number of people will be alive but unfree. After limited nuclear devastation, the possibility of free institutions remains, although social unrest and economic disorder may make this possibility fairly remote. If Soviet domination is to be regarded as an evil worse than nuclear devastation, then it must be because of the greater certainty that unfreedom will be experienced by those who live while domination persists, or because of the distribution of deaths and suffering that results. If the fact that citizens of the United States—rather than citizens of other countries—are more likely to die is not morally relevant (Hardin, in Chapter 2, may hold otherwise), experienced unfreedom is the sole moral consideration for regarding Soviet domination as the worse of the two evils.

Stalinism may not be the worst-case result of unilateral disarmament, however. Another possibility is that Soviet control would be incomplete, marked by recurrent efforts to consolidate control along the lines of Soviet policy in Eastern Europe. In this scenario, political and economic instability might be greater than with successful domination. Efforts to prevent rearmament in the United States or to stamp out the technological capacity that makes rearmament possible also could be expected. Incomplete hegemony thus might include more unfreedom, loss of life, and economic suffering than full domination. But it still does not risk evils of the range and scale of nuclear devastation.

Nuclear devastation thus is the outcome in which harms are more widely distributed. Arguably, it is also the outcome that involves more basic harms, for experienced unfreedom is the only worse feature of nuclear devastation, and life itself is necessary for the experience of freedom or unfreedom. We should choose the policy with the best chance of avoiding this outcome. Nuclear threats indeed may be this policy. For example, a unilateral disarmament policy by the United States might provide other countries with more incentive than they now have to develop their own nuclear capacities. The resulting proliferation might increase nuclear instability and the chances of nuclear war. But if nuclear threats are not the best way of avoiding nuclear war, it would be wrong to choose them on the ground that they have an (unknown) greater probability of avoiding the lesser evil of Soviet world domination.

References

Gauthier, David. 1984. "Deterrence, Maximization, and Rationality." *Ethics* 94:474–495.

Hardin, Russell. 1983. "Unilateral Versus Mutual Disarmament." *Philosophy and Public Affairs* 12:236–254.

Kavka, Gregory. 1983. "Doubts About Unilateral Nuclear Disarmament." *Philosophy and Public Affairs* 12:261–265.

Lackey, Douglas. 1982. "Missiles and Morals: A Utilitarian Look at Nuclear Deterrence." *Philosophy and Public Affairs* 11:189–231.

———. 1983. "Disarmament Revisited: A Reply to Kavka and Hardin." *Philosophy and Public Affairs* 12:261–265.

10

The Immorality of Nuclear Deterrence

Richard Werner

> When we think about the future of the world, we always have in mind
> its being at the place where it would be if it continued to move as we see
> it moving now. We do not realize that it moves not in a straight line, but
> in a curve, and that its direction constantly changes.
>
> **—Ludwig Wittgenstein**

It has become fashionable of late to refer to the paradoxes of deterrence.
We are told that the consequences of a nuclear war are so formidable
that we are morally justified in doing whatever is necessary to prevent
one. Consequently, according to this view, teleological moral theories[1]
can justify the practice of nuclear deterrence.[2]

So, the argument continues, it is paradoxical, but not fallacious, to
hold that the best way to prevent a nuclear war is to threaten waging
a nuclear war. It is paradoxical, but not fallacious, to hold that one is
morally justified in threatening and thereby intending to wage a nuclear
war if one's cause is world peace, justice, and freedom. It is paradoxical,
but not fallacious, to believe that the best way to decrease the number
of nuclear weapons and thereby to increase world stability is to build
more nuclear weapons.

I suspect that labeling a seeming contradiction a "paradox" is merely
a philosopher's gambit for protecting a favored belief from refutation. It
is, I fear, a gambit steeped in bad faith, designed to save one's
worldview from an all too drastic yet necessary revision. I will argue
that the teleological arguments currently being used to justify deterrence
are unsound. They are unsound for the simple reason that we lack
adequate evidence to conclude that deterrence has better consequences
than various other alternatives, including unilateral disarmament. In so

doing, I hope to reveal the inherent ideological commitments of such arguments.

On the other side of the moral coin, some deontologists[3] have argued that we can concoct plausible moral principles that justify nuclear deterrence in some possible world.[4] Unfortunately, these same deontologists fail to inform us whether the actual world is among the possible worlds in which deterrence is justified. In my arguments I am not concerned with possible worlds that bear little or no resemblance to our own world. Nor am I concerned with all logically possible counterexamples. I suspect that one can find any practice, including intentional nuclear war or nuclear deterrence, justified in some possible world and that one can find logically possible counterexamples to any principle or claim, moral or otherwise. But a moral theory, if it is to be a *moral* theory, must be practical; it must guide our actions in the actual world.[5] Hence, I conclude that talk of justifying deterrence in some merely possible world is, at best, an interesting exercise in intellectual masturbation.[6]

Every philosophical argument rests on some unproven assumptions. Among mine is the unproven assumption that a nuclear war, even a limited nuclear war, will have devastating consequences for humanity.[7] My assumption is unproven because no one knows what the consequences of such a war will be, until we have one. Yet the best science of the time clearly supports my assumption.[8] Both the Pentagon and its counterpart in the USSR have embraced these same conclusions but have concluded that they do not imply a change in deterrence policy.[9] Based on these scientific arguments, I will assume that even a limited nuclear war of any significance will result in the end of civilization as we know it and that a total war, at the very least, will return us to the state of nature.

One last point before we turn to our central questions. Appeals to emotion are generally considered anathema in philosophical arguments, regardless of the fact that their subtle use in such arguments is ubiquitous. I find the bifurcation between reason and emotion not only sexist in origin and design, but simply false and dangerous. Such a bifurcation rests on the deeply criticized notion of some value-neutral, Archimedean point from which one can "see" matters *sub specie aeternitatis* and from which one is to make and evaluate sound arguments.[10] It is in large part because the dichotomy between reason and emotion is illusory that no such point exists. If reason is not the slave of the passions, it is certainly no better than its handmaiden. Thus, I will not trade in the usual false consciousness of cleverly concealing emotional appeals. Mine will be obvious and, I hope, intertwined with sound arguments.

So, then, let us turn to the central question of the morality of deterrence debate. Can we be justified in threatening nuclear war in order to deter nuclear war? Surely if nuclear war is as heinous as the experts claim, we are justified in doing whatever is necessary to prevent one—even threatening to engage in such a war.

On Kantian grounds, the answer to this question is clear. As Kant correctly indicated, we normally can control our intentions, but we have far less control of the consequences of our actions. By Kantian lights, the person who attempts murder but does not succeed is as guilty as the successful murderer. The negligent but lucky driver who fortuitously avoids an accident is as guilty as those upon whom fortune does not smile.[11] One is responsible for what one intends to do rather than for the consequences of one's actions.

Moreover, according to the Kantian, we are to assess our intentions in terms of two categorical imperatives. First, we must be willing to universalize our actions. We must be willing to be on the receiving as well as the giving end of our actions. We must be willing to allow all others to act as we intend to act. Second, we must treat all innocent persons, including ourselves, as ends and never as means merely. Because, for the Kantian, innocent persons are autonomous, rational agents, to treat them as ends or in simpler language to respect them as persons, we must treat them as any autonomous, rational agent desires to be treated. That is, if we desire to influence their behavior we are to appeal to them rationally, humanly, and not by coercing their wills through threat or violence. Thus we are to treat innocent persons in a manner in which it is reasonable to believe that they themselves would consent to be treated after attempts at rational persuasion. Further, we are never to use persons merely as instruments in our pursuit of some goal, no matter how high or lofty the goal may be. Hence, the threat or use of violence against innocents as well as the exploitation or domination of innocents would be condemned on Kantian grounds.

Accordingly, even the conditional intention to use nuclear weapons only if they are used against one would seem to violate Kantian morality. Should the intent be acted upon, vast numbers of innocent persons would be killed, maimed, and injured as a mere means by national leaders whose ends would be those of war or ideology. Moreover, the very practice of deterrence uses these same innocent noncombatants[12] as a nation's means of preventing nuclear attack and of forcing concessions from one's adversaries whenever possible.[13] It is the innocent noncombatants who are intentionally targeted and threatened, either directly or indirectly,[14] by the practice of deterrence. It is they who are wronged by the present practice of deterrence. Hence, in two clear senses, deterrence would seem to directly violate Kantian morality, particularly the notion of respect for persons.[15]

Yet it has been argued that the conditional intention to wage nuclear war if attacked does not entail that one *intends* to wage nuclear war *when* one is attacked. As with similar fallacies in modal logic, the intentional operator ranges over the entire conditional. Thus one cannot correctly perform *modus ponens* on the conditional when the consequent is fulfilled. Hence the antecedent, the intention to wage nuclear war, does not follow as a conclusion even when the consequent is fulfilled.[16]

Logically, this is a fine point. But what does it mean in the actual world? The only plausible interpretation one can attach to it would be that of a "nuclear bluff." That is, the commander in chief of either of the superpowers could bluff with respect to her intention to wage nuclear war, if attacked. When the attack occurs, she simply will not respond, for it would be immoral and probably pointless to do so. Nevertheless, in order for deterrence to be effective, she must act as though she has every intention of using nuclear weapons in response to an attack.[17]

Although such a scenario might make for a decent science fiction story, in the real world it simply is implausible if not impossible. It is implausible because if the bluff is discovered by the other side, it would make nuclear war more likely and nuclear blackmail almost a certainty. The likelihood of containing such a secret for decades or even centuries seems extremely remote. White House and Kremlin leaks spring daily. Spies abound. In addition, the continuity of such a plan from one administration to the next cannot be assured.

Such a scenario is impossible because of the command and control problems that develop during a nuclear war.[18] Unless the commander in chief has revealed the bluff strategy to submarine and bomber captains as well as to commanders of missile silos, the probability is very high that several of these will decide to "use them or lose them" when they realize that a nuclear war is underway and that communications have been destroyed. Revealing the bluff to the requisite number of people would increase the likelihood of a leak almost to a certainty.

But, one might respond, even if all that you say is correct, the commander in chief can still bluff in the required manner and thereby not intend a nuclear war. As long as the commander in chief does not intend a nuclear response, even if she knows that one will occur, she is not culpable. Hence, the bluff is morally justified even if your scenario is correct.

If one knows that by bluffing one increases significantly the odds of nuclear war in the long run, while almost assuring retaliation by one's forces should an attack occur from the other side, in what sense does one *not* intend to use one's nuclear arsenal? The Kantian morality may be deontological, but it does not allow for universal idiocy concerning expected outcomes of actions.[19]

At any rate, this first line of argument against deterrence could be dismissed as a red herring, yet the Kantian argument against deterrence still would stand.[20] Consider the second line of argument previously mentioned. Right now each superpower is threatening violently to kill, maim, and torture hundreds of millions of innocent noncombatants as a mere means toward the twin ends of preventing the other from launching a nuclear attack and of forcing political concessions whenever possible. What is most important for our purposes is that they do so today and have done so for more than thirty-five years. It is unreasonable to conclude that the innocent civilians of the two superpowers would consent to such treatment, even after attempts at rational persuasion. I know that I, and those who share my beliefs, would not. Each superpower is intentionally treating innocent persons as a mere means toward its own ends of power and ideology.

Such behavior is an unequivocal violation of the Kantian notion of respect for persons, of the second formulation of the categorical imperative. Morally, it is on a par with threatening the lives and well-being of innocent third parties merely as a means of forcing another person to bend to our wills. It is blackmail that uses innocent others as the bait. It is hostage taking that uses innocent others as the hostages. One needs only to recall the public outcry against the Iranian government when the U.S. Embassy was taken hostage and used as blackmail against the United States to appreciate the attitude toward international hostage taking and blackmail. Yet the logic of deterrence rests on the same sort of sinister behavior.[21] I conclude that one cannot morally justify nuclear deterrence on Kantian grounds, regardless of one's analysis of conditional intentions.

Let us turn our attention to consequentialist theories. Gregory Kavka has argued that teleological moral theories justify one in framing the conditional intentional to wage nuclear war in order to prevent nuclear war from occurring *if* the expected consequences of so doing are the best.[22] Yet it is not obvious that the present world bears much resemblance to Kavka's reckoning.

Given a teleological moral theory we must consider the effects not merely on the United States but also on the USSR and all other nations and persons. In the present world, as Bertrand Russell was fond of arguing, unilateral disarmament almost certainly will assure that *total* war does not occur. If total nuclear war threatens all life, while unilateral disarmament diminishes that threat considerably (that is, diminishes both its likelihood and its bad consequences should it occur) consequentialist thinking would seem to rule against deterrence as the morally best means of defense. If only one superpower has nuclear weapons, the probability of the occurrence of total nuclear war is diminished considerably. Given that there could be no retaliatory strikes by the disarmed side and given that the number of weapons available would be diminished by about one-half, only lesser nuclear wars are likely.

Further, it would seem to be in the interests of the sole nuclear power to use its weapons sparingly, if at all, should the other side disarm. There is little point in occupying an economically destroyed, highly radiated nation covered with rotting corpses and diseased rodents and insects. This is even more obvious when one considers that the burning cities caused by a nuclear war could pump enough dark, oily, sooty smoke into the upper atmosphere to envelope the Northern Hemisphere with an opaque shroud for a couple of months or more, blocking out the sun and radically cooling the land by as much as 40 degrees centigrade. Sulfuric acid, asbestos fibers, and radiation would rain down on the earth for years. Holes in the ozone layer, punched by the nuclear blasts, would allow the sun's radiation to pass unimpeded to the earth's surface, thereby causing death, genetic mutation, and cancer across the globe.[23] The user of nuclear weapons can be expected to suffer so severely from even a limited nuclear attack against another nation that it is not unreasonable to believe that the user's own attack would be deterred by the expected consequences of the attack.

Nuclear blackmail, involving a few surgical strikes, may be more likely should one side unilaterally disarm, but, again, it would be irrational for the attacker to cause anything approaching the destruction of even a limited war. Accordingly, the negative effects of such attacks would be far lower than those of total war, thus more than offsetting the increased probability.

It has been argued by some, including Kavka,[24] that unilateral disarmament would risk not only lesser Soviet nuclear strikes but also worldwide domination by the Soviets. In combination, so the argument goes, the two smaller threats times their higher probability of occurrence is not orders of magnitude different from the greater threat of total nuclear war times the much lower probability of its occurrence should the United States maintain its present deterrence policy.

Now I do not claim to know that unilateral disarmament is optimific on utilitarian grounds, although I suspect that it is.[25] As Kavka himself puts it,

> Reliable estimates of the probabilities and utilities of the relevant possible outcomes are not available. Hence, in comparing nuclear deterrence and unilateral disarmament, the utilitarian seems trapped between the Scylla of a smaller risk of a worse disaster (that is, full-scale nuclear war) and the

Charybdis of a greater risk of a smaller disaster (that is, a nuclear strike or Soviet domination via blackmail).[26]

My point is a simple one. I do not think that anyone knows whether unilateral disarmament or present deterrence policy has the best foreseeable consequences for all persons. We lack the means to predict the future with sufficient accuracy concerning such global policy decisions. We lack the means to accurately assign probabilities to the expected outcomes of various possible lines of action.[27] We do have a great deal of speculation concerning the expected outcomes of the various alternatives, but little by way of warranted assertions.

Let me explain. There is a complicated dialectical equilibrium that normally occurs between one's theoretical understanding of foreign affairs and the events of foreign affairs themselves. As a result, the facts of the matter concerning the choice between deterrence and unilateral disarmament are rendered opaque. Each side of the debate, and there are far more than two, is supported by a coherent network of beliefs that is equally capable of explaining available past and most future events as well.[28]

The idea of a crucial experiment to adjudicate the differences is nearly impossible because each view interprets the event that is the experiment so as to render the event consistent with the given view.[29] The available behavioral evidence concerning the superpowers is consistent with many diverse interpretations of the events of foreign affairs.[30] Determining which interpretation is correct is normally out of the question because it involves being privy to a great deal of past or present top secret information or unavailable future information concerning how decisions are made, how policy is set, and what the intentions are of the superpowers. As a result, the facts as we know them severely underdetermine the choice of theory. The known facts are far too thin to allow us to choose rationally which theory of foreign affairs is maximally explanatory or best.

It is perhaps for this reason that debates concerning the past and future intentions of the superpowers are so frustrating. Not only do different yet coherent interpretations of the behavior and intentions of the superpowers come into play, but so do personality differences concerning benefit/risk assessment and benefit/risk response. As Thomas Kuhn has indicated, when a dispute is nonadjudicable for reasons of conflicting paradigms, rational persuasion quickly gives way to emotive attempts to coax, cajole, or intimidate. The ideologies of the nuclear hawk and nuclear dove are examples of such incommensurable systems of belief.[31]

Accordingly there is no point to prolonged debates concerning the utilitarian merits of deterrence versus unilateral disarmament. The rounds of points and counterpoints that inevitably occur in such debates reach ever deeper into the realms of speculation and fantasy. In these realms, one's prior commitments hold sway concerning what one judges the foreseeable consequences of U.S. or Soviet actions to be. If we unilaterally disarm, will the Soviets enslave humanity under the bitter yoke of communism? If the balance of terror continues for the next ten years, will we have a nuclear holocaust? For the next one hundred years? One thousand years? Although speculation and fantastic scenarios run rampant, I doubt that we have the requisite information to make warranted assertions on these matters. Lacking such justified beliefs, how are we to compare the odds and evils of these two alternatives? As Kavka alludes, we seem to be caught between a rock and a hard place. Utilitarian theory is not only unhelpful in such instances; it is utterly useless as a guide to action. Hence, it is otiose for determining the morality of deterrence policy.[32]

All that I have said here concerning the difficulty of arriving at warranted assertions concerning the future consequences of nuclear arms policy applies as well to game-theoretic analyses and utilitarianism. Unless we know which type of game we are playing in the actual world, be it "chicken," "prisoner's dilemma," or whatever, the theory is useless in practice. We cannot know which game we are playing unless we understand correctly both Soviet intentions and the facts of the matter at a given time, as well as the probabilities of pursuing various courses of action. As indicated, it is just this sort of knowledge we lack.[33]

Game-theoretic approaches suffer from another problem. While the logic of game theory is ahistorical, the problem of deterrence is historical. Let me use the prisoner's dilemma as an example. According to the prisoner's dilemma, at any given time in history, total nuclear disarmament would appear to be an irrational move.[34] But it seems clear that as the arms race accelerates, so do the risks of nuclear war. New weapons add new destabilizing situations. Changes in administrations make treaties irrelevant. Risky global adventurism destabilizes relationships between the superpowers. The neocolonial ambitions of each of the superpowers create an eventual zero-sum problem for natural resources, cheap labor, and land. Meanwhile, the chances increase for nuclear blackmail from those exploited in underdeveloped nations. Yet the logic of the prisoner's dilemma ignores the increase in the risk of nuclear war.[35]

The illogic of this mismatch of an ahistorical method with a historical problem is too compelling to be ignored. The choice can be stated rather simply. Are we to accept an ever-increasing risk of nuclear war, or are we to take a large initial risk that slowly diminishes to zero over time?

The calculation of consequences, the assignment of actual risks and benefits, and the other unknowns involved make any attempt at meaningful calculations into an exercise in futility.

But there is another problem with game-theoretic approaches that further muddies the waters. Most of the considerations are not utilitarian at all. As with Hobbesian analyses, the arguments are prudential rather than moral. Each side is to adopt that course of action that will maximize, in some sense, the realization of its own national interest. Each nation is to be concerned directly only with the effects upon its own citizenry, not with the effects upon everyone. As such, game-theoretic and Hobbesian arguments fail to accommodate the notion that ethics takes a universal point of view, which, many have argued, is the sine qua non of morality.[36] So, I conclude, both game-theoretic and Hobbesian arguments can be dismissed in considerations of the morality of deterrence.

My point is not mere skepticism concerning our ability to predict future events. I am rather committed to the view that the future will resemble the past and that nature is uniform. Neither is it my intention to argue that morality is fundamentally subjective because it is ideologically embedded. Careful scrutiny will reveal that it is the casting of a theoretical net over the events of superpower relations in foreign affairs that is severely underdetermined by the facts. This factual point—and nothing about the ideological embeddedness of morality—plays center stage in my arguments. Quite simply, one's choice of theory concerning superpower relations in foreign affairs is based as much on one's ideological commitments as on fact. The immorality of deterrence is more obvious than the facts that are summoned to argue the issue of deterrence on strict consequentialist grounds.

I am not advocating the absurd view that all theories of foreign affairs are equally good. Common sense allows us to see that many such theories are defective, and for a variety of reasons. For instance, conspiracy theories of the John Birch type can be dismissed because they are nonfalsifiable, while simplistic versions of the evil empire view are dismissable because they fail to apply the same moral categories to U.S. behavior as are applied to Soviet behavior. Yet the choice of the best theory is still severely underdetermined by the facts. Consequently, the debate between nuclear hawks and nuclear doves cannot be adjudicated on purely factual grounds or considerations if one is to settle the issue.

What I do mean to argue is that on matters of foreign affairs we lack anything approaching a legitimate science. Accordingly, attempts to rest utilitarian and prudential considerations upon the claims of political scientists and strategists probably will do more harm than good on such issues as deterrence. If I am correct, then by consequentialist lights we are justified in dismissing strict consequentialist arguments concerning the morality of deterrence. One might expect such a dismissal to be optimific.

Consider the gross failures of U.S. foreign policy in the postwar era. Even though U.S. foreign policy has been based upon political realism and on the notion that the United States primarily should pursue its national interest and has relied consistently upon the minds of the "best and the brightest" to do so, few admit to feeling safer or more secure in the world community today than they did in the 1940s. What appeared to be in the national interest prior to Soviet development of nuclear weapons is not. What appeared to be in the national interest in Vietnam, in Iran, or in Nicaragua is not. What appeared to be in the national interest in pursuing the Anti-Ballistic Missile Treaty is not. The examples can be multiplied almost without end.[37] As with William Haber in Ursula LeGuin's *The Lathe of Heaven,* we lack the wisdom, if not the hubris, to turn successfully our dreams into reality. Consequently, our attempts all too often result in reality being turned into a nightmare.

But, one might argue, even if your analysis is correct and we do not know which course of action will have the best consequences, we do know that deterrence policy has prevented nuclear war to date. Why deal in hypothetical cases when we know that deterrence works?

Even this is an overstatement. All we know is that we have engaged in an arms race and that nuclear war has not occurred. Now it may be that the arms race has deterred a nuclear war, or it may be, as recent literature suggests, that nuclear deterrence has little to do with post–World War II peace.[38] Until about twenty years ago the Soviets did not have the capacity to wage nuclear war against the United States. Prior to that, it is pointless to argue that deterrence worked because one cannot deter another from doing what it cannot do. In addition, the geopolitical balance of power established after World War II may have been so stable that it, rather than nuclear arms, is responsible for the prevention of a nuclear war.[39] Present deterrence policy, rather than being a success, may be a paradigm of the post hoc fallacy.

Further, the argument that we should not change deterrence because it has worked heretofore is actually a very weak argument from analogy. Insofar as there are changes in the strategic arsenals or war-fighting strategy of the superpowers, changes in the leadership of the superpowers, changes in the membership of the nuclear club, changes in the global balance of power, changes in the causes of international tension, or any one of a number of changes around the globe the analogy between the past and the future is weakened. Notice that all the parameters I have mentioned have changed dramatically during the last two decades. As the analogy weakens, so does the logical strength by which we can draw the conclusion of the argument. Who among us is willing to trust the lives of hundreds of millions, indeed to trust civilization as we know it, to the slender thread of a severely weakened inductive argument?

Richard Wasserstrom makes similar points.[40] In many contexts, the assumption that because an equilibrium has existed in the past it will continue to exist in the future is foolish and mistaken. For example, we know that were we continuously to increase the volume of air in a balloon, it would be extremely foolish to suppose that we could count on the balloon remaining intact just because it has not burst so far. The facts of deterrence clearly are compatible with the balloon model. Thus, we are left in a state of bewilderment concerning whether it is reasonable to project the success of deterrence into the future. One can reasonably conclude that the absence of war between the superpowers is because sufficient pressure or level of crisis has not yet been attained to burst the nuclear balloon; this absence is not the result of some equilibrium between threat and nonuse. Richard Nixon's statement that he seriously considered using nuclear weapons on four occasions of heightened international tension during his presidency lends even more plausibility to such a conclusion.

So I conclude that we cannot successfully use strict consequentialist moral theory to determine the morality of deterrence policy. That is, we cannot rest our moral arguments on the consideration of foreseeable future consequences, if we are to evaluate successfully the morality of deterrence. The foreseeable consequences of our actions are far too murky to be used in consequentialist calculations, given the gravity of the decision involved. We simply cannot assign probabilities or values to expected outcomes with the degree of warrant needed to successfully use strictly teleological moral theories on this topic. Similar arguments can be used to dismiss prudential arguments concerning the national interest. Thus consequentialism is rendered otiose on matters of deterrence because what we cannot speak about with warrant we should pass over in silence.[41]

But still, one suspects that from the point of view of human rights, a nation has a right of self-defense. The right of self-defense seems to be a prerequisite for the maintenance of any human rights. Without guarantees of one's rights, they are meaningless. What better guarantee can there be of one's rights than the entitlement to defend them against standard threats?[42]

Traditionally, self-defense has had a strict meaning. One may defend oneself and others against an attack. One may endanger the life of the attacker(s) *only* if it is reasonable to believe that doing so is the *sole* available means of preventing danger to one's own life or to the lives of others. Further, the right of self-defense is the right to defend life by threatening *only* the life of the attacker(s), *not* by threatening the lives of innocent third parties. Clearly, the logic of nuclear deterrence as self-defense parallels the specious reasoning of threatening to kill innocent third parties as a means of preventing attack against oneself. Thus, I conclude that deterrence cannot be justified as a legitimate right of self-defense.[43]

But still the point can be made, as it has been by philosophers as diverse in their moral views as Robert Nozick, Thomas Nagel, and Richard Brandt, that exceptions to otherwise absolutely binding moral rules may have to be allowed in order to prevent catastrophe.[44] Obviously, nuclear holocaust would qualify as a catastrophe. Thus, we are justified in doing whatever is necessary to prevent a nuclear war—including threatening one, taking hostages, and using blackmail if that is needed.

Given our previous discussion, it should be obvious that many questions are begged here. It is not obvious nor has it been shown that deterrence policy is the best means of preventing a nuclear holocaust. Indeed, it has not even been shown that it is a means to prevent a nuclear holocaust. It is arguable that the best means to prevent nuclear holocaust is unilateral disarmament. Accordingly, deterrence cannot be justified by appeal to catastrophe.

What are we to make of the arms race and the various alternatives to it that have been posed? How are we to assess which will have the best consequences overall? Should the United States unilaterally disarm while adopting a posture of civilian defense[45] and encouraging our allies to do the same? Should we pursue unilateral nuclear disarmament while building our conventional forces and alliances around the world? Should we seek a bilateral nuclear weapons freeze?[46] Should we adopt a policy of no first use? Of build-down? A 50 percent across-the-board cut in nuclear weapons by all nations that possess them? Arms control agreements that allow nuclear buildups but put upper limits on warheads and launchers? Should we continue our policy of containment with respect to communism? Should we continue to use the arms race as the main tool in our policy of containment? Or should we pursue the nuclear arms race wholeheartedly in an attempt to force the Soviets into a new round of arms buildup that will destroy their domestic economy, cause the populace to revolt, and bring an end to communism? If the opportunity presents itself where the odds of successfully launching a counterforce strike are high, ought we to strike first? What are the acceptable risks in order to attain such a successful first strike? Ten million? Twenty million? Forty million? As previously argued, I do not think we have the means even to begin answering such questions. How then can we morally and practically assess deterrence and its alternatives?

In such cases we must appeal to deontological notions of morality because appeals to consequences are useless. It is my contention that any plausible deontological theory will contain elements of the Kantian morality, particularly the first and second formulations of the categorical imperative, although probably not the Kantian rigorism associated with perfect duties. Further, Kantian morality clearly condemns deterrence policy as the immoral intention to use others as a mere means to one's ends. As such, I conclude that the policy of nuclear deterrence is, quite simply, indefensible on moral grounds and also is immoral.

What are we to do? First and foremost we should fulfill our Kantian duty to condemn morally the policy of nuclear deterrence and the arms race it attempts to justify. Beyond that we should confront, accept, and *act* in the fact of the existential uncertainties that surround this issue. We also should accept and embrace the prospect that one's adversary in arguments concerning what is to be done to attain nuclear disarmament as safely and quickly as possible may be correct. As such, intelligent action and tolerance both are required.

But what are we to do? As Robert Holmes writes, "William James once wrote that faith in certain facts may help to bring those facts into existence. So, we might say, with the power of nonviolence."[47] It is here that one finds an answer to our dilemma. To date, neither one of the superpowers has actively pursued an end to deterrence. Each has made a variety of proposals concerning how to slow or even stop the arms race, but neither really has attempted to rid the world of nuclear weapons.

I propose that the United States begin immediately to fulfill our Kantian duty by taking the first steps toward nuclear disarmament. It has been argued by many, including Admiral Rickover, father of the nuclear navy, that the United States can safely and successfully devoid itself of land-based nuclear weapons and still have a credible deterrent against the USSR.[48] The United States would be left with approximately five thousand warheads on nuclear submarines, an overkill of about twelve.[49] These warheads lack the accuracy, at least at present, to be used as first-strike weapons. But because of their lack of precision, they are highly effective as retaliatory weapons, as a deterrent to nuclear attack. Their use guarantees masive destruction because they cannot be guided precisely to target. As the sole means of nuclear deterrence, they constitute a proverbial doomsday machine. Contrary to the self-serving fears of many strategists, the existential deterrence the maintenance of such warheads would generate should deter any rational actor from a first strike. Also, nuclear submarines presently are invulnerable to attack, unlike land-based weapons, and probably will remain so for at least the remainder of this century. By removing land-based nuclear weapons, the United States also would remove the Soviet incentive to target them.

To do more initially would be to endanger the lives of innocent persons across the globe because doing more may not deter Soviet nuclear blackmail or attack. Accordingly, to do more at this time involves treating persons outside the Soviet Union as mere means. To do less would involve continuing the present spiraling arms race and the immoral use of innocent noncombatants in the USSR. It also is important to stress that my proposal is a first step on the road to disarmament. Admittedly, my proposal would not allow the United States to practice extended deterrence, but I know of no moral argument to justify the practice.

While removing our land-based nuclear weapons, the U.S. government could encourage the Soviets to match its move with one that they believed to be parallel. We could ask them to choose their own response as a sign of good faith. We could ask for parallel actions by other nuclear nations and pledges of nondevelopment by nonnuclear nations. Meanwhile, we could be doing all that we can to build trust between the superpowers and among the rest of the nations of the world. We could inform the world that our move is to be the first step in total disarmament and encourage all other nations to join us. Clearly, all this would have to be done slowly, carefully, and with great openness and humanity toward the Soviets. At first, they would not believe us, just as we would not believe them. But if we honestly pursued our goal while treating them with the due respect all persons deserve, we may be able to convince them of our own integrity and that the policy of deterrence is evil and irrational. We would have broken the mutual distrust and hatred that fuel the arms race.

My argument is based on hope. But if my arguments concerning the opacity of the future consequences of weapons policy come to anything, they should establish that *all* proposals concerning the nuclear future, including maintaining the status quo, are based on hope. Heretofore our hopes have been based on worst-case reasoning.[50] As a result, in far too many cases, our fear and hatred have created a self-fulfilling prophecy. In far too many cases the worst case has come to pass because we acted as though we expected it and thereby brought it to pass. Fear and hatred have been reified. Distrust has been elevated to outright paranoia. Each side has become the other's worst nightmare.

Suppose that instead of basing policy on worst-case reasoning the U.S. government opted to base its policy on moral ideals. Suppose that we take a humane understanding of the Kantian Kingdom of Ends as that ideal. Suppose that we guide our actions not by fear and hatred but by trust and love, not by moral weakness but by moral strength, not by war but by peace. My belief is that the path to a sane and livable world is based on the best of humanity, not the worst. For if our worst-case reasoning indeed has produced a self-fulfilling prophecy, then one might expect that by basing our future actions on the best of humanity, these, too, may make possible the closer realization of our ideals.

At the same time, I offer my proposal as an experiment. It is a relatively safe one. It can be revoked at any time. But it may reveal future possibilities that, had the United States maintained the status quo, would have seemed simply utopian. There is only one way to know, finally, if the United States can live in peace with the Soviets and that is to attempt some such experiment. If it is attempted with the right intentions and the United States gives the Soviets the time and encouragement to follow its lead, it may be able to build a better world, one where love is more possible. One where nuclear weapons are confined to textbooks and museums. One where children can live their lives free from the fears and hatred generated by the constant preparation for nuclear holocaust. If there is some way to get there from here without increasing dramatically the long-term risk of nuclear destruction, then it is a risk well worth taking. In light of the existential uncertainties that confront us, I can think of no better proposal. If, however, nuclear war is truly inevitable, then I prefer to suffer the evil rather than to do it—especially given that all of us in the Northern Hemisphere will be the victims of such a war at any rate.

We would do well to keep before us one of the central insights of both existentialism and ethical pragmatism. Our choices reveal not only who we are as individuals, but also help to create a new future self. Likewise, our choices reveal not only who we are as a society of people, but who we are to become. Our choice of a nonnuclear future must be made in view of this broader, more signficant, and more hopeful perspective and in light of the fact that we live in a world beset with existential uncertainty concerning the outcomes of our actions. Yet the choice also must be made in light of the fact that we bear the responsibility for what that future will be and that we owe it to our children to make that world as safe and as sane as possible. For when all the words are done and the choice is made, "the only reality is in action."[51]

Notes

I thank Jeffrey Eaton, Trudy Govier, Russell Hardin, Robert Holmes, Elizabeth Ring, James Ring, Robert Simon, and Eric Werner for their thoughtful comments and criticisms on earlier versions of this chapter. I thank the co-editors of the "Special Issue on Ethics and Nuclear Deterrence," *Ethics,* 95 (1985), for including me among the participants at the conference at the Aspen Institute, Aspen, Colorado, Labor Day Weekend, 1985. My own thoughts on deterrence and, accordingly, this chapter have profited greatly from that meeting. I thank especially the Center for Dewey Studies, which supported me with a John Dewey Senior Fellowship while much of the work for the chapter was undertaken. Versions of this chapter were presented at the APA, Meetings of Concerned Philosophers for Peace, Chicago, Illinois, April 1983; the University of Rochester Interdisciplinary Conference on "War and Morality," October 1983; Notre Dame University, AMINTAPHIL Conference on "War, Peace, and Disarmament," November 1984; International Conference on "Issues in Deterrence," Inter-University Centre of Postgraduate Studies, Dubrovnik, Yugoslavia, June 1985.

1. By a teleological moral theory I mean a normative ethical theory that determines the rightness and wrongness of actions by considering solely the value of the consequences of action.

2. Gregory Kavka, "Some Paradoxes of Deterrence," *Journal of Philosophy* 75 (1978):285–302, presents a view similar to the one sketched. Kavka argues that the value of the consequences involved in deterrence policy decisions is so high that for anyone other than a strict deontologist consideration of consequences would override any deontological considerations.

3. By a deontological moral theory I mean a normative ethical theory that does not consider the rightness and wrongness of action to be determined solely by the value of the consequences of action.

4. See, for instance, William H. Shaw, "Nuclear Deterrence and Deontology," *Ethics* 94 (1984), pp. 248–260.

5. R. M. Hare, *Freedom and Reason* (Oxford, 1963); and William K. Frankena, "The Concept of Morality," *The Definition of Morality,* ed. G. Wallace & A.D.M. Walker (London, 1970), pp. 146–173.

6. For similar reasons I will assume occasionally that present nuclear policy entails in arms race. Logically, the two are distinct. Historically, they never have been separated. In fact, deterrence policy always has entailed arms racing between the superpowers. I see no reason to believe that the two will be separated in fact in any of our probable futures.

7. By total nuclear war, I mean a war that involves, if not preemptive strikes, strikes such that the superpowers use large percentages of their strategic nuclear stockpiles. By limited nuclear war, I mean a nuclear war between the superpowers designed to be far less than total and to have a distinct military or political target the attainment of which is incompatible with total war. A counterforce strike would be a paradigm of a limited nuclear war. By nuclear blackmail, I mean the attempt by a nuclear power to force concessions from an opponent that does not possess or will not use nuclear weapons.

8. See Ruth Adams and Susan Cullen, eds., *The Final Epidemic* (Chicago, 1981); Office of Technology Assessment, U.S. Congress, *The Effects of Nuclear War* (Washington, D.C., May 1979); "The Prompt and Delayed Effects of Nuclear War," *Scientific American* 241 (1979):35–47; R. P. Turco, et al., "Nuclear Winter: Global Consequences of Multiple Nuclear Explosions," *Science* (Dec. 23, 1983).

9. Thomas Powers, "How to Destroy Ourselves Without Even Trying," *Washington Post National Weekly Edition,* April 15, 1985, pp. 23–24.

10. Richard Rorty, *Philosophy and the Mirror of Nature* (Princeton, 1979).

11. See Holly Goldman, "Culpable Ignorance," *Philosophical Review* (Oct. 1983):543–571, for a defense of this view.

12. In George Mavrodes, "Conventions and the Morality of War," *Philosophy and Public Affairs* 4 (1975):117–131, Mavrodes argues that the laws of war are

best understood as analogous to conventions or rules of the road and that the distinction between combatants and noncombatants is anything but a clear one. As such, like conventions of the road, the distinction is justified only to the degree that it minimizes social costs. Consequently, if one side ignores the distinction, the other is justified in also ignoring it. There are, I believe, two excellent responses to this view in print, even though neither mentions Mavrodes. See Jeffrie G. Murphy, "The Killing of the Innocent," *The Monist* 57 (1973):527–536; and Richard Wasserstrom, "War, Nuclear War, and Nuclear Deterrence: Some Conceptual and Moral Issues," *Ethics* 95 (1985):424–444, but particularly pp. 430–433.

13. It is important to realize that the actual practice of nuclear deterrence by the superpowers extends far beyond merely threatening to use nuclear weapons to prevent a nuclear attack. Strict deterrence rests on threatening to use nuclear weapons only as a means of preventing nuclear attack. Extended deterrence includes strict deterrence as well as threatening to use nuclear weapons whenever their military use can be translated into political advantage. Hence, the U.S. policy of threatening to use nuclear weapons should the Soviets invade Europe with conventional weapons is an example of extended deterrence. Similarly, the Cuban missile crisis and the 1973 Arab-Israeli war are examples where the United States successfully threatened to use nuclear weapons to force concessions from the Soviets. Much of the philosophical literature reads as though present U.S. deterrence policy is justified, if limited deterrence is justifiable—which is clearly a non sequitur.

14. The distinction between counterforce and countervalue targeting is largely irrelevant. A 1978 study of Soviet civil defense planning by the Arms Control and Disarmament Agency suggested that a U.S. retaliatory strike during a major nuclear war would target 80 percent of Soviet cities of more than 25,000 in population. Moscow would be hit with up to sixty warheads, Leningrad with forty or more, and the next eight largest cities with an average of thirteen each. All of these are *military* targets. *Washington Post National Weekly Edition,* April 15, 1985, p. 24.

15. I take Kantian morality to include *both* the first and second formulations of the categorical imperative. Hence it will not do to argue that deterrence can be justified on Kantian grounds as long as one is willing to universalize the practice of deterrence. One also would need to show that deterrence does not treat innocent noncombatants as mere means, insofar as it is they who are targeted, either directly or indirectly, by the practice of deterrence.

16. Kavka, "Some Paradoxes of Deterrence," makes similar points. See Wasserstrom, "War, Nuclear War, and Nuclear Deterrence," particularly note 10, who argues that there is no "univocal, stable context within which to address the question of the morality of a conditional intention to use nuclear weapons."

17. I am assuming that seems obvious, if one knows at time t that one will not do x at time t+1, then one cannot truly *intend* at time t to do x at time t+1. However, one can still bluff that one intends to do x at time t+1.

18. See Nigel Calder, *Nuclear Nightmares* (NY, 1980), Chap. 4; and "Nuclear War: Communications Clobbered," *Economist* (May 15, 1982).

19. For similar reasons I find the Catholic just-war theory unconvincing. In many contexts, such as the one just mentioned, it seems to be mere sophistry to argue that one does not intend that the known and clearly foreseen consequences are catastrophic. Morally significant intentions are broader than the unduly narrow intentions allowed by the doctrine of double effect. Indeed, I am not convinced that, phenomenologically speaking, one can make sense of the narrow intentions that double effect entails. Such intentions seem to rest on the deeply criticized Cartesian-Lockean notion of the mind as a glassy essence having its own "mind's eye" that "sees" what it intends to do as an idea in the mind.

20. See Jeff McMahan, "Deterrence and Deontology," and Gerold Dworkin, "Nuclear Intentions," *Ethics* 95 (1985):517–536 and 445–460, who make similar points.

21. Whether nuclear deterrence is literally a legal case of blackmail or hostage taking is irrelevant to the moral point I am making. What is relevant is that on Kantian grounds, such behavior is clearly immoral. See Steven Lee, "The Morality of Nuclear Deterrence: Hostage Holding and Consequences," *Ethics* 95 (1985):549–566.

22. Kavka, "Some Paradoxes of Deterrence" and Gregory Kavka "Deterrence, Utility, and Rational Choice," *Theory and Decision* 12 (1980):41–60.

23. See note 8.

24. Kavka, "Doubts About Unilateral Disarmament," *Philosophy and Public Affairs* 12 (1983):255–260.

25. See Douglas P. Lackey, "Missiles and Morals: A Utilitarian Look at Nuclear Deterrence," *Philosophy and Public Affairs* 11 (1982)189–231, who defends the view that utilitarianism prescribes unilateral disarmament; and the challenge and response, Russell Hardin, "Unilateral Versus Mutual Disarmament," Kavka, "Doubts About Unilateral Disarmament," and Douglas P. Lackey, "Disarmament Revisited: A Reply to Kavka and Hardin," same issues, pp. 236–265.

26. Kavka, "Doubts About Unilateral Disarmament," p. 225. Kavka, "Deterrence, Utility and Rational Choice," attempts to reconcile the paradox in favor of deterrence policy. See the debate between Georges Bernard, "Deterrence, Utility, and Rational Choice—A Comment"; and Kavka, "Deterrence and Utility Again: A Response to Bernard," *Theory and Decision* 14 (1982):89–97 and 99–102. Their central differences concerning U.S.-Soviet relations are nonadjudicable for reasons I will begin to describe.

27. See Robert Goodin, "Disarmament as a Moral Certainty," *Ethics* 95 (1985):641–658, who argues that we have no justification for claims concerning the probability of nuclear war or whether particular moves will increase or decrease the probability of nuclear war.

28. The debate among Lackey, Hardin, and Kavka, "Doubts About Unilateral Disarmament," is enlightening on this point. See also, Jan Narveson, "Getting on the Road to Peace: A Modest Proposal," *Ethics* 95 (1985):589–605, who elaborates two distinctly different ideologies in far greater detail than I do.

29. See Lackey, Hardin, and Kavka concerning U.S. restraint with nuclear weapons during the U.S. atomic monopoly, China's role in the balance of terror, the effectiveness of conventional arms as a substitute for nuclear weapons, and

so on. The Quine-Duhem thesis is operative with a vengeance in the theoretical world of superpower relations.

30. See Sanford Gottlieb, *What About the Russians?* (Northfield, Mass.: Educators for Social Responsibility, 1982), for a discussion and comparison of a few of these interpretations.

31. Again, the aforementioned debate is instructive, as are the endless debates among supporters of these positions as found in the mass media.

32. Although I cannot delve deeper into the issue here, I suspect that utilitarian theories generally suffer from the same problem with respect to many social issues—for example, capital punishment, affirmative action, and economic justice.

33. Hardin, "Unilateral Versus Mutual Disarmament," who defends the game-theoretic approach, acknowledges the difficulties inherent in both the transmission of information and the understanding of intent between the superpowers. As Lackey, "Missiles and Morals," indicates, these apply to unilateral disarmament as well as to deterrence policy.

34. Actually, as Douglas Lackey argues, what the prisoner's dilemma prescribes depends on how we assign values to the different options and their outcomes; see "Ethics and Nuclear Deterrence," *Moral Problems,* ed. James Rachels, 3rd ed. (New York, 1979), pp. 426–441. But in actual use, the values in fact are assigned so as to make total disarmament a less than optimific outcome. See Leo Groarke, "Nuclear Arms Control: Eluding the Prisoner's Dilemma," *Nuclear War: Philosophical Perspectives,* ed. Michael Fox and Leo Groarke (New York, 1985).

35. Although versions of the prisoner's dilemma exist that attempt to accommodate the history of the arms race, how is one to verify that the accommodation of history by such logics is accurate? Here one suspects that the advocates of game theory are victims of the illusion that such logics are ahistorical, that they view the world *sub specie aeternitatis* rather than being historically and culturally embedded themselves.

36. See Peter Singer, *Practical Ethics* (Cambridge, 1979), p. 10ff; and Frankena, "The Concept of Morality."

37. See Robert Holmes, "Political Realism," presented at the AMINTAPHIL Conference on War, Peace, and Disarmament, Notre Dame University, November 1984.

38. Marc Catudal, *Nuclear Deterrence: Does It Deter?* (London, 1984).

39. One may question how much "peace" the postwar period has seen. If nuclear arms are considered to be partly responsible for the so-called peace of the period, ought they not, by parity of reasoning, to be considered partly responsible for all the wars?

40. See Wasserstrom, "War, Nuclear War, and Nuclear Deterrence," p. 442, including the balloon example that follows.

41. I should indicate that on most moral matters I consider myself a deontologist of the pluralist variety, for example, Ross or Frankena. However, when consideration of consequences becomes otiose, the pluralist must turn to the deontological side of pluralism to render a moral judgment. Admittedly, a

consequentialist could agree with my arguments yet conclude that, morally speaking, nothing is to be decided about deterrence. But this allows deontological pronouncements to be made on deterrence unimpeded by the teleologist's counters. It also runs counter to the insight that morality, by its very nature, is to be action guiding (see note 5)—especially if I am correct in thinking that the determination of consequences is a general problem for teleologists.

42. See Henry Shue, *Basic Rights* (Princeton, 1980), for a similar analysis of rights.

43. See Thomas Donaldson, "Nuclear Deterrence and Self-Defense," *Ethics* 95 (1985):537–548, for a deeper consideration of this issue.

44. Kavka, "Some Paradoxes of Deterrence," p. 288, n. 4.

45. Robert Holmes, "The Sleep of Reason Brings Forth Monsters," *Harvard Magazine* (1983):56A–56H; Gene Sharp, *Exploring Nonviolent Alternatives* (Boston, 1970); and Martin Benjamin, "Pacifism for Pragmatists," *Ethics* 83 (1973): 196–213.

46. Randall Forsberg, "A Bilateral Nuclear-Weapon Freeze," *Scientific American* 247 (1982):52–61.

47. Holmes, "The Sleep of Reason," p. 56H.

48. James Sterba, "How to Achieve Nuclear Deterrence Without Threatening Nuclear Destruction," *The Ethics of War and Nuclear Deterrence,* ed. James Sterba (Belmont, Calif., 1984), pp. 155–168; Lackey, "Ethics and Nuclear Deterrence"; Groarke, "Nuclear Arms Control."

49. This is based on former Secretary of Defense McNamara's estimates of the "overkill ratio," U.S. Joint Committee Defense Production, "Economic & Social Consequences of a Nuclear Attack on the US," 8/78, pp. 23–24. Approximately four hundred warheads produce damage equal to an overkill of one, according to the 1978 estimate. Present estimates of warheads can be found in *The Defense Monitor* 13 (1984). According to these estimates, the United States has approximately eleven thousand deliverable strategic warheads while the Soviets have about nine thousand. About five thousand, or one-half of the U.S. warheads are on nuclear submarines.

50. Narveson, "Getting on the Road to Peace."

51. Quotation attributed to Jean Paul Sartre.

Selected Bibliography

Benjamin, Martin. 1973. "Pacifism for Pragmatists." *Ethics* 83:3.

Chomsky, Noam. 1979. *Towards a New Cold War.* New York: Pantheon Books.

Cohen, Avner, and Lee, Steven, eds. 1984. *Nuclear Weapons and the Future of Humanity.* Totowa, N.J.: Rowman & Allanheld.

Fox, Michael, and Groarke, Leo, eds. 1985. *Nuclear War: Philosophical Perspectives.* New York: Peter Lang.

Gray, Colin, and Payne, Keith. 1980. "Victory Is Possible." *Foreign Policy* (Summer).

Gottlieb, Sanford. 1982. *What About the Russians?* Northfield, Mass.: Educators for Social Responsibility.

Halliday, Fred. 1983. *The Making of the Second Cold War.* New York: Schocken Books.

Hardin, Russell, John J. Mearsheimer, Gerald Dworkin, and Robert E. Goodin, eds. 1985. "Symposium on Ethics and Nuclear Deterrence." *Ethics* 95:3.

Holmes, Robert L. 1983. "The Sleep of Reason Brings Forth Monsters." *Harvard Magazine* (March-April).

James, William. 1882. "The Sentiment of Rationality." John J. McDermott, ed., *The Writings of William James.* New York: Modern Library, 1968.

Kissinger, Henry. 1957. *Nuclear Weapons and Foreign Policy.* New York: Harper & Row.

Lackey, Douglas P. 1984. *Moral Principles and Nuclear Weapons.* Totowa, N.J.: Rowman & Allanheld.

Sagan, Carl. 1983. "Nuclear Winter and Climatic Catastrophe." *Foreign Affairs* (Winter):2.

Sharp, Gene. 1985. *National Security Through Civilian-Based Defense.* Omaha, Neb.: Association for Transarmament Studies.

Sterba, James, ed. 1984. *The Ethics of War and Nuclear Deterrence.* Belmont, Calif.: Wadsworth Publishing.

Turco, R. P., O. B. Toon, T. P. Packerman, J. B. Pollack, and Carl Sagan. 1983. "Nuclear Winter: Global Consequences of Multiple Nuclear Explosions." *Science* (December 23).

Yergin, Daniel. 1977. *Shattered Peace: The Origins of the Cold War and the National Security State.* Boston: Houghton Mifflin.

PART THREE

Nationalism and the Prospects for Peace

Introduction to Part Three

Diana T. Meyers

The chapters in Part 3 raise questions about the viability of a world of independent nation states pursuing their respective interests. Each chapter defends constraints on realpolitik. Michael Doyle argues that liberal principles can provide the basis for peace among liberal states and for extending peaceful relations to presently nonliberal states. Diana Meyers doubts the efficacy of liberal principles in sustaining peace and stresses the dangers of elevating national security to the status of an overriding moral imperative. Avner Cohen contends that the doctrine of political realism is inadequate to address the problems nuclear weapons present. Sidney Axinn defends world government as a way out of the impasse that the deployment of nuclear weaponry has created. Although these authors differ with respect to the solutions they advocate, they concur in recognizing the bankruptcy of an international order composed of power-hungry, self-aggrandizing nation-states.

In "Liberal Institutions and International Ethics," Michael Doyle asks whether liberalism—with its concern for individual freedom, political participation, private property, and equality of opportunity—might provide a sound basis for a lasting world peace. Doyle begins by reviewing Schumpeter's thesis that democratic capitalism leads to peace and Machiavelli's contention that the passion for liberty leads to republican imperialism. Doyle finds both theories wanting. He claims that an adequate theory must account for two liberal legacies in the area of international relations: (1) "the pacification of foreign relations among liberal states" and (2) "imprudent aggression [against nonliberal states] by the liberal state." Doyle maintains that Kant's philosophy of history and international relations makes sense of these historical trends.

Kant holds that a variety of forces combine to bring about liberal states and that a variety of institutions and mechanisms operate within and among liberal states to ensure peace among them. For example, "asocial sociability" supports the emergence of republican governments because democratic institutions empower people to defend and advance their own interests while gaining the benefits of social cooperation. Similarly, democratic institutions reduce the probability of war because the people who must fight the wars have a voice in public policy. Whereas the implementation of civil rights in liberal states sustains an attitude of mutual respect among them because each perceives the legitimacy of the others, the failure of nonliberal states to implement these rights contributes to an atmosphere of suspicion and hostility between liberal and nonliberal states. Doyle maintains that the principles that Kant enunciates provide a plausible explanation of the history of peaceful relations among liberal states as well as the history of bellicose relations between liberal and nonliberal states. Furthermore, Doyle maintains that Kant's views can help set the agenda for a liberal foreign policy. Doyle's recommendations include the following: (1) U.S. national security should be the primary concern in relations with the USSR, but arms control and expanded trade also should be sought; (2) arms should be sold to the People's Republic of China; and (3) policy vis-à-vis the Third World should be calibrated to reflect each state's commitment to liberal principles. By remaining realistically vigilant yet adhering to liberal principles in foreign policy, liberal states can extend the liberal alliance and enhance the prospects of enduring peace.

In "Kant's Liberal Alliance: A Permanent Peace?" Diana Meyers questions the tenability of a Kantian political science as a basis for peace. Meyers finds Kant's view of history somewhat paradoxical. Although he recognizes that the historian cannot assume that human events move steadily in any direction, at the same time Kant holds that history is progressive. The resolution of this paradox lies in part in Kant's epistemological contention that people must understand history from the standpoint of their own needs for security and freedom—and hence must understand their past as a movement toward peace—and in part in his observation that people had been moved by the events of the French Revolution to seek social improvement—hence there is empirical evidence that people can control the course of history. Meyers expresses doubts about both claims. But Kant goes on to urge that self-interest operating through democratic institutions promotes peace. However, Meyers notes that democracy does not give the majority control of public policy in any straightforward way and that election outcomes do not necessarily reflect the interests of the electorate.

Still, it seems that liberal states have maintained a peaceful alliance, and it is necessary to ask whether they have done so, as Kant and Doyle believe, as a result of the constraints that publicity imposes on public officials, the mutual esteem in which liberal states hold one another, and the moral duty to promote peace. Meyers suggests that liberal politicians have learned to evade the constraints of publicity and that common economic interests may be more fundamental than mutual esteem with respect to the liberal alliance. Can Kant's (and, following Kant, Doyle's) dual duty to preserve the liberal state while restraining state aggression for the sake of peace secure perpetual peace? Meyers contends that as long as national survival is given moral priority, this aspect of Kant's duty is likely to overwhelm the pacific aspect and undermine the prospects of peace.

Avner Cohen's chapter, "Reflections on Realism in the Nuclear Age," raises further questions about the tenability of political realism in today's military context. Cohen focuses his discussion on relations between the superpowers, that is, on relations between a liberal and a nonliberal state. He maintains that "the rise of nuclear weapons has turned out to negate the fundamental logic of realism." Thus, Cohen takes exception to Doyle's contention that realpolitik should be the foundation of U.S. policy toward the Soviet Union.

Cohen begins by rehearsing the history of U.S. public debate regarding nuclear weaponry. Although the use of atomic bombs to destroy Hiroshima and Nagasaki precipitated a pacifistic demand for enforced disarmament in the wake of World War II, the thrust of this movement was blunted quickly. By the late 1940s, political realism had gained the upper hand, and the arms race was in full swing. Cohen observes that despite their incompatibility with our most fundamental moral intuitions, nuclear weapons and the regime of mutual deterrence nevertheless attained legitimacy through force of circumstance. It was not until the 1980s that nuclear policy and its background of international power politics was questioned seriously.

In the remainder of his chapter Cohen argues that both nuclear war and nuclear deterrence are incompatible with political realism. Cohen's position is that politics and war are "by-products of civilization," but that the unpredictability of nuclear war threatens to destroy civilization. Hence, nuclear war cannot serve the purposes of realpolitik. Moreover, Cohen rejects the contention that nuclear deterrence protects humanity from nuclear war. On the contrary, the logic of political realism entails that the international balance of power is unstable, and because there is no reason to believe that the policy of nuclear deterrence has defused conflict to date, we must assume that nuclear weapons will be used eventually. Cohen concludes that pacifistic recommendations for world government and international control of nuclear materials are utopian. Instead, he maintains, we must accept the system of sovereign nation-states and seek to delegitimize the regime of nuclear deterrence from within that framework.

Sidney Axinn develops the themes of the hazards that national security poses to peace in terms of the individual's relation to the state. In "Loyalty and the Limits of Patriotism," Axinn argues that national loyalties are outmoded by present-day military realities. Axinn begins by criticizing Oldenquist's account of loyalty. Oldenquist holds that loyalties are necessary to morality and that acting loyally often is good. Axinn counters that loyalty to one's own group often goes hand in hand with hatred of other groups and that acting on loyalties is often immoral. Axinn then develops an account of loyalty in which sacrifice plays a central role. For Axinn, loyalty always involves sacrifice to a beneficiary. Loyalty can be absolute or conditional, but if one is unwilling to make any sacrifice, one is not loyal. Accordingly, patriotism is the willingness to sacrifice for the sake of one's country. But how much sacrifice of this sort is reasonable? Against Avner Cohen, Axinn argues that national loyalties exact too high a sacrifice in the nuclear age. Because patriotism entails risking global destruction, Axinn advocates transferring our loyalties from nation-states to a world government. Whereas Doyle contends that independent nation-states can achieve a lasting peace, Axinn maintains that the logic of loyalties makes world government necessary for peace.

11

Liberal Institutions and International Ethics

Michael W. Doyle

We often have been told that promoting freedom will produce peace. In a speech before the British Parliament in June 1982, President Reagan proclaimed that governments founded on a respect for individual liberty exercise "restraint" and "peaceful intentions" in their foreign policy. He then announced a "crusade for freedom" and a "campaign for democratic development."[1]

In making these claims the president joined a long list of liberal theorists (and propagandists) and echoed an old argument: The aggressive instincts of authoritarian leaders and totalitarian ruling parties make for war. Liberal states, founded on such individual rights as equality before the law, free speech and other civil liberties, private property, and elected representation, are fundamentally against war, this argument asserts. When the citizens who bear the burdens of war elect their governments, wars become impossible. Furthermore, citizens appreciate that the benefits of trade can be enjoyed only under conditions of peace. Thus the very existence of liberal states, such as the United States, Japan, and their European allies, makes for peace.

Building on some of my earlier work and on a growing literature in international political science, I reexamine the liberal folklore that the president retold for us. I look at three distinct theoretical traditions of liberalism, attributable to three theorists: Schumpeter—a brilliant explicator of the liberal pacifism the president invoked; Machiavelli—a classical republican whose glory is an imperialism we often practice; and Kant.[2]

An earlier version of this paper was published as "Liberalism and World Politics" in *American Political Science Review,* vol. 80, no. 4, December 1986, pp. 1152–1169. Reprinted by permission of the American Political Science Association and the author.

Despite the contradictions of liberal pacifism and liberal imperialism, I find with Kant and other democratic republicans that liberalism does leave a coherent legacy on foreign affairs. Liberal states are different. They indeed are peaceful. But they also are prone to make war, as the United States and its "freedom fighters" are now doing, not so covertly, against Nicaragua. Liberal states, as Kant argues they would, have created a separate peace. They also, as he fears they might, have discovered liberal reasons for aggression.

I conclude by returning to policy. Is there a coherent alternative, for liberals, to both the isolationism of pacifism and the imperialism of the "crusade for freedom"?

Liberal Pacifism

There is no canonical description of liberalism. What we tend to call liberal resembles a family portrait of principles and institutions, recognizable by certain characteristics—for example, individual freedom, political participation, private property, and equality of opportunity— that most liberal states share, although none has them all. Joseph Schumpeter clearly fits within this family when he considers the international effects of capitalism and democracy.

Schumpeter's "Sociology of Imperialisms," which was published in 1919, makes a coherent and sustained argument concerning the pacifying effects of liberal institutions and principles.[3] Unlike some of the earlier liberal theorists, who focused on a single feature (such as trade)[4] or failed to examine critically the arguments they were advancing, Schumpeter sees the interaction of capitalism and democracy as the foundation of liberal pacifism, and he tests his arguments in a sociology of historical imperialisms.

He defines imperialism as "an objectless disposition on the part of a state to unlimited forcible expansion."[5] Excluding imperialisms that are mere "catchwords" and objectful imperialisms (for example, defensive), he traces the roots of objectless imperialism to three sources, each an atavism. Modern imperialism resulted from the combined impact of a "war machine," warlike instincts, and export monopolism.

Once necessary, the war machine later developed a life of its own and took control of a state's foreign policy. "Created by the wars that required it, the machine now created the wars it required."[6] Thus, Schumpeter tells us, the army of ancient Egypt, created to drive the Hyksos out of Egypt, took over the state and pursued militaristic imperialism. Like the later armies of the courts of absolutist Europe, it fought wars for the sake of glory and booty, for the sake of warriors and monarchs—wars *gratia* warriors. A warlike disposition, elsewhere called "instinctual elements of bloody primitivism," is the natural ideology of a war machine. It also exists independently;[7] the Persians, Schumpeter says, were a warrior nation from the outset.

Under modern capitalism, export monopolists, the third source of modern imperialism, push for imperialist expansion as a way to expand their closed markets. But the absolute monarchies were the last clearcut imperialisms. Nineteenth century imperialisms merely represented the vestiges of the imperialisms created by Louis XIV and Catherine the Great. Thus the export monopolists are an atavism of the absolute monarchies, for they depend completely on the tariffs imposed by the monarchs and their militaristic successors for revenue.[8] Without tariffs, monopolies would be eliminated by foreign competition.

Modern (nineteenth-century) imperialism, therefore, rests on an atavistic war machine, militaristic attitudes left over from the days of monarchical wars, and export monopolism, which is nothing more than the economic residue of monarchical finance. In the modern era, imperialists gratify their private interests. From the national perspective, their imperialistic wars are objectless.

Schumpeter's theme now emerges. Capitalism and democracy are forces for peace. Indeed, they are antithetical to imperialism, and the further development of capitalism and democracy means that imperialism inevitably will disappear.

Capitalism produces an unwarlike disposition; its populace is "democratized, individualized, rationalized."[9] The people's daily energies are absorbed in production. The disciplines of industry and the market train people in "economic rationalism"; the instability of industrial life necessitates calculation. Capitalism also "individualizes"; "subjective opportunities" replace the "immutable factors" of traditional, hierarchical society. Rational individuals demand democratic governance.

Democratic capitalism leads to peace. As evidence, Schumpeter claims that (1) throughout the capitalist world an opposition has arisen to "war, expansion, cabinet diplomacy"; (2) contemporary capitalism is associated with peace parties; and (3) the industrial worker of capitalism is "vigorously anti-imperialist." In addition, (4) the capitalist world has developed the means of preventing war, such as the Hague Court; and (5) the least feudal, most capitalist society—the United States—has demonstrated the least imperialistic tendencies (for example, the United States left more than half of Mexico unconquered in the war of 1846–1848).[10]

His explanation for liberal pacifism is quite simple. Only war profiteers and military autocrats gain from wars. No democracy would pursue a minority interest and tolerate the high costs of imperialism. When free trade prevails, "no class" gains from forcible expansion: "Foreign raw materials and food stuffs are as accessible to each nation as though they were in its own territory. Where the cultural backwardness of a region makes normal economic intercourse dependent on colonization it does not matter, assuming free trade, which of the 'civilized' nations undertakes the task of colonization."[11]

Schumpeter's arguments are difficult to evaluate. In partial tests of quasi-Schumpeterian propositions, Michael Haas discovers a cluster that associates democracy, development, and sustained modernization with peaceful conditions.[12] But J. D. Singer and M. Small discover that there is no clearly negative correlation between democracy and war in the period 1816–1965—the period that would be central to Schumpeter's argument.[13]

Later in his career, in *Capitalism, Socialism, and Democracy*, Schumpeter acknowledges that "almost purely bourgeois commonwealths were often aggressive when it seemed to pay—like the Athenian or the Venetian commonwealths."[14] But he sticks to his (pacifistic) guns, restating the view that capitalist democracy "steadily tells . . . against the use of military force and for peaceful arrangements, even when the balance of pecuniary advantage is clearly on the side of war which, under modern circumstances, is not in general very likely."[15] Recently, a study by R. J. Rummel of "libertarianism" and international violence is the closest test that Schumpeterian pacifism has received.[16] "Free" states (those enjoying political and economic freedom) have considerably less conflict at the level of economic sanctions or above (more violent) than "nonfree" states. The free, the partly free (including the democratic socialist countries such as Sweden), and the nonfree accounted for .24, .26, and .61 of the violence respectively.

These correlations are impressive but not conclusive for the Schumpeterian thesis. The data set is limited, in this test, to 1976–1980. It includes (for example) the Soviet-Afghan war, the Vietnamese invasion of Cambodia, China's invasion of Vietnam, and Tanzania's invasion of Uganda, but just misses the U.S., quasi-covert intervention in Angola (1975) and the not so covert U.S. war against Nicaragua (1981–). More importantly, the data set excludes the Cold War period with its numerous interventions and the long history of colonial wars (the Boer War, the Spanish American War, the Mexican Intervention, and so on) that marked the history of liberal, including democratic, capitalist states.

The discrepancy between the warlike history of liberal states and Schumpeter's pacifistic expectations highlights three extreme assumptions. First, his "materialistic monism" leaves little room for noneconomic objectives, whether espoused by states or individuals. Neither glory, prestige, ideological justification, nor the pure power of ruling shapes policy. These nonmaterial goals leave little room for positive-sum gains, such as the comparative advantages of trade. Second, his states are the same. The political life of individuals seems to have been homogenized at the same time as the individuals were "rationalized, individualized, and democratized." Citizens, capitalists, and workers, both rural and urban, seek material welfare. Schumpeter presumes that no one wants to rule. He also presumes that no one is prepared to take those measures (such as stirring up foreign quarrels to preserve a domestic ruling coalition) that enhance one's political power, despite detrimental effects on mass welfare. Third, just as domestic politics are homogenized, so world politics, too, is homogenized. Materially monistic and democratically capitalist, states evolve toward free trade and liberty together. Countries differently constituted seem to disappear from Schumpeter's analysis. "Civilized nations" govern "culturally backward *regions*." These assumptions are not shared by Machiavelli's theory of liberalism.

Liberal Imperialism

Machiavelli argues that not only are republics not pacifistic, they are the best form of state for imperial expansion. Establishing a republic fit for imperial expansion is, moreover, the best way to guarantee the survival of a state.

Machiavelli's republic is a classical mixed republic. It is not a democracy, which he thought would degenerate quickly into a tyranny, but it is characterized by social equality, popular liberty, and political participation.[17] The consuls serve as "kings," the senate as an aristocracy managing the state, and the people in the assembly as the source of liberty and strength.

Liberty results from the "disunion"—the competition and necessity for compromise required by the division of powers among senate, consuls, and tribunes (the last representing the common people). Liberty also results from the popular veto. The powerful few, Machiavelli says, threaten tyranny because they seek to dominate; the mass demands not to be dominated and its veto thus preserves the liberties of the state.[18] But because the people and the rulers have different social characters, the people need to be "managed" by the few to avoid having their recklessness overturn or their fecklessness undermine the ability of the state to expand.[19] Thus the senate and the consuls plan expansion, consult oracles, and employ religion to manage the resources that the energy of the people supplies.

Strength, indeed imperial expansion, results from the way liberty encourages increased population and property, which grow when the citizens know that their lives and goods are secure from arbitrary seizure. Free citizens equip large armies and provide soldiers who fight for public glory and the common good because they in fact are their own.[20] Thus, if you seek the honor of having your state expand, Machiavelli advises, you should organize it as a free and popular republic like Rome, rather than as an aristocratic republic like Sparta or Venice. Expansion thus calls for a free republic.

"Necessity"—that is, political survival—calls for expansion.[21] If a stable aristocratic republic is forced by foreign conflict "to extend her territory, in such a case we shall see her foundations give way and herself quickly brought to ruin." If domestic security, on the other hand, prevails, "the continued tranquillity would enervate her, or provoke internal disensions, which together, or either of them separately, will apt to prove her ruin."[22]

Hence liberal imperialism. We are lovers of glory, Machiavelli announces. We seek to rule or at least to avoid being oppressed. In either case, we want more for ourselves and our states than just material welfare (materialistic monism). Because other states with similar aims thereby threaten us, we prepare ourselves for expansion. Because our fellow citizens threaten us if we do not allow them either to satisfy their ambition or to release their productive energies through imperial expansion, we expand.

There is considerable historical evidence for liberal imperialism. Machiavelli's (Polybius's) Rome and Thucydides's Athens both were imperial republics in the Machiavellian sense.[23] The historical record of numerous interventions support Machiavelli's argument.[24] But the current record of liberal pacifism, weak as it is, calls some of Machiavelli's insights into question. To the extent that the modern populace actually controls (and thus unbalances) the mixed republic, its diffidence may outweigh elite (senatorial) aggressiveness.

We can conclude either that (1) liberal pacifism at last has taken over with the further development of capitalist democracy, as Schumpeter predicts it would; or (2) that the mixed record of liberalism—pacifism and imperialism—indicates that some liberal states are Schumpeterian democracies while others are Machiavellian republics. But before we accept either conclusion, we must consider a third apparent regularity of modern world politics.

Liberal Internationalism

Modern liberalism carries with it two legacies. They affect liberal states, not separately, according to whether they are pacifistic or imperialistic, but simultaneously.

The first of these legacies is the pacification of foreign relations among liberal states.[25] During the nineteenth century, the United States and

Great Britain engaged in nearly continual strife. But after the Reform Act of 1832 widened the representation of the British Parliament, Britain and the United States negotiated their disputes despite, for example, British grievances against the North's blockade of the South, with which Britain had close economic ties. Despite severe Anglo-French colonial rivalry, liberal France and liberal Britain formed an entente against illiberal Germany before World War I. In 1914–1915, Italy, the liberal member of the Triple Alliance with Germany and Austria, chose not to fulfill its treaty obligations under the Triple Alliance to support its allies. Instead, Italy joined in an alliance with Britain and France that prevented it from having to fight other liberal states and then declared war on Germany and Austria. Despite generations of Anglo-American tension and Britain's wartime restrictions on U.S. trade with Germany, the United States leaned toward Britain and France from 1914 to 1917, before entering World War I on their side.

Beginning in the eighteenth century and slowly growing since then, a zone of peace, which Kant called the "pacific union," was established among liberal societies. (More than forty liberal states currently make up the union. Most are in Europe and North America, but they can be found on every continent. See Table 11.1.)

Here the predictions of liberal pacifists (and President Reagan) are borne out: Liberal states do exercise peaceful restraint, and a separate peace exists among them. This separate peace provides a solid foundation for the crucial U.S. alliances with the liberal powers (the North Atlantic Treaty Organization [NATO], the U.S.-Japanese alliance, the Australia-New Zealand-United States alliance). This foundation appears to be impervious to the quarrels with allies that bedeviled the Carter and Reagan administrations and offers the promise of a continuing peace among liberal states. Thus, the increasing number of liberal states announces the possibility of global peace this side of the grave or world conquest.

But liberalism also carries with it a second legacy—international imprudence.[26] Peaceful restraint only seems to work in the liberals' relations with other liberals. Liberal states have fought numerous wars with nonliberal states. In a widely circulated, published list of overt international wars waged between 1816 and 1980,[27] Melvin Small and David Singer have shown that every one of these was fought between a liberal and a nonliberal nation. Many of these wars have been defensive, and thus prudent by necessity. Liberal states have been attacked and threatened by nonliberal states that do not exercise any special restraint in their dealings with liberal states. Authoritarian rulers stimulate and respond to an international political environment in which conflicts of prestige, interest, and pure fear of what other states might do all lead

TABLE 11.1 Liberal Regimes and the Pacific Union[a]

Period	Regime	Total Number
18th century	Swiss Cantons[b] United States[b] 1776– French Republic 1790–1795	3
1800–1850	Swiss Confederation United States France 1830–1849 Belgium 1830– Great Britain 1832– Netherlands 1848– Piedmont 1848– Denmark 1849–	8
1850–1900	Switzerland United States Belgium Great Britain Netherlands Piedmont–1861 Italy 1861– Sweden 1864– Greece 1864– Denmark–1866– Canada 1867– France 1871– Argentina 1880– Chile 1891–	14
1900–1945	Switzerland United States Great Britain Sweden Canada Greece–1911, 1928–1936 Italy–1922– Belgium–1940 Netherlands–1940 Argentina–1943 France–1940 Chile–1924, 1932 Australia 1901– Norway 1905–1940 New Zealand 1907– Colombia 1910–1949 Denmark 1914–1940 Poland 1917–1935	

Table 11.1 (cont.)

Period	Regime	Total Number
	Germany 1918–1932 Austria 1918–1934 Estonia 1919–1934 Finland 1919– Uruguay 1919– Costa Rica 1919– Czechoslovakia 1920–1939 Ireland 1920– Latvia 1922–1934 Mexico 1928– Lebanon 1944–	29
1945[c]–	Switzerland United States Great Britain Sweden Canada Australia New Zealand Finland Ireland Mexico Uruguay–1973; Chile–1973; Lebanon–1975 Costa Rica–1948, 1953– Iceland 1944– France 1945– Denmark 1945– Norway 1945– Austria 1945– Brazil 1945–1954, 1955–1964 Belgium 1946– Luxemburg 1946– Netherlands 1946– Italy 1946– Philippines 1946–1972 India 1947–1975, 1977– Sri Lanka 1948–1961, 1963–1977, 1978– Ecuador 1948–1963, 1979– Israel 1949– West Germany 1949– Peru 1950–1962, 1963–1968, 1980– El Salvador 1950–1961 Turkey 1950–1960, 1966–1971	

Table 11.1 (cont.)

Period	Regime	Total Number
	Japan 1951–	
	Bolivia 1956–1969	
	Colombia 1958–	
	Venezuela 1959–	
	Nigeria 1961–1964, 1979–	
	Jamaica 1962–	
	Trinidad 1962–	
	Senegal 1963–	
	Malaysia 1963–	
	South Korea 1963–1972	
	Botswana 1966–	
	Singapore 1965–	
	Greece 1975–	
	Portugal 1976–	
	Spain 1978–	
	Dominican Republic 1978–	49

[a]I have drawn up this approximate list of Liberal Regimes according to the four institutions described as essential: market and private property economies; polities that are externally sovereign; citizens who possess juridical rights; and "republican" (whether republican or monarchical), representative government. This latter includes the requirement that the legislative branch have an effective role in public policy and be formally and competitively, either potentially or actually, elected. Furthermore, I have taken into account whether male suffrage is wide (that is, 30 percent) or open to "achievement" by inhabitants (for example, to poll-tax payers or householders) of the national or metropolitan territory. Female suffrage is granted within a generation of its being demanded; and representative government is internally sovereign (for example, including and especially regarding military and foreign affairs) as well as stable (in existence for at least three years).

[b]There are domestic variations within these liberal regimes. For example, Switzerland was liberal only in certain cantons; the United States was liberal only north of the Mason-Dixon line until 1865, when the country became liberal throughout. These lists also exclude ancient "republics" because none appears to fit Kant's criteria. See Stephen Holmes, "Aristippus in and out of Athens," *American Political Science Review* 73, no. 1 (March 1979).

[c]This selected list excludes liberal regimes with populations less than 1 million.

Sources: Arthur Banks and W. Overstreet, eds., *The Political Handbook of the World, 1980* (New York: McGraw-Hill, 1980); Foreign and Commonwealth Office, *A Year Book of the Commonwealth 1980* (London; HMSO, 1980); *Europa Yearbook, 1981* (London: Europa, 1981); W. L. Langer, *An Encyclopedia of World History* (Boston: Houghton Mifflin, 1968); Department of State, *Country Reports on Human Rights Practices* (Washington, D.C.: Government Printing Office, 1981); and *Freedom at Issue,* no. 54 (Jan.–Feb. 1980).

states toward war. War and conquest thus have characterized the careers of many authoritarian rulers and ruling parties from Louis XIV and Napoleon to Mussolini's fascists, Hitler's Nazis, and Stalin's communists.

But imprudent aggression by the liberal state also has characterized many of these wars. Both France and Britain fought expansionist wars throughout the nineteenth century. The United States fought a similar war with Mexico in 1846–1848, wages a war of annihilation against the American Indians, and intervened militarily against sovereign states many times before and after World War II. Liberal states invade weak nonliberals states and display exceptional degrees of distrust in their dealings with powerful nonliberal states.[28]

Neither realist (statist) nor Marxist theory accounts well for these two legacies. Neither the logic of the balance of power nor of international hegemony explains the separate peace maintained for more than one hundred fifty years among states sharing one particular form of governance—liberal principles and institutions. Balance-of-power theory expects, indeed is premised upon, flexible arrangements of geostrategic rivalry that include preventive war. Hegemonies wax and wane, but the liberal peace holds. Marxist "ultraimperialists" expect a form of peaceful rivalry among capitalists, but only liberal capitalists maintain peace. Leninists expect liberal capitalists to be aggressive toward nonliberal states but also (and especially) expect them to be imperialistic toward fellow liberal capitalists.[29]

Kant's theory of liberal internationalism helps us understand these two legacies. "Perpetual Peace," written in 1795, predicts the ever-widening pacification of the liberal pacific union, explains that pacification, and at the same time suggests why liberal states are not pacific in their relations with nonliberal states. Kant argues that perpetual peace will be guaranteed by the ever-widening acceptance of three "definitive articles" of peace. When all nations have accepted the definitive articles in a metaphorical "treaty" of perpetual peace he asks them to sign, perpetual peace will have been established.[30]

The First Definitive Article requires that the civil constitution of the state be republican. By republican Kant means a political society that has solved the problem of combining moral autonomy, individualism, and social order. A private property and market-oriented economy partially addressed that dilemma in the private sphere. The public, or political, sphere was more troubling. His answer was a republic that preserved juridical freedom—the legal equality of citizens as subjects—on the basis of a representative government with a separation of powers. Juridical freedom is preserved because the morally autonomous individual is by means of representation a self-legislator making laws that apply to all citizens equally, including her- or himself. Tyranny is avoided because the individual is subject to laws she or he does not administer.[31]

Liberal republics will progressively establish peace among themselves by means of the "pacific union" described in the Second Definitive Article of the Eternal Peace. The pacific union is limited to "a treaty of the nations among themselves" that "maintains itself, prevents wars, and steadily expands." The world will not have achieved the "perpetual peace" that provides the ultimate guarantor of republican freedom until "very late and after many unsuccessful attempts." Then right conceptions of the appropriate constitution, great and sad experience, and goodwill will have taught all the nations the lessons of peace. Not until then will individuals enjoy perfect republican rights or the full guarantee of a global and just peace. But in the meantime, the "pacific union" of liberal republics "steadily expands," bringing within it more and more republics (despite republican collapses, backsliding, and disastrous wars) and thus creating an ever-expanding separate peace.[32] The pacific union is neither a single peace treaty ending one war nor a world state or state of nations. The first is insufficient; the second and third are impossible or potentially tyrannical. Kant develops no organizational embodiment of this treaty, and presumably he does not find institutionalization necessary. He appears to have in mind a mutual nonaggression pact, perhaps a collective security agreement, and the cosmopolitan law set forth in the Third Definitive Article.[33]

The Third Definitive Article of the Eternal Peace establishes a cosmopolitan law to operate in conjunction with the pacific union. The cosmopolitan law "shall be limited to conditions of universal hospitality." In this Kant calls for the recognition of the "right of a foreigner not to be treated with hostility when he arrives upon the soil of another [country]," which "does not extend further than to the conditions which enable them [the foreigners] to attempt the developing of intercourse [commerce] with the old inhabitants." Hospitality does not require extending either the right to citizenship to foreigners or the right to settlement, unless the foreign visitors would perish if they were expelled. Foreign conquest and plunder also find no justification under this right. Hospitality does appear to include the right of access and the obligation of maintaining the opportunity for citizens to exchange goods and ideas, without imposing the obligation to trade (a voluntary act in all cases under liberal constitutions).[34]

Perpetual peace, for Kant, is an epistemology, a condition for ethical action, and (most importantly) an explanation of how the "cunning of nature" will produce "a harmony from the very disharmony of men against their will."[35] Understanding history requires an epistemological foundation, for without a teleology, such as the promise of perpetual peace, the complexity of history would overwhelm human understanding.[36] But perpetual peace is not merely a heuristic device with which to interpret history. It is guaranteed, Kant explains in "On the Guarantee of Perpetual Peace," to result from humans fulfilling their ethical duty or, failing that, from a hidden plan. Peace is an ethical duty because it is only under conditions of peace that all humans can treat each other as ends.[37]

In order for this duty to be practical, Kant needs, of course, to show that peace in fact is possible. The widespread sentiment of approbation that he saw aroused by the early success of the French revolutionaries showed him that we indeed can be moved by ethical sentiments with a cosmopolitan reach.[38] This does not mean, however, that perpetual peace is certain ("prophesyable"). Even the scientifically regular course of the planets could be changed by a wayward comet striking them out of orbit. Human freedom requires that we allow for much greater reversals in the course of history. In fact, we must anticipate the possibility of backsliding and destructive wars (although these will serve to educate nations to the importance of peace).[39]

But, in the end, our guarantee of perpetual peace does not rest on ethical conduct, as Kant emphasizes.

> Now we face the question which concerns the essential point in accomplishing eternal peace: what does nature do in relation to the end which man's reason imposes as a duty, in order to favor thus his *moral intent*? In other words: how does nature guarantee that what man ought to do according to the laws of freedom, but does not do, will be made secure regardless of this freedom by a compulsion of nature which forces him to do it? . . . And if I say of nature: she wants this or that to take place, it does not mean that she imposes a *duty* to do it—for that only noncompulsory practical reason can do—but it means that nature itself does it, whether we want it or not (*facta volentem ducunt, nolentem tradunt*).[40]

The guarantee thus rests, Kant argues, on the probable behavior not of moral angels but of "devils, if only they have intelligence." In explaining the sources of each of the three definitive articles of the perpetual peace, Kant then tells us how we (as free and intelligent devils) could be motivated by fear, force, and calculated advantage to undertake a course of actions whose outcome we can reasonably anticipate to be perpetual peace. But although it is possible to conceive of the Kantian road to peace in these terms, Kant himself recognizes and argues that social evolution also makes the conditions of moral behavior less onerous, and hence more likely.[41] In tracing the effects of both social and moral development, he builds an account of why liberal states do maintain peace among themselves and of how the pacific union will expand (and by implication, has expanded). He also explains how these republics would engage in wars with nonrepublics and therefore suffer the "sad experience" of wars that an ethical policy might have avoided.

The first source derives from a political evolution, from a constitutional law. Nature (providence) has seen to it that human beings can live in all the regions where they have been driven to settle by wars. (Kant, who once taught geography, reports on the Lapps, the Samoyeds, the Pescheras.) "Asocial sociability" draws people together to fulfill needs for security and material welfare as it drives them into conflicts about the distribution and control of social products. This violent natural evolution tends toward the liberal peace because "asocial sociability" inevitably leads toward republican governments and republican governments are a source of the liberal peace.

Republican representation and separation of powers are produced because they are the means by which the state is "organized well" to prepare for and meet foreign threats (by unity) and to tame the ambitions of selfish and aggressive individuals (by authority derived from representation, general laws, and nondespotic administration). States that are not organized in this fashion fail. Monarchs thus encourage commerce and private property in order to increase national wealth and cede rights of representation to their subjects in order to strengthen their political support or to obtain willing grants of tax revenue.[42]

Kant shows how republics, once established, lead to peaceful relations. He argues that once the aggressive interests of absolutist monarchies are tamed and once the habit of respect for individual rights is engrained by republican government, wars would appear as the disaster to the people's welfare that he and other liberals think them to be.

> If, as is necessarily the case under the constitution, the consent of the citizens is required in order to decide whether there should be war or not, nothing is more natural than those who have to decide to undergo all the deprivations of war will very much hesitate to start such an evil game. For the deprivations are many, such as fighting oneself, paying for the cost of the war out of one's own possessions, and repairing the devastation which it costs, and to top all the evils, there remains a burden of debts which embitters the peace and can never be paid off on account of approaching new wars. By contrast, under a constitution where the subject is not a citizen and which is therefore not republican, it is the easiest thing in the world to start a war. The head of state is not a fellow citizen but owner of the state, who loses none of his banquets, hunting parties, pleasure castles, festivities, etc. Hence he will resolve upon war as a kind of amusement on very insignificant grounds and will leave the justification to his diplomats, who are ever ready to lend it an air of propriety.[43]

Yet these domestic republican restraints do not end war. If they did, liberal states would not be warlike, which is far from the case. These restraints do introduce republican caution, Kant's "hesitation," in place of monarchical caprice. Liberal wars are fought only for popular, liberal purposes. The historical liberal legacy is laden with popular wars fought to promote freedom, protect private property, or support liberal allies against nonliberal enemies. Kant regards these wars as unjust and warns liberals of their susceptibility to these wars.[44] To see how the pacific union removes the occasion of wars among liberal states and not wars between liberal and nonliberal states, we need to shift our attention from constitutional law to international law, Kant's second source.

Complementing the constitutional guarantee of caution, international law adds a second source—a guarantee of respect. The separation of nations that asocial sociability encourages is reinforced by the development of separate languages and religions. These further guarantee a world of separate states—an essential condition needed to avoid a "global, soulless despotism." Yet, at the same time, languages and religions also morally integrate liberal states "as culture progresses and men gradually come closer together toward a greater agreement on principles for peace and understanding."[45] As republics emerge (the first source) and as culture progresses, an understanding of the legitimate rights of all citizens and of all republics comes into play; and this, now that caution characterizes policy, sets up the moral foundations for the liberal peace. Correspondingly, international law highlights the importance of Kantian publicity. Domestically, publicity helps ensure that the officials of republics act according to the principles they profess to hold just and according to the interests of the electors they claim to represent. Internationally, free speech and the effective communication of accurate conceptions of the political life of foreign peoples are essential to establish and preserve the understanding on which the guarantee of respect depends. In short, domestically just republics, which rest on consent, presume foreign republics to be consensual, just, and therefore deserving of accommodation. The experience of cooperation helps engender further cooperative behavior when the consequences of state policy are unclear but (potentially) mutually beneficial. At the same time, liberal states assume that nonliberal states, which do not rest on free consent, are not just. Because nonliberal governments are in a state of aggression with their own people, their foreign relations become for liberal governments deeply suspect.

Lastly, cosmopolitan law adds material incentives to moral commitments. The cosmopolitan right to hospitality permits the "spirit of commerce" sooner or later to take hold of every nation, thus impelling states to promote peace and to try to avert war. Liberal economic theory holds that these cosmopolitan ties derive from a cooperative international division of labor and free trade according to comparative advantage. Each economy is said to be better off than it would have been under autarky; each thus acquires an incentive to avoid policies that would lead the other to break these economic ties. Given that keeping markets open rests upon the assumption that the next set of transactions also will be determined by prices rather than coercion, a sense of mutual security is vital to avoid security-motivated searches for economic autarky. Thus avoiding a challenge to another liberal state's security or even enhancing each other's security by means of alliance naturally follows economic interdependence.

A further cosmopolitan source of liberal peace is that the international market removes difficult decisions of production and distribution from the direct sphere of state policy. A foreign state thus does not appear directly responsible for these outcomes; states can stand aside from, and to some degree above, these contentious market rivalries and be ready to step in to resolve crises. The interdependence of commerce and the international contacts of state officials help create crosscutting transnational ties that serve as lobbies for mutual accommodation. According to modern liberal scholars, international financiers and transnational and transgovernmental organizations create interests in favor of accommodation and have ensured by their variety that no single conflict sours an entire relationship.[46] Conversely, a sense of suspicion, such as that characterizing relations between liberal and nonliberal governments, can lead to restrictions on the range of contacts between societies. This can increase the prospect that a single conflict will determine an entire relationship.

No single constitutional, international, or cosmopolitan source is alone sufficient, but together (and only together) they plausibly connect the characteristics of liberal polities and economies with sustained liberal peace. Alliances founded on mutual strategic interest among liberal and nonliberal states have been broken, economic ties between liberal and nonliberal states have proven fragile, but the political bonds of liberal rights and interests have proven a remarkably firm foundation for mutual nonaggression. A separate peace exists among liberal states.

But in their relations with nonliberal states, liberal states have not escaped from the insecurity caused by anarchy in the world political system considered as a whole. Moreover, the very constitutional restraint, international respect for individual rights, and shared commercial interests that promote peace among liberal states tend to exacerbate conflicts in relations between liberal and nonliberal societies.

Kant's liberal internationalism, Machiavelli's liberal imperialism, and Schumpeter's liberal pacifism rest on fundamentally different views on the nature of humans, the state, and international relations. Schumpeter's citizens are rationalized, individualized, and democratized. They also are homogenized, pursuing material interests "monistically." Because their material interests lie in peaceful trade, they and the democratic state they control are pacifistic. Machiavelli's citizens are splendidly diverse in their goals but are fundamentally unequal in them as well; his citizens seek to rule or fear being dominated. In extending the rule of the dominant elite or avoiding the political collapse of their state, each calls for imperial expansion. Kant's citizens are diverse in their goals but also are individualized, rationalized, and capable of appreciating moral equality and thus of treating other individuals as ends rather than as means. The Kantian state thus is governed publicly according to law, as a republic. Kant's is the state that solves the problem of governing individualized equals whether they are the "rational devils" he says we often find ourselves to be or the·ethical agents we can and should become. Republics show us how

> to organize a group of rational beings who demand general laws for their survival, but of whom each inclines toward exempting himself, and to establish their constitution in such a way that, in spite of the fact that their private attitudes are opposed, these private attitudes mutually impede each other in such a manner that their public behavior is the same as if they did not have such evil attitudes.[47]

Unlike Machiavelli's republics, Kant's republics are capable of achieving peace among themselves because they exercise democratic caution and because they are capable of appreciating the rights (derived from moral equality) of foreign individuals. Unlike Schumpeter's capitalist democracies, Kant's republics, as well as the United States, remain in a state of war with nonrepublics because these liberal republics on occasion are prepared to promote democratic interests and protect the rights of individuals overseas against governments that in liberal terms do not have the right to represent their citizens, even though these wars may cost more than the economic return they generate. Perpetual peace, Kant says, is the endpoint of the hard journey his republics will take. The promise of perpetual peace, the violent lessons in wars the republics will suffer first, and the experience of a partial peace; these are proof of the need for and the possibility of world peace. They thus are the ground for ethical citizens and statesmen to assume the duty of striving for peace.

A Liberal Foreign Policy for the United States?

No country lives strictly according to its political ideology, and few liberal states are as hegemonically liberal as the United States.[48] Even in the United States, certain domestic interests and actors derive their sense of legitimacy from sources other than liberalism. The state's national security bureaucracy, isolated from domestic politics, reflects an approach to politics among nations that tends to fall into the realist, national interest frame of reference. Certain Western European states and Japan have more syncretic and organic sources of a "real" national interest. But in the United States, and in other liberal states to a lesser degree, public policy derives its legitimacy from its concordance with liberal principles. Policies not rooted in liberal principles generally fail to sustain long-term public support.

This leads to a foreign policy dilemma: Liberal principles are a firm anchor of the most successful zone of international peace yet established but also are a source of conflicted and confused foreign policy toward the nonliberal world. Improving policy toward the nonliberal world by introducing steady and long-run calculations of strategic and economic interest is likely to require political institutions that are inconsistent with both a liberal policy and a liberal alliance: for example, an autonomous executive branch or a predominance of presidential and military actors in foreign policy so as to obtain flexible and rapid responses to changes in the strategic and economic environment. In peacetime, such "emergency" measures are unacceptable in a liberal democracy. Moreover, they would break the chain of stable expectations and the mesh of private and public channels of information and material lobbying that sustain the pacific union. In short, completely resolving liberal dilemmas may not be possible without threatening liberal success.

The goal of concerned liberals therefore must be to reduce the harmful impact of the dilemmas without undermining the successes. Although there can be no simple formula for an effective liberal foreign policy (its methods must be geared toward specific issues and countries), liberal legacies do suggest guidelines for liberal policymaking that contrast quite strikingly with the simple advocacy of maximizing the national interest.

First, if "publicity" makes radically inconsistent policy impossible in a liberal republic, then policy toward the liberal and the nonliberal world should be guided by general liberal principles. Liberal policies thus must attempt to promote liberal principles abroad: to secure basic human needs, civil rights, and democracy and to expand the scope and effectiveness of the world market economy. Important among these principles, Kant argues, are some of the "preliminary articles" from his treaty of perpetual peace: extending nonintervention by force in internal affairs of other states to nonliberal governments and maintaining a scrupulous respect for the laws of war.[49] These, as J. S. Mill argues, follow from the fact that if a foreign state is needed to free another people, it also is likely to impose its own foreign dependence. But these principles also imply a right to support liberty by defending states threatened by external aggression and to intervene against foreigners attempting to crush a popular rebellion striving to achieve a free government.[50] Furthermore, powerful and weak, hostile and friendly nonliberal states must be treated according to the same standards. There are no special geopolitical clients, no geopolitical enemies other than those judged to be such by liberal principles. Therefore, the United States, as a liberal state, must have no liberal enemies and no unconditional alliances with nonliberal states. This policy is as radical in conception as it sounds. It requires abandoning the national interest and the balance of power as guidelines to policy. The interests of the United States must be consistent with its principles.

Second, given contemporary conditions of economic interdependence, a liberal foreign policy could employ economic warfare to lead an imperialistic, liberal crusade against communism and against Third World authoritarians of the left or the right. This policy also could lead to a withdrawal into isolationism, pacifism, and a defense of only one principle: the right of the United States to territorial integrity and political independence. Both policies are consistent with liberal principles—liberal states, although obliged to offer hospitality to foreigners, are not obliged to trade, and liberal states, although they have the right to support liberty under certain circumstances, have no duty to do so. But these policies neither promote security in a nuclear age nor enhance the prospects for meeting the needs of the poor and oppressed. To avoid the extremist possibilities of its abstract universalism, U.S. liberal policy must be constrained further by a geopolitical budget. Here the realists' calculus of security provides a benchmark of survival and prudence from which a liberal policy that recognizes national security as a liberal right can navigate. This benchmark consists of prudent policies toward the most significant, indeed the only, strategic threat the United States faces—the USSR. Once the realists define what the United States must do and how much it must invest to have a prudent policy toward the USSR, the liberals then can take over again, defining more supportive and interdependent policies toward those countries more liberal than the USSR and defining more constraining and more containing policies toward countries less liberal than the USSR.

Third, specific features of liberal policy will be influenced by whether voting citizens choose to be governed by a laissez faire or by a social democratic administration. But both liberalisms should take into account more general guidelines to a prudent, liberal foreign policy, such as those that follow.[51]

In relations with the USSR, a prudent set of policies calls for rejecting subversion—a cold war, liberal crusade—as unjustified, while offering moral and diplomatic support to those within the Soviet Union striving to improve human rights. Instead, mutually beneficial arrangements should be accepted to the extent they do not violate liberal principles or favor long-run Soviet interests over the long-run interests of the United States and the liberal world. Arms control would be central to this, as would the expansion of civilian trade. The United States will encounter difficulties when its liberal allies can gain economic benefits from trade deals (for example, the sale of computer technology) that might in the long run favor the USSR. These situations may be exceptionally difficult to resolve diplomatically because assessments of strategic advantage tend to be uncertain and because the particular nature of the benefits (say, sales of grain as opposed to sales of computers) can influence the assessment of the strategic risks entailed. Liberals also will need to ensure that ties of dependence on the USSR (such as the gas pipeline) are not a major constraint on liberal foreign policy by equalizing the import costs of energy and by assuring alternative sources in an emergency. Given the Soviet Union's capacity to respond to bottlenecks imposed by the West, there will be few occasions (fortunately for the coherence of the liberal alliance) when an embargo would unambiguously hamper the Soviet Union and help the liberal alliance.[52]

In relations with the People's Republic of China (PRC), similar liberal principles permit trade that includes arms sales to a state no more restrictive of its subjects' liberty but much less restrictive of the liberty of foreign peoples than is the USSR. But strategic temptations toward a further alliance should be curbed. Such an alliance would backfire, perhaps disastrously, when liberal publics confront policymakers with the Chinese shadows of antiliberal rule.

Arms control, trade, and accommodation toward nonliberal Third World nations must be measured first against a prudent policy toward the Soviet Union and then should reflect the relative degrees of liberal principle that their domestic and foreign policies incorporate. Although U.S. policy should be directed by liberal principles, it should free itself from the pretension that by acts of will and material benevolence the United States can replicate itself in the Third World. The liberal alliance should be prepared to have diplomatic and commercial relations as it does with the USSR with every state that is no more repressive of liberal rights than is the USSR. For example, North Korea and Mozambique might receive PRC-level relations; Vietnam, with its foreign incursions, and Angola, with its internal ethnic conflict, Soviet-level relations. Being one of the few states that deny the legal equality of its subjects, South Africa should be treated as Amin's Uganda and Pol Pot's Khmer Republic should have been, in a more containing fashion than is the USSR. No arms should be traded, investment should be restricted with a view to its impact on human rights, and trade should be limited to humanitarian items that do not contribute to the longevity of apartheid.

Elsewhere, the liberal world should be prepared to engage in regular trade and investment with all Third World states no more restrictive of liberty than is the PRC, and this could include the sale of arms not sensitive to the actual defense of the liberal world in regard to the USSR. Furthermore, the liberal world should take additional aid measures to favor Third World states attempting to address the basic needs of their own populations and seeking to preserve and expand the roles of the market and democratic participation. Much of the potential success of this policy rests on an ability to preserve a liberal market for Third World growth; for the market is the most substantial source of Third World accommodation with a liberal world whose past record includes imperial oppression. To this should be added mutually beneficial measures designed to improve Third World economic performance, such as export earnings insurance, export diversification assistance, and technical aid.

Liberals should persevere in attempts to keep the world economy free from destabilizing, protectionist intrusions. Although intense economic interdependence generates conflicts, it also helps to sustain the material well-being underpinning liberal societies and to promise avenues of development to Third World states with markets that are currently limited by low income. Discovering ways to manage interdependence when rapid economic development has led to industrial crowding (at the same time as it retains massive numbers of the world's population in poverty) will call for difficult economic adjustments at home and institutional innovations in the world economy. These innovations may even require more rather than less explicit regulation of the domestic economy and more rather than less planned disintegration of the international economy. Under these circumstances, liberals will need to ensure that those suffering losses, such as from market disruption or restriction, do not suffer a permanent loss of income or exclusion from world markets. Furthermore, to prevent these emergency measures from becoming a spiral of isolationism, liberal states should undertake these innovations only by international negotiation and only when the resulting agreements are subject to a regular review by all the parties.[53]

Above all, liberal policy should strive to preserve the pacific union of similarly liberal societies. It is currently of immense strategic value (as the political foundation of both NATO and the Japanese alliance) and also is the single best hope for the evolution of a peaceful world. Liberals therefore should be prepared to defend and formally ally with authentically liberal, democratic states that are subject to threats or actual instances of external attack or internal subversion.

Strategic and economic realists are likely to judge this liberal foreign policy to be either too much of a commitment or too little. The realists may argue that through a careful reading of the past one can interpret in a clear fashion a ranked array of present strategic and economic interests. Strategically beneficial allies, whatever their domestic system, should be supported. The purposes of power must be to maximize power. Global ecologists claim an ability to foresee future disasters that we should be preparing for now by radical institutional reforms.

But liberals always have doubted their ability to interpret the past or predict the future accurately and without bias. Liberalism has been an optimistic ideology of a peculiarly skeptical kind. Liberals assume individuals to be both self-interested and rationally capable of accommodating their conflicting interests. Liberals have held that principles such as rule under law, majority rule, and the protection of private property that follow from mutual accommodation among rational, self-interested people are the best guide to present policy. These principles preclude taking advantage of every present opportunity. They also discount what might turn out to have been farsighted reform. The implicit hope of liberals is that the principles of the present will engender accommodating behavior that avoids past conflicts and reduces future threats. As the realists and global ecologists have warned, the gamble has not always paid off in the past (as in accepting a Sudeten separatism) and is not guaranteed to work in the future (for example, in controlling nuclear proliferation or pollution). But liberalism cannot politically sustain nonliberal policies. Liberal policies rest upon a different premise and can be accepted by a liberal world in good faith and sustained by the electorates of liberal democracies.

In responding to the demands of their electorates, liberal states also must ascribe responsibility for their policies to their citizenry. The major costs of a liberal foreign policy are borne at home. Not merely are a policy's military costs at the taxpayers' expense, but a liberal foreign policy requires adjustment to a less controlled international political environment, which thus is a rejection of the status quo. The home front becomes the frontline of liberal strategy.[54] Tolerating more foreign change requires a greater acceptance of domestic change. Not maintaining an imperial presence in the Persian Gulf calls for a reduction of energy dependence. Accepting the economic growth of the Third World may require trade and industrial adjustment. The choice is between preserving liberalism's material legacy at the cost of liberal principles or accepting the costs of adjusting to a changing world in order to preserve liberal principles.

Notes

1. President Reagan's speech is printed in the *New York Times*, June 9, 1982.

2. This chapter draws on my "Kant, Liberal Legacies, and Foreign Affairs," Parts 1 and 2, *Philosophy and Public Affairs* 12, nos. 3-4 (Summer and Fall 1983), and on "Why Democracies Are Prone to Fight Dictators," *Wall Street Journal*, August 25, 1983. I thank the publishers for allowing me to use material from those articles here. I also would like to thank Marshall Cohen, Diana Meyers, and Jerome Schneewind for critical suggestions that helped me improve this chapter.

3. Joseph Schumpeter, "The Sociology of Imperialism," *Imperialism and Social Classes* (Cleveland: World Publishing Co., 1955), pp. 3-98. This discussion draws on parts of the "Introduction" to Part 2 of my *Empires* (Ithaca, N.Y.: Cornell University Press, 1986).

4. See, for example, Montesquieu, *Spirit of the Laws* I, Book 20, chap. 1.

5. Schumpeter, op. cit., p. 6.

6. Ibid., p. 25.

7. Ibid., pp. 25-32.

8. Ibid., pp. 82-83.

9. Ibid., p. 68.

10. Ibid., pp. 95-96.

11. Ibid., pp. 75-76.

12. Michael Haas, *International Conflict* (New York: Bobbs-Merrill, 1974), pp. 464-465.

13. M. Small and J. D. Singer, "The War-proneness of Democratic Regimes," *The Jerusalem Journal of International Relations* 50, No. 4 (Summer 1976).

14. J. Schumpeter, *Capitalism, Socialism, and Democracy* (New York: Harper Torchbooks, 1950), pp. 127-128.

15. Ibid., p. 128. Schumpeter notes that testing this proposition is likely to be very difficult, requiring "detailed historical analysis." But the bourgeois attitude toward the military, the spirit, and the manner by which bourgeois societies wage war and the readiness with which they submit to military rule during a prolonged war are "conclusive in themselves" (p. 129).

16. R. J. Rummel, "Libertarianism and International Violence," *Journal of Conflict Resolution* 27, no. 1 (March 1983):27-71.

17. N. Machiavelli, *The Prince and the Discourses* (New York: Modern Library, 1950), Bk I, Chap. 2, p. 112. See Quentin Skinner, *Machiavelli* (New York: Hill and Wang, 1981), Chap. 3, for a thorough analysis of the *Discourses*.

18. Machiavelli, ibid. Bk. I, Chap. 5, p. 122.

19. Ibid., Bk. I, Chap. 53, pp. 249-250.

20. Ibid., Bk. II, Chap. 2, p. 287.

21. Ibid., Bk. I, Chap. 6, p. 129.

22. Ibid., Bk. I, Chap. 6, p. 129.

23. Thucydides, *The Peloponnesian War* (Baltimore, Md.: Penguin, 1954). See especially Book VI, the debate on the expedition to Sicily.

24. Raymond Aron, *The Imperial Republic*, Frank Jellinek, trans. (Englewood Cliffs, N.J.: Prentice-Hall, 1973).

25. In a reference brought to my attention by Ferdinand Hermens, Clarence Streit, in *Union Now: A Proposal for a Federal Union of the Leading Democracies* (New York: Harpers, 1938), seems to have first pointed out (in modern foreign relations) the empirical tendency of democracies to maintain peace among themselves, and he made this the foundation of his proposal for a (non-Kantian) federal union of the fifteen leading democracies of the 1930s (pp. 88, 90–92). D. V. Babst, "A Force for Peace," *Industrial Research* (April 1972):55–58, performed a quantitative study of this phenomenon of "democracies." R. J. Rummel did a similar study of "libertarianism" (in the sense of laissez faire) focusing on the postwar period in R. J. Rummel, op. cit., which drew on an unpublished study (Project no. 48) noted in Appendix I:7.5 of Rummel's *Understanding Conflict and War*, vol. 4 (Beverly Hills, Calif.: Sage, 1979), p. 386. I use "liberal" in a wider (Kantian) sense in my discussion of this issue in "Kant, Liberal Legacies, and Foreign Affairs: Part 1." In that article, I survey the period from 1790 to the present and find no war among liberal states.

26. David Hume discusses this meaning of "imprudent vehemence" in "Of the Balance of Power" in *Essays: Moral, Political, and Literary* (Oxford: Oxford University Press, 1963), pp. 346–347.

27. *Resort to Arms* (Beverly Hills, Calif.: Sage Publications, 1982), pp. 79–80. The list is reprinted in my "Liberalism and World Politics," *American Political Science Review* 80, no. 4 (December 1984), pp. 1165–1166.

28. For a discussion of the historical effects of liberalism on colonialism, the U.S.-Soviet Cold War, and post–World War II interventions, see Doyle, "Kant, Liberal Legacies, and Foreign Affairs: Part 2" and the sources cited there.

29. See the survey of theories in Bruce Russett, "The Mysterious Case of Vanishing Hegemony" *International Organization* 39, no. 2 (Spring 1985):207–231, that discusses various explanations of the liberal, capitalist, or Western peace. I criticized these competing explanations in ibid.

30. Three important sources that focus on Kant's international theory are Kenneth Waltz, "Kant, Liberalism, and War," *American Political Science Review* 56, no. 2 (June 1962); Stanley Hoffmann, "Rousseau on War and Peace" in his *The State of War* (New York: Praeger, 1965); and Pierre Hassner, "Immanuel Kant," in *History of Political Philosophy*, ed. by L. Strauss and J. Cropsey (Chicago: Rand McNally, 1972). I have benefited from their analyses and from those that follow herein and, more generally, from Karl Friedrich, *Inevitable Peace* (Cambridge, Mass.: Harvard University Press, 1948); F. H. Hinsley, *Power and the Pursuit of Peace* (Cambridge: Cambridge University Press, 1967), Chap. 4; W. B. Gallie, *Philosophers of Peace and War* (Cambridge: Cambridge University Press, 1978), Chap. 1; George A. Kelly, *Idealism, Politics, and History* (Cambridge: Cambridge University Press, 1969); Susan Shell, *The Rights of Reason* (Toronto: University of Toronto Press, 1980); Howard Williams, *Kant's Political Philosophy* (Oxford: Basil Blackwell, 1983); and Patrick Riley, *Kant's Political Philosophy* (Totowa, N.J.: Rowman and Allanheld, 1983).

31. Kant's republican constitution is described in Kant, "Perpetual Peace," *The Philosophy of Kant*, ed. by Carl Friedrich (New York: Modern Library, 1949),

various translators, p. 437; and analyzed by Riley, ibid., Chap. 5. (The Friedrich edition is the source cited for essays by Kant unless otherwise noted.)

32. Kant, "Idea for a Universal History," in Friedrich, *The Philosophy of Kant*, p. 123. The pacific union follows a process of "federalization" such that it "can be realized by a gradual extension to all states, leading to eternal peace." This interpretation contrasts with those cited in n. 29. I think Kant means that the peace would be established among liberal regimes and would expand by ordinary political and legal means as new liberal regimes appeared. By a process of gradual extension the peace would become global and then perpetual; the occasion for wars with nonliberal states would disappear as nonliberal regimes disappeared.

33. Kant's "Pacific Union," the *foedus pacificum*, thus is neither a *pactum pacis* (a single peace treaty) nor a *civitas gentium* (a world state). He appears to have anticipated something like a less formally institutionalized League of Nations or United Nations. One could argue that these two institutions in practice worked for liberal states and only for liberal states. But no specifically liberal "pacific union" was institutionalized. Instead liberal states have behaved for the past one hundred eighty years as if such a Kantian pacific union and treaty of perpetual peace had been signed. This follows Riley's views of the legal, not the organizational, character of the *foedus pacificum*.

34. Kant, "Perpetual Peace," pp. 444–447.

35. Kant, the fourth principle of the "Idea for a Universal History," p. 120.

36. See the ninth principle of the "Idea for a Universal History," pp. 129–131.

37. See Jeffrie Murphy, *Kant: The Philosophy of Right* (New York: St. Martins, 1970), Chap. 3.

38. This is established in the "Contest of the Faculties" where Kant discusses ethical sentiments, Hans Reiss, ed., *Kant's Political Writings* (Cambridge: Cambridge University Press, 1970), pp. 181–182. This passage was drawn to my attention by Bonnie Honig and Diana Meyers. The following paragraphs have benefited from the arguments of Yirmiahu Yovel, *Kant and the Philosophy of History* (Princeton, N.J.: Princeton University Press, 1980); and William Galston, *Kant and the Problem of History* (Chicago: Chicago University Press, 1975).

39. Kant, "Idea for a Universal History," p. 124.

40. Kant, "Perpetual Peace," p. 452.

41. Kant, "Contest of the Faculties," nos. 9–10, where Kant discusses the increase in the "quantity" of moral action resulting from the socialization achieved by a republican constitution. This point is explained in Kelly, op. cit., pp. 106–113.

42. See Hassner, op. cit., pp. 583–586 for a systematic analysis of the factors leading to republicanism.

43. Kant, "Perpetual Peace," p. 438.

44. See Kant's discussion of European relations with the Bedouins, ibid., p. 446.

45. Kant, ibid., p. 454.

46. Karl Polanyi, *The Great Transformation* (Boston: Beacon Press, 1944), Chaps. 1–2; and Samuel Huntington and Z. Brzezinski, *Political Power: USA/*

USSR (New York: Viking Press, 1963, 1964), Chap. 9. See Richard Neustadt, *Alliance Politics* (New York: Columbia University Press, 1970), for a detailed case study of interliberal politics.

47. Kant, "Perpetual Peace," p. 453. For a comparative discussion of the political foundations of Kant's ideas, see Judith Shklar, *Ordinary Vices* (Cambridge, Mass.: Harvard University Press, 1984), pp. 232–238.

48. Louis Hartz, *The Liberal Tradition in America* (New York: Harcourt, Brace, and World, 1953). The United States is one of the few liberal states whose leading political factions (parties) are liberal. Others have shared or competitive factions: aristocratic or statist-bureaucratic factions contesting more centrally liberal factions.

49. See Kant's "Preliminary Articles" in "Perpetual Peace," pp. 431–436.

50. J. S. Mill contends that rights of nonintervention do not extend to "barbarous" peoples, hence his justification of nineteenth-century imperialism. But even a liberal imperialist of a Millian persuasion now would accept that the right to nonintervention should extend to the contemporary Third World. Because the criteria set forth in "Civilization" (commercialization and public security) now are met by almost all nations (Pol Pot's regime in Cambodia, however, might be considered one exception), Mill would find that we no longer have "barbarous nations" requiring imperial rule. See J. S. Mill, "Civilization," and "A Few Words on Nonintervention," in *Essays on Literature and Society*, ed. by J. Schneewind (New York: Collier, 1965). Michael Walzer, *Just and Unjust Wars* (New York: Basic Books, 1977), has reformulated and revised the major liberal propositions concerning the justice of wars and justice in wars. A thorough legal and moral-historical argument against intervention can be found in R. J. Vincent, *Nonintervention and International Order* (Princeton, N.J.: Princeton University Press, 1974). For political and philosophical treatments of the question of intervention, see Charles Beitz, *Political Theory and International Relations* (Princeton, N.J.: Princeton University Press, 1979); and David Luban, "Just War and Human Rights," *Philosophy and Public Affairs* 9, no. 2 (Winter 1979).

51. For a contemporary application of liberal views that shares a number of positions with the policies suggested here, see Richard Ullman, "The Foreign World and Ourselves: Washington, Wilson, and the Democrat's Dilemma," *Foreign Policy* (Winter 75/76); and Stanley Hoffmann, *Duties Beyond Borders* (Syracuse, N.Y.: Syracuse University Press, 1981), Chaps. 2–4. For a coherent exposition of a liberal foreign policy that has helped inform my views on this entire question, see Marshall Cohen, "Toward a Liberal Foreign Policy," in *Liberalism Reconsidered*, ed. D. MacLean and C. Mills (Totowa, N.J.: Rowman and Allanheld, 1983).

52. See *the Economist* study of Soviet technology (June 1981) and an extensive literature on the use of economic sanctions, including F. Holtzman and R. Portes, "Limits of Pressure," *Foreign Policy* (Fall 1978).

53. These and similar policies can be found in Fred Hirsch, Michael Doyle, and Edward Morse, *Alternatives to Monetary Disorder* (New York: McGraw-Hill, 1977); and in C. Fred Bergsten et al., "The Reform of International Institutions," and Richard N. Cooper et al., "Towards a Renovated International System"

(Triangle Papers 11 and 14), both in *Trilateral Commission Task Force Reports: 9–14*, ed. Trilateral Commission (New York: New York University Press, 1978).

54. See Robert Paarlberg, "Domesticating Global Management," *Foreign Affairs* 54 (April 1976), for an explication of what this would involve in current policy formation.

Selected Bibliography

Beitz, Charles. *Political Theory and International Relations*. Princeton, N.J.: Princeton University Press, 1979.

Cohen, Marshall, "Toward a Liberal Foreign Policy." Ed. D. MacLean and C. Mills. *Liberalism Reconsidered*. Totowa, N.J.: Rowman and Allanheld, 1983.

Doyle, Michael W. "Kant, Liberal Legacies, and Foreign Affairs," Parts 1 and 2. *Philosophy and Public Affairs* 12, nos. 3–4 (Summer and Fall 1983).

Hassner, Pierre. "Immanuel Kant." Ed. L. Strauss and J. Cropsey. *History of Political Philosophy*. Chicago: Rand McNally, 1972.

Hoffmann, Stanley. "Rousseau on War and Peace." *The State of War*. New York: Praeger, 1965.

Kant, Immanuel. "Perpetual Peace" and "Idea for a Universal History with a Cosmopolitan Intent." *The Philosophy of Kant*, ed. Carl Friedrich. New York: Modern Library, 1949.

Machiavelli, Niccolo. *The Prince and the Discourses*. New York: Modern Library, 1950.

Rummel, Rudolph J. "Libertarianism and International Violence." *Journal of Conflict Resolution* 27, no. 1 (March 1983):27–71.

Schumpeter, Joseph. "The Sociology of Imperialism." *Imperialism and Social Classes*. Cleveland: World Publishing Co., 1955, pp. 3–98.

Small, Melvin, and J. D. Singer. "The War-proneness of Democratic Regimes." *The Jerusalem Journal of International Relations* 50, no. 4 (Summer 1976).

Ullman, Richard. "The Foreign World and Ourselves: Washington, Wilson, and the Democrats Dilemma," *Foreign Policy* (Winter 75/76).

Waltz, Kenneth. "Kant, Liberalism, and War." *American Political Science Review* 56, no. 2 (June 1962).

Yovel, Yirmiahu. *Kant and the Philosophy of History*. Princeton, N.J.: Princeton University Press, 1980.

12

Kant's Liberal Alliance: A Permanent Peace?

Diana T. Meyers

Michael Doyle argues that Kant's theories of international relations and history have been borne out by events. As Kant expected, the number of liberal states has increased, and these states have not fought one another. Thus, it seems that global peace and justice are within reach. Whatever the merits of this projection, we confront a worrisome interim period, and we must ask whether Doyle's Kantian political science provides a tenable guide to policy for the intervening period and a reasonable basis for optimism in regard to the ultimate outcome. To deal with these questions, I shall first examine Kant's philosophy at some length and then consider Doyle's use of it.

Kant warns that the empirical discipline of history concerns people, whose dual nature—a mix of good and evil—bars the historian from assuming that the future must resemble the past.

> Even if it were found that the human race as a whole had been moving forward and progressing for an indefinitely long time, no one could guarantee that its era of decline was not beginning at that very moment, by virtue of the physical character of our race. And conversely, if it is regressing and deteriorating at an accelerating pace, there are no grounds for giving up hope that we are just about to . . . take a turn for the better, by virtue of the moral character of our race. (CF, p. 180)

In view of these concessions to common sense, we must ask how Kant reaches the startling conclusion that "providence" is guiding human affairs in the direction of liberalism and peace (PP, p. 106). In other words, what leads Kant to believe, after all, that history is progressive?

Kant gives two main arguments for this thesis. The first comes at the end of his "Idea for a Universal History." There, after wondering how future generations will grasp the complexities of their past and cope with its immensity, Kant affirms that they will study history from the standpoint of their own concerns (IUH, p. 25). These generations will frame the problem of history as the "question of what the various nations and governments have contributed to the goal of world citizenship and what they have done to damage it" (IUH, p. 26). Our needs being what they are—we need freedom and security—and events being what they are—a vast welter of disconnected details—we are obliged to orient historical inquiry in terms of the concept of peace. That is, we must regard history as a process of gradual pacification in order to make sense of domestic and international political relations.

Still, it is somewhat mysterious why Kant should suppose that history must be so congenial to human interests. The fact that people need peace does not imply that peace eventually will prevail. Furthermore, the idea of a cyclical history of peace and war seems as comprehensible as a linear history moving toward peace. In a later essay, Kant answers these objections.

In "The Contest of the Faculties," Kant contends that the key question is whether we have any solid reason to believe that people are able to bring about their own improvement (CF, p. 181). As evidence that people are capable of doing so, he cites the "universal yet disinterested sympathy for one set of protagonists [the French revolutionaries] against their adversaries" (CF, p. 182). This fervent consensus of opinion, declares Kant, "can never be forgotten" because "it has revealed in human nature an aptitude and power for improvement" (CF, p. 184) and also because the ideal that has stirred this response is "too momentous, too intimately interwoven with the interests of humanity and too widespread in its influence . . . for nations not to be reminded of it when favourable circumstances present themselves" (CF, p. 185; also see IUH, p. 13, for Kant's stress on the collective nature of this capacity for improvement).

Kant's position is a complex blend of moral and empirical views. He begins by noting that people in fact are disposed to applaud the principles of the French Revolution, which celebrated individual dignity and popular sovereignty. Then he suggests that this behavior presupposes a concept of humanity with rich implications for history and politics. Enthusiasm for French republicanism would be nonsensical if people collectively could not control their history, but collective autonomy can be manifest fully only in a pacific union. Because Kant believes that such natural capacities "are destined to evolve completely to their natural end," it follows that peace is the end of history (IUH, p. 12). Still, the free yet pacific community of nations that Kant finds implicit in liberal sentiment is not an experienced reality. Rather, it is an idea without which our understanding of historical phenomena would remain fragmentary. More-over, it is an idea upon which principles of political morality are founded.

Later, I shall take up Kant's moral claims that people ought to instate governments that respect personal liberty and that they ought to seek peace among nations. What I want to focus on now is his injection of a telos into history on the strength of popular endorsement of the French Revolution. Let us suppose that Kant is right that "true enthusiasm is always directed towards the *ideal*" (CF, p. 183). In other words, let us agree that a widespread eruption of popular sentiment in response to a public event is emblematic of auspicious political attitudes (CF, p. 183). What follows in regard to the probable course of history?

I would suggest that the U.S. bombing of Hiroshima and Nagasaki in 1945 was an event comparable in certain important respects to the French Revolution. It was portentious, and, once the war was over, the disinterested response to this action was strong and virtually unanimous. If we set aside the debate about whether these nuclear attacks were militarily necessary and concentrate on the moral response they inspired, it appears that people generally came to feel appalled at the monstrousness of the destruction. I would urge further that the strength and the generality of this condemnation have grown in the intervening decades. Can we conclude that because this incident "can never be forgotten," we are safe from nuclear holocaust? Surely not. If not, we also cannot accept Kant's claim that popular solidarity with the French Revolution guarantees the eventual achievement of lasting peace.

To see why Kant's argument for the ultimate triumph of peace fails, it is necessary to examine his account of the forces that propel history. Kant is no Pollyanna. He discounts the importance of morality as an explanatory factor in public affairs and relies, instead, on self-interest (PP, p. 113). Yet, in Kant's consoling view, self-interest operates in both the political and the economic arenas to advance the cause of peace.

Briefly, Kant holds that people need a coercive public authority to guarantee their personal freedom and their property rights. But given that not all political arrangements are equally satisfactory from the standpoint of self-interest, people are spurred to agitate for political reform. Broadly speaking, this is why Kant sees historical significance in the sympathetic response to the French Revolution: It presages a restructured conception of self-interest that henceforth must shape history. More particularly, Kant maintains that people need to gain control of the state's war-making capacity because they typically bear the brunt of war (PP, p. 94). He also points out that commerce cannot flourish in the midst of international instability or crisis (PP, p. 114). Thus, self-interest supports the rise of liberal democracy; liberal democracy allows a self-interested citizenry to limit its government's military options, thereby compelling its government to pursue diplomatic settlements; and ultimately a global pacific union emerges.

The critical assumption in this line of argument is that liberal democratic constitutions provide mechanisms through which aggregated self-interest is translated into national policy. But this assumption is flawed in two respects. First, state bureaucracies are not passive sensors of public opinion. Certainly, they take public opinion into account in the formation of policy and in the dissemination of propaganda, but public opinion is by no means the sole input into government decisionmaking. Whether we call the state's handling of popular sentiment "leadership" or "manipulation," it is clear that government filters (or distorts) individual self-interest. Thus, liberal democracy does not in any straightforward way place state action under the control of majority interests. Second, even if we could devise a political apparatus that automatically would convert public opinion into matching public policy, this apparatus merely would register perceived self-interest. Because we often are mistaken individually as well as collectively about where our real interests lie, this pure procedural agency could not ensure the eventual achievement of peace. Because political rhetoric often distracts people from issues that really affect their interests and because political relations mesh personal self-interest with the national interest, expressed preferences may militate toward or away from peace.

I have argued that Kant's claim that peace is the end of history is highly dubious if it is taken to mean that circumstances will conspire to bring about an enduring peace. History is intelligible without this supposition. Indeed, history may be obscured by this supposition. Moreover, the forces at work in politics hardly encourage optimism. If liberal democracy is the only possible conduit for collective autonomy, collective autonomy need not bring about peace. Thus, Kant's attempt to depict "those events whose a priori possibility suggests that they will in fact happen" seems misguided (CF, p. 177). Nevertheless, Doyle argues that history tends to confirm Kant's view, the philosophical weakness of this view notwithstanding. I do not propose to contest Doyle's facts. So far as I know, liberal states by and large have maintained peaceful relations. However, I would like to raise some questions about the dynamic underlying this concord.

According to Doyle, democratic constraints prevent governments from hotheadedly plunging into wars and ensure that wars are fought only for the sake of "popular, liberal purposes" (LIIE, p. 199). Because democratic regimes are obliged to justify their activities publicly, they are deterred from pursuing policies that betray announced principles and concerns (LIIE, p. 199). Thus, liberal ideology and institutions combine to engender reciprocal respect among liberal states and to suppress animosities among them.

My first difficulty with this account is that it exaggerates both the efficacy of publicity and the rigidity of liberal ideology. Looking first at the public scrutiny Doyle says liberal state policies are subject to, I would venture that this exposure does not greatly constrain liberal foreign policy. U.S. leaders are notorious for mouthing liberal rationales to gain support for policies that are anything but liberal. For example, three presidents during the course of a decade claimed to be fighting in Vietnam in defense of freedom and democracy, but the regimes the United States propped up in fact were authoritarian and corrupt. If publicity makes liberal states cautious about entering wars, it also makes them duplicitous in justifying military actions. The case of the Vietnam War exhibits this tendency and illustrates my doubts about the power of a free press and an informed public to keep liberal governments in check. Although this example concerns liberal policy vis-à-vis a nonliberal state, I see no reason to suppose that official duplicity could not serve just as well to rationalize an attack on a bothersome liberal state. Nevertheless, duplicity is not always necessary in liberal politics. Because politicians have an uncanny genius for advocating incoherent doctrines without jeopardizing their careers in the least, it often is the case that no policy is incompatible with politicians' expressed beliefs, and therefore publicity cannot restrict their options. Thus, my suspicion is that liberal ideology and institutions play a very minor part in the maintenance of peaceful relations among liberal states.

But Doyle does not depend exclusively on liberal political arrangements to account for interliberal relations. He grants that shared economic interests are necessary adjuncts to liberal principles if a pacific union is to last (LIIE, p. 199–200). This leads me to wonder how important to peace are liberalism and the mutual esteem in which Doyle says liberal states hold each other. Have communist states clashed because communist theory allows ideological disputes to explode on the battlefield or because of ancient geopolitical rivalries that have yet to be eased? Do liberal states of a social welfare stripe and those of a conservative stripe tolerate one another because they all are basically committed to human rights or because they cannot afford to fight? In this connection, it is worth noting that when liberal ideology conflicts with economic interests, this ideology can prove conveniently elastic. For example, respect for democratic procedures did not prevent the United States from sabotaging Allende's government. Although it is undeniable that various circumstances have supported a liberal peace, it seems entirely possible that circumstances could so favor a different ideology in the future.

At this point, it could be objected that I have taken Kant's protestations that morality is not a potent historical force too literally. As a result, I may have overlooked the moral weight of Kant's idea of peace and, with it, an important dimension of Doyle's argument. Let me return to Kant's theory before assessing Doyle's normative views.

Some of Kant's assertions about the likelihood of peace are very modest, indeed. Near the end of "Perpetual Peace," he states that we can only be sufficiently sure of peace to know that we are morally obliged to pursue it (PP, p. 114). Elsewhere, he comments, "What duty requires is that we act in accordance with the Idea of such an end [perpetual peace], even if there is not the slightest theoretical probability that it is feasible, as long as its impossibility cannot be demonstrated either" (MEJ, p. 128). In passages like these, Kant seems bent on exhorting politicians to abandon prudential calculation and to embrace the categorical imperative. The morality of peace thus seems to assume paramount status.

Kant's appeal to a historical telos undoubtedly is intended to outflank realism in international affairs and is a strategy for introducing values into the conduct of international relations without placing undue faith in the probity of politicians. I already have argued that Kant's institutional program cannot harness self-interest so as to ensure peace. I shall conclude by asking whether Kant's conception of peace as an Idea of history succeeds in combining morality with political realism without collapsing the former into the latter.

I think that Kant underestimates the voraciousness of political realism. He sensibly holds that history can be predicted only when the forecaster is in a position to control the events divined (CF, p. 177). Accordingly, in his remarks on the French Revolution's reverberations, Kant stresses the idea of autonomous social improvement (CF, p. 181). But once Kant has posited what he calls "unsocial sociability" as the prime force in history, it is not clear that moral autonomy is left sufficient scope to offset belligerent forces.

Officials of liberal democratic states have a duty, in Kant's view, to perpetuate their political systems, for these political systems are the seedbeds from which peace springs. Also, officials of authoritarian states have a complementary duty to reform their political institutions—and thus, by liberalizing them, to move toward peace—but they do not have a duty to dissolve the sovereignty of these institutions, for the social contract should not be abrogated (PP, p. 86). How does Kantian morality constrain these various official pursuits of the national interest?

Very little, if at all, I would hazard. Kant forbids standing armies and deficit spending for military purposes (PP, pp. 87–88). But these prohibitions do not require immediate compliance (PP, p. 90). Thus, it is the responsibility of public officials to balance their duties to defend their respective states against their duties to disarm them, and the latter are plainly secondary. A more exacting rule with which Kant prescribes immediate and full compliance enjoins nonintervention in the domestic affairs of other states (PP, p. 89). Yet despite its relative stringency, this precept proves to be quite weak. If rebels have effectively divided a foreign state, Kant thinks that supporting one side is not a form of intervention (PP, p. 89). The gaping dimensions of this loophole become evident if we recall that this qualification would authorize most of the U.S. military adventures since World War II. Only two of Kant's provisions seem to sharply curb unbridled nationalism. During a war, states must abstain from cruel or treacherous tactics that would undermine any possible peace (PP, p. 89). When hostilities cease, no party to the treaty is entitled to reserve the option of recommencing the fight (PP, p. 85). Yet in insisting that states ought not submit to a global government that would enforce these treaties and deprive the relevant states of the excuse to fight, Kant must allow for the possibility of betrayal and therefore the moral permissibility of renewed defensive war (PP, p. 100).

Doyle's recommendations for liberal foreign policy comport with Kant's international morality. Doyle begins by proposing that we stop dividing the world into geopolitical clients and enemies on the basis of realpolitik considerations (LIIE, p. 203). But after characterizing his proposal as a radical departure from conventional thinking, Doyle makes some major concessions to the realists. Calculations of national interest must set "a prudent policy toward the USSR," and policy regarding "nonliberal Third World nations must first be measured against a prudent policy toward the Soviet Union" (LIIE, pp. 203, 204). But what does it take to satisfy prudence? To what extent are superpower politics, the arms race, and support for anticommunist dictatorships to continue? Only when prudence is satisfied is U.S. foreign policy to be governed by liberal principles. Although Doyle urges that the United States associate itself with reasonably liberal regimes, dissociate itself from oppressive regimes, and disregard economic cleavages in choosing its friends, he also maintains that these requirements are contingent upon national security.

Kant and Doyle give the goal of national survival a moral imprimatur. However, this objective is a disturbingly consuming one. Although there is room for debate about which policies are most conducive to national security and the most fruitful policies may turn out to be more benign than political leaders generally have thought, the argument here is an instrumental, not a moral, one. Moreover, the realist can argue with some persuasiveness that however safe a liberal state may seem to be now, it cannot exclude the possibility of reversals and must not miss any opportunity to strengthen its position. In this view, misplaced confidence and relaxed vigilance are antithetical to national security. The realist's contention that national security altogether eclipses moral choice in the international sphere seems to me a doubtful one. Nevertheless, it is clear that if this goal is given moral priority, as Kant and Doyle do, it narrowly circumscribes the role of other moral principles, consigns these principles to the periphery of foreign policy, and leaves most decisions in the hands of military and diplomatic gamesmen. Evidently, Kantian international morality overlaps with realism to such an extent that morality cannot be counted on to make the world safe for peace. We already have seen that self-interest in conjunction with liberal institutions does not ensure this result. Consequently, I conclude that Kant's philosophy and Doyle's elaboration on it afford us little hope of lasting peace.

References

CF: "The Contest of the Faculties." Immanuel Kant, *Kant's Political Writings*, ed. Hans Reiss. (Cambridge: Cambridge University Press, 1970).

IUH: "Idea for a Universal History from Kant on History from a Cosmopolitan Point of View." Immanuel Kant, *Kant on History*, ed. Lewis White Beck. (Indianapolis, Ind.: Bobbs-Merrill, 1963).

LIIE: "Liberal Institutions and International Ethics." Michael W. Doyle, Chapter 11 in this book.

MEJ: *The Metaphysical Elements of Justice*. Immanuel Kant. (Indianapolis, Ind.: Bobbs-Merrill, 1965).

PP: "Perpetual Peace." Immanuel Kant, *Kant on History*, ed. Lewis White Beck. (Indianapolis, Ind.: Bobbs-Merrill, 1963).

13

Reflections on Realism in the Nuclear Age

Avner Cohen

The nuclear revolution has distinct, *emergent* features.[1] The invention of nuclear weapons is one of those unique thresholds in human history at which a distinctly new causal factor emerges, whose actual and symbolic consequences transcend its original historical context.[2] With the advent of nuclear weapons a new predicament was in the making, a predicament whose emergent features can be discerned only *in hindsight*, decades after its birth.[3] The predicament came into being as technology was pushed to its limits. As it turned out, those emergent features overwhelmed the very political, strategic, and moral presuppositions that had initiated the nuclear revolution in the first place. Political Man was left much behind Technological Man.

Indeed, throughout much of the nuclear age our political culture has tended to deny the predicament, or at least to minimize its significance.[4] Concerns about the *legitimacy* of nuclear weapons for the most part were subdued and quiet. As the Hobbesian "state of nature" image of international relations continued to govern our political thinking, the regime of nuclear deterrence emerged as the only option available to us. Although it was recognized at the outset that nuclear weapons no longer had the qualities of genuine weapons, we have been driven to think about them and, even worse, to treat them as legitimate instruments of superpower politics. Because it is impossible to "disinvent" nuclear weapons, we must learn how to live with them. This is the essence of the argument in favor of nuclear deterrence.

Realism is the philosophical framework that supposedly justifies the political legitimacy of "living with nuclear weapons."[5] Realism is as old as the practice of international relations itself. Versions of realism can be traced to Thucydides, Machiavelli, and Hobbes, as well as to many twentieth-century international relations theorists. Realism begins with the thesis that substantial differences exist between domestic politics and international politics; the former is about *authority*, and the latter is about *power relations*. In the absence of a supreme authority to impose law and order over sovereign states, international relations are the manifestation of the anxiety involved in the Hobbesian "state of nature." In the words of a renowned contemporary realist, while national politics "is the realm of authority, of administration, and of law, international politics is the realm of power, struggle and accommodation."[6] For the realist, "this was true in Thucydides's time as it was in Renaissance Italy. It has been true in Europe since at least the seventeenth century, and it is true of the entire world today."[7] Nuclear deterrence is the epitome of realism in the nuclear age.

It is against the realism of "living with nuclear weapons" that I address this chapter. Indeed, realism as a theory of international relations has been under attack on normative-philosophical grounds in recent years by a number of political theorists.[8] The reasons for my criticism of nuclear realism, however, are quite different and separate from the general moral case against realism put forward by these theorists. The arguments I will develop here are derived directly from the emergent features of the nuclear predicament itself, the ways in which the rise of nuclear weapons has turned out to negate the fundamental logic of realism. The nuclear predicament brings realism to a reductio ad absurdum and negates the very political framework that is supposed to justify it.

The Nuclear Age: A Brief Retrospect

The end of World War II created a moment, not unlike the one that came after World War I, of historical anticipation. There was a sense of political revolution in the air. The lesson of the war was clear and indisputable, but this time with added urgency. If civilization is to survive, it cannot tolerate another Great War. War is now a threat to civilization itself. There must be a way, a political way, to liberate humanity once and for all from the horrors of Great War. It is either war or civilization. Radical politics appeared then as the only solution to this emerging recognition. Anything less than a full abolition of the institution of war, so went the popular sentiment, would be just a waste of the historical opportunity.

More than any single event, however, the dropping of the bomb on Hiroshima and Nagasaki as the final act of the war shaped this anticipation of a forthcoming political revolution.[9] Nothing could have made the case for restructuring world politics stronger than the testimony of Hiroshima and Nagasaki. With Hiroshima and Nagasaki all had changed. These names immediately became the symbol of the need for the establishment of a new world: a world free of war. "Civilization and humanity can now survive only if there is a revolution in mankind's political thinking," as the *New York Times* editorial put it only a day after Hiroshima.[10]

Nuclear pacifism overnight became the focus of worldwide political anticipation. Although the new sentiment was clearly pacifist in its radical call to outlaw the institution of war altogether, it did not stem from the traditional philosophical origins of pacifism.[11] The main impetus behind nuclear pacifism was the newly formed scientists movement, which later evolved into the American Federation of Atomic Scientists. For the scientists, nuclear pacifism was the only possible realism of the nuclear age. "Time is short," they argued, "and survival is at stake."[12] This new situation was for some even a source of optimism, as if "a glimmer of hope appeared in the darkness."[13]

Because the bomb changed everything, old realism built upon sovereign states now must yield to nuclear pacifism. It is important to see the intrinsically realistic reasoning behind the call for the establishment of world government: "Equal and sovereign power units can never, under any circumstances, under any conditions, coexist peacefully."[14] Even though the idea of extending sovereignty to the world community had attracted the attention of pacifists, visionaries, and theorists for a long time, the bomb made the issue politically alive and relevant. The argument for nuclear pacifism was based not just on abstract morality but on realistic prudence as well. "We cannot afford the luxury of national rivalry and jealousy running wild in a world that holds the atom bomb."[15] National sovereignty became obsolete in the nuclear age. Nuclear pacifism, enforced by an internationalist regime of disarmament, appeared the only politically and morally adequate response to the challenge of the bomb. Farewell to old Hobbesian realism was the name of the new anticipation.

Nuclear pacifism, however, predates August 1945. Along with the bomb itself, the worries about it also were conceived within the Manhattan Project. Even before the bomb was fully assembled, let alone tested, a number of prominent scientists voiced their moral and political qualms about the long-term implications of "nucleonics." The Franck Report on the social and political implications of atomic energy, written to the secretary of war in June 1945 by a group of scientists from the Metallurgical Laboratory in Chicago headed by physicist James Franck, is one of the early comprehensive statements about the unique nature of the emerging predicament.[16] Although the primary concern of the report was the immediate future—if and how to use the bomb in the war against Japan—the reasoning behind it was based exclusively on long-term considerations of the significance of the bomb. The report urged the United States to weigh using the bomb against Japanese cities in light of its long-term moral and political implications. "These considerations," the report stated, "make the use of nuclear bombs for an early unannounced attack against Japan inadvisable."[17]

In making the case against dropping the bomb, the report laid down the most fundamental facts of the nuclear age.

1. *Discontinuity*: "In the past, science has often been able to provide new methods of protection against new weapons of aggression it made possible, but it cannot promise such efficient protection against the destructive use of nuclear power."[18]
2. *Proliferation*: "Nuclear weapons cannot possibly remain a 'secret weapon' at the exclusive disposal of this country for more than a few years."[19]
3. *Invulnerability*: "In no other type of warfare does the advantage lie so heavily with the aggressor."[20]

On the basis of these emerging facts the report outlined a course of action—banning the bomb through an effective mechanism of international control. In fact, this meant establishing a new world order, a non-Hobbesian one, based on the existence of a sovereign world authority. "Among all the arguments calling for an efficient international organization for peace, the existence of nuclear weapons is the most compelling one."[21] The choice the report presents is simple, yet radical: either international control or a deadly nuclear arms race. In clearcut language the report warns that "unless an effective international control of nuclear explosives is instituted, a race for nuclear armaments is certain to ensue following the first revelation of our possession of nuclear weapons to the world."[22] This unprecedented situation in human history also places unique moral and political responsibility on the nation that developed the bomb first.

Although the initial recommendation of the report against dropping the bomb on Japanese cities was rejected, its moral and political concerns shaped the entire agenda for the forthcoming open nuclear debate (1945–1947).[23] In retrospect, the debate was about *legitimacy*: Should we allow the bomb to enter the sphere of *realpolitik*, or should we change the nature of international politics itself in order to ban the bomb. Traditional pacifists, atomic scientists, and world federalists all joined forces in the effort to ban the bomb. The focus of the debate was on the world government concept.[24] "A world authority and an eventual world state are not just *desirable* in the name of brotherhood, they are *necessary* for survival."[25] The either-or attitude, *One World or None* to use a title of a popular book as an example, typified the basic sentiment of the antinuclear movement of the late 1940s. Nuclear pacifism was conceived by its advocates as possible only within an abolitionist framework—a world government authority that would outlaw war. This pacifist attitude was implicit even in the Baruch Plan, the official U.S. proposal for nuclear disarmament, whose declared goal was not merely banning the bomb but eliminating the political institution of war altogether.[26]

Alas, this unique goal never materialized. The first nuclear debate was short-lived and, ultimately, politically ineffective. Within less than five years the political climate changed entirely. As the Cold War heightened the political reality in 1947–1948, the antinuclear sentiment began to lose its popular base. Antinuclear activism was transformed into moral apathy and indifference. The new political climate was no longer receptive to the postwar abolitionist sentiment. The failure of the Baruch Plan at the United Nations (1946–1947), along with the rapid deterioration in the relations between the emerging postwar superpowers, undermined the desire to establish an internationalist (non-Hobbesian) political order. When the Soviets exploded their atomic bomb in August 1949 and President Truman subsequently responded with the decision to initiate a crash program to develop the H-bomb, the call to control the bomb by international mechanism already was dead.[27]

By the late 1940s Hobbesian realism reasserted itself in world politics as forcefully as ever. A radically new political order emerged out of the ashes of the war, with little resemblance to the old European regime of the previous three centuries. Europe was no longer split into a multitude of loose and short-term political coalitions—the epitome of the Hobbesian state of nature. Instead, Europe was divided along bipolar ideological and geographical lines of East and West. Yet the new order was still a version of power politics in the realistic fashion. In such a world the idea of nuclear disarmament was out of touch with the political reality and very soon became just a rhetorical point in the war of propaganda between the superpowers. Only by way of hindsight can we now speculate, forty years after, about if and how things could have been different.

Perhaps the most regrettable historical mistake was the legitimation given to the nuclear regime. As the modest U.S. nuclear monopoly of the years 1945–1948 gave way (through a number of crash programs) to an aggressively growing complex of nuclear forces based, in the mid-1950s, on overkill capacity, the debate about legitimacy became more and more a dead issue. The nuclear regime gained its de facto legitimacy status in the 1950s with almost no debate at all. Nuclear weapons gained a technical victory. The victory was simply the by-product of the growing presence of nuclear weapons, a matter of bureaucratic momentum.[28]

This also is true about the doctrine of nuclear deterrence. By default the doctrine of nuclear deterrence was ready to emerge in the late 1950s as the age's new article of faith, and it did. The doctrine of nuclear deterrence came along to provide a realistic rationale for a new political reality that from a moral standpoint defies (and offends) our most fundamental intuitions. Nuclear deterrence provides the strategic legitimacy for the existence of overkill. "Living with nuclear weapons" soon would become the new realistic slogan. After all, if nuclear weapons cannot be eliminated, as the realists argued, then we should use their apocalyptic presence to prevent their actual use. This soon would become the paradigm of realistic prudence in the nuclear age.

In the early 1960s the world witnessed, once again, a new wave of public concern about nuclear weapons. But this debate, to a large extent a European phenomenon, was quite different from its predecessor.[29] The focus of the debate was no longer on the fundamental issue of legitimacy (although the issue was raised), but rather on the more limited issues of atmospheric testing and security arrangements in Europe. This debate, too, was short-lived. The great irony is that it was an outcome of the Cuban missile crisis—the Partial Test Ban Treaty (1963) and the installation of the hotline—that helped to dissipate this new wave of nuclear anxiety.

The outcome of this debate determined the fate of the next two decades. Nuclear realism prevailed. Nuclear weapons no longer were perceived in apocalyptic terms and became utterly mundane, a normal feature of abstract superpower politics. Apart from sporadic islands of nuclear protests, the general public seemed to accept the wisdom of nuclear realism. We seemed to "stop worrying and learned to love the bomb," just as the subtitle of the film *Dr. Strangelove* suggests. The public became morally reconciled and politically accustomed to the bomb's presence. As happened in other quarters of modernity, nuclear weapons were left almost exclusively in the hands of professionals, nuclear strategists, and systems analysts.

The inevitable intellectual result of these complex sociohistorical developments was a growing split between the strategic and the moral discourses about nuclear weapons, leaving the latter alienated from the mainstream of the nuclear debate. In the age of mutual assured destruction (MAD), strategic prudence stands on one side and morality on the other. Although MAD seemed to offend our basic moral intuitions, we also believed it was decisive in preventing nuclear war. Consequently, the moral perspective split along two lines. While the moral categorical objection to nuclear deterrence had virtually no room within the policymaking debate (for example, Walter Stein), the just-war revisionists advocating some moral legitimacy to nuclear deterrence were driven to deny the essence of the nuclear revolution—its discontinuity with the past (for example, Paul Ramsey). Their apologetic enterprise led them to support counterforce nuclear strategies as a way to mold nuclear weapons into the traditional modes of just-war thinking.[30] But neither the nuclear pacifists nor the advocates of Counterforce had much impact on the moral consciousness of the public at large.

In the early 1980s, however, the situation was reversed dramatically. Although no immanent global crisis seemed to be on the horizon, anxiety about nuclear weapons and the risk of war reached new peaks. The new scientific findings associated with the "nuclear winter" theory and the continuing lack of significant progress in the area of arms control have fueled further a growing antinuclear sentiment. Almost overnight the risk entailed by the continuing reliance on nuclear deterrence is perceived as no longer morally and politically acceptable.[31]

Four decades after its birth the regime of nuclear weapons seems to be facing its first crisis of *legitimacy*. A sense of historical awakening, a kind of nuclear *Zeitgeist*, shapes a new type of public consciousness. If anything, this is what the current nuclear debate is all about.

On Nuclear War: An Updated Argument

The historical narrative presented so far assumes that Hobbesian realism has become inadequate and obsolete in the nuclear age. But why is this so? The basic argument for this claim, I think, has been with us from the very early stage of the nuclear age (for example, the Franck Report) and has to do with the recognition of the uniqueness of nuclear weapons—the sui generis nature of the nuclear regime. In its very essence this intuition was true then as it is true now. Yet in retrospect it seems that only from the perspective of the present debate can we better understand it. The old argument about the relation between nuclear war and civilization probably overstated the case *then*, and it would overlook the case *now*. There is a need, therefore, to reconstruct the basic argument and to update it in light of the present strategic circumstances.

To understand the nuclear predicament we are in, one should reflect on how the rise of nuclear weapons has upset the intimate relation between civilization and war. Consider the very phenomenon of war. In contrast to all other forms of domestic violence, war is linked closely with the purposes of an organized society. War as an *institution* is distinguished by its political significance. As the anthropologist B. Malinowski puts it in his classical definition, war is "an armed contest between two independent political communities by means of an organized military force in pursuit of national or tribal policy."[32]

To rephrase it somewhat differently, one can account for the conceptual difference between war and other forms of domestic violence by appeal to the notion of *authority*. Authority is the necessary mark of any society;

there is no social institution without it. "Authority means not only a charter for deciding and balancing the opposing claims, but also power to enforce such decisions. The beginning of law, of authority, and of sanctions exists at the lowest levels of culture."[33] Naturally, from the perspective of society itself domestic violence is regarded as deviant, criminal, and illegal; it defies law and authority in its very nature. But war is very different. From the society's vantage it is neither deviant nor criminal. War takes place in an area distinguished by the absence of authority "for deciding and balancing the opposing claims." If domestic violence is a violation of the law, war occurs where there is no law. A genuine war bears the mark of political authority. The violence on the battlefield, by contrast to domestic violence, receives its legitimacy from within the warring community. The act of declaring war, a ritual essential to the institution of war, symbolizes very clearly the link with authority.

In tracing the historical origins of the institution of war, the link between war and politics becomes apparent. It lies in the origin of civilization itself.[34] Malinowski puts much weight on this point. "If we insist that war is a fight between two independent and politically organized groups, war does not occur at a primitive level."[35] War became more than just sporadic acts of pugnacity within those conflict situations peculiar to politicized societies. Hence, both politics and war are by-products of the rise of civilization. As Thucydides clearly teaches us, ever since the formation of the political regime based on sovereign city-states, the institution of war always has been with it. Here is the origin of the Hobbesian image of international relations.

But with the rise of nuclear weapons everything has changed. The very fundamentals of this Hobbesian logic are called into question. The delicate relationship between civilization and war now has reached a full dialectical turn. War, born out of the emergence of civilization, has developed in the nuclear age into a threat to all civilized life. What was "invented" jointly with the "invention" of politics now threatens the very existence of power politics itself. Nuclear war comes to negate the very essence of the institution of war—its essential link with politics.

This claim is not a new one. In its essence it already was presented at the first early debate. Yet in itself this claim is not enough to demonstrate the radical discontinuity between nuclear weapons and modern conventional means of total war. What makes the possibility of nuclear warfare so different—politically, strategically, and morally—from all other kinds of warfare humanity has known before? The answer, I think, lies not so much in the unprecedented extent of the actual devastation that any single nuclear bomb is bound to leave (as was argued early on), but rather in the unprecedented uncertainty that any crossing of the nuclear threshold would bring about. Contemporary nuclear weapons systems have unique features whose strategic and moral significance is irreducible to the physical properties of a single A-bomb. These are the emergent features of the nuclear revolution that I mentioned earlier.

Nuclear war is utterly sui generis due to our unprecedented ignorance about the ways that nuclear weapons can be put to use and the unpredictable consequences that their use may bring about. To cross the nuclear threshold is "to take a leap into the vast unknown," to quote Robert McNamara. At that point all preplanned strategic doctrines (when, where, why, how, and which nuclear weapons ought to be used) fade into irrelevance. One thing, however, is quite clear: No matter what nuclear war might be, it would *not* (and cannot) be the kind of rule-governed practice that typifies the traditional institution of war. This element of unpredictability is the most basic emergent feature of the nuclear revolution. This unpredictability is not a property of the hardware itself, but rather of the entire organization of nuclear deterrence. The moral and prudential consequences of this unpredictability have not yet been appreciated fully.

One may object to this reasoning by stressing the continuity of nuclear warfare with previous types of warfare. After all, any eruption of large-scale violence, such as major war, is bound to produce waves of chaos, disorder, and unpredictability. Indeed, Clausewitz's appeal to the unpredictability of war constitutes one of the defining features of his ideal form of war: "In war more than anywhere else in the world, things happen differently to what we had expected, and look differently when near, to what they did at a distance."[36] Yet there is a qualitative difference between the kinds of unpredictability associated with conventional wars and those invoked by nuclear weapons.

One way to demonstrate this qualitative difference is by an appeal to what Thomas Donaldson has called "technological recalcitrance"—the tendency of contemporary nuclear weapons systems to be highly recalcitrant to the intentions of their users.[37] The more advanced and technologically sophisticated the system becomes, the less room it provides for full human control. Nuclear weapons systems rely so heavily on hair-trigger mechanisms for their operation and are so quick in response that they create a built-in tendency to crisis instability.[38] This emergent feature undermines the possibility of long deliberations by decisionmakers at times of crisis.

The problem of technological recalcitrance is manifested particularly in the area known as command, control, communication, and intelligence (C^3I). Operations of nuclear forces must rely heavily on adequate functioning of C^3I. If a nuclear deterrent posture is to be credible, there must be reliable operational procedures to verify nuclear attack and the extent of damage inflicted as well as to communicate retaliatory orders.

But the incredible speed and destructive power of modern nuclear weapons systems raise grave doubts regarding the possibility of C³I to function in a nuclear war environment.[39] Let me briefly mention five points of concern relating to this problem.

1. an unprecedented reliance on highly sophisticated and complex nonhuman elements (for example, computers and sensors) of C³I along the entire chain of command
2. a drastic temporal compression of the formerly distinct levels of political and military decisionmaking
3. unprecedented institutionalized pressures for a very rapid use of nuclear weapons at time of crisis, lest the opportunity to use them at all be lost permanently ("use them or lose them")
4. the impossibility of testing the proper functioning of the entire system prior to its actual use
5. the highly vulnerable structure of the C³I systems in the face of nuclear attack, which increases the likelihood that plans for "limited nuclear exchange" would turn into an all-out nuclear catastrophe.

The lesson is general. In past wars weapons for initiating war were relatively accident-free, and even if accidents did occur the stake was never that high. But this is very different now that the survival of civilization is at stake. Today's technologically recalcitrant systems raise the unprecedented possibility of initiation of nuclear war by error or miscalculation at time of crisis. Technologically recalcitrant systems not only tend to increase crisis instability, but also have the propensity to frustrate, even to foreclose, political options of control during war.[40] In the absence of any experience with nuclear war, no one can responsibly claim to know whether or how such war could be managed, controlled, or concluded.[41]

In summing up, the unmanageability of nuclear warfare calls into question one of the essential aspects of realism's view of the institution of war—its rationality. Thus, nuclear war loses any moral justification as well as any rational and prudential sense.

Nuclear Deterrence: Hobbesian Realism Revisited

So far my argument has focused almost entirely on the issue of nuclear war. I argued that nuclear war is utterly incompatible with the very institution of war and no longer fits the political order that makes war possible, that is, Hobbesian realism. But I have said very little about nuclear deterrence, a deliberately war-*preventive* policy. After all, has not the very existence of nuclear overkill prevented the actual use of those weapons? Shouldn't we be thankful for a policy that not only strengthened the nuclear taboo in world politics, but actually has made the possibility of any Great War between the superpowers unthinkable?

For roughly three decades the doctrine of nuclear deterrence has been sold as the embodiment of the new realistic wisdom of the nuclear age (at least until the appearance of the Strategic Defense Initiative rhetoric). Nuclear deterrence, as its advocates maintain, is above all a doctrine of *self*-deterrence. This makes it very different from all past deterrent postures.[42] The theory of nuclear deterrence, as developed by theoreticians in the late 1950s and 1960s (for example, Halperin, Smoke, Schelling, and Kaufman), provided both the strategic rationale and the political legitimacy for the capacity for overkill.[43] Deterrence, in its reflection of the new realism of the nuclear age, is presented as the political mechanism that ensures, promotes, and enforces the nuclear taboo. Given that presumably it is impossible to "disinvent" nuclear weapons, a credible and stable posture of mutual nuclear deterrence is the only guarantee in the nuclear age against the horrors of nuclear war.[44] For the advocates of nuclear realism, judgments about nuclear war and about nuclear deterrence are two separate issues; the absurdity of the former does not imply a similar conclusion for the latter.

، This nuclear realism, however, is logically and morally flawed. Just as nuclear war negates our basic intuitions about war politics and civilization, so the regime of nuclear deterrence runs afoul of our intuitions about political realism. The crux of the argument, according to Hobbesian realism, is the essential link that exists, and *must* exist, between deterrence and war. Even if the moral lesson of the nuclear age has become clear and indisputable due to nuclear deterrence, as its ardent supporters argue, it is still insufficient to provide us with the kind of "moral certitude" we deserve against the possibility of nuclear holocaust.[45] It is inherent in the logic of Hobbesian realism that situations of major crisis may occur that force one to resort to force. The hard fact is that as long as there are nuclear weapons in a Hobbesian world, they may well be used. Indeed, what is unique about current nuclear weapons systems is that their presence alone at time of crisis may be destabilizing. No one can calculate the impact of the uncertainty and anxiety involved in managing nuclear crisis. Even the most strategically stable posture of nuclear deterrence at peacetime would not constitute an adequate comfort at time of major crisis.

The link between nuclear deterrence and realism is a fundamental problem. The institution of nuclear deterrence is but an affirmation of the mighty grip of Hobbesian realism on our political thinking. In the "state of nature" that typifies international relations the only language that prevails is the language of power relations. Each sovereign state is free to take whatever it sees fit to protect, maintain, and promote its national security interests. The Hobbesian predicament is ultimately a constant state of insecurity. Hence, deterrence is an ever-present product of the Hobbesian system and is the parallel of the ever-present threat of aggression that typifies that system.

Furthermore, viewed from the perspective of any member state in a Hobbesian world order, deterrence is always more than just an isolated threat of retaliation; it is a system of threats, commitments, strategic doctrines, and the like that constitute the entire national security policy of a state. Viewed from the perspective of the entire international system, deterrence is the ever-present regulatory mechanism of order and stability among sovereign states. In this broad sense, deterrence is the by-product of the ever-prevailing condition of the Hobbesian regime, a condition expressed via the old truth that peace is achieved only by preparing for war. Deterrence is the instrument that keeps political conflicts stable. It contains conflicts within the boundaries of threats only, defines the power boundaries among participants in a given world order, and determines the harm a state risks in defying those boundaries. If the threats are successful, they are neither executed nor tested—they simply deter.[46]

This analysis brings to light the severe limits of deterrence in a Hobbesian world. Above all, there is no comfort that deterrence would *not* fail at some point in the future. On the contrary, the failure of the deterrence system is inevitable in the long run, due to the nature of political power as seen from the realistic view. Because political power itself is fluctuating, the international system is fundamentally dynamic. In essence, no Hobbesian world order arrangements ever can be fully stable or final.

Another reason why deterrence is inherently fallible has to do with the fact that deterrent postures are communicative acts. The way deterrent postures are understood is necessarily *interpretive* in nature. The notorious problem of the "hermeneutic circle," typical of any interpretive act, is not absent in politics. The political meaning assigned to an isolated deterrent threat depends on the entire interpretation of the opponent's foreign and defense policy (that is, intentions, interests, policies, commitments, and so forth). As such, deterrence is not only liable to misinterpretations and miscalculations in ways that may lead unexpectedly to its failure, but systematic biases of all kinds in fact are inevitable.[47] The lesson of this is clear and simple: As long as we continue to rely on the mechanism of deterrence, the phenomenon of war cannot be excluded.[48]

Is there a nonutopian way out of this predicament?

Beyond Nuclear Deterrence:
Toward Delegitimization of Nuclear Weapons

With this question our discussion is shifted finally from the realm of theory to the realm of the politically feasible. Is there a politically feasible way out of this predicament? Such a move, to be sure, is not a simple one because it is not exactly clear what kind of action follows from the denouncement of nuclear deterrence or from the retrospective admission that the regime of nuclear deterrence should have never been brought into existence. The hard facts are that nuclear weapons were introduced some four decades ago, and ever since they have gained further political legitimacy. Nuclear deterrence is now the key foundation in our global security arrangement. Any proposal for change must address these hard facts—that is, it must offer a politically acceptable alternative to the current policy of nuclear deterrence. We simply cannot place ourselves now at the point where we were four decades ago.

These hard facts of the nuclear age tend to make any purely moral judgments on nuclear deterrence politically awkward.[49] To recognize that the existence of nuclear deterrence is an offense to our moral sensibilities is not enough; one should be able to translate that moral aversion into a policy-oriented proposal, and most moral theorists fail at this difficult task. Morally motivated proposals often appear prudentially and politically irresponsible and hence irrelevant.[50]

So we are back with the question of the boundaries of the politically possible, that is, with the philosophical question of realism. After all, what is politically possible is determined largely by how we normatively view the nature of the international arena. It is for this reason that I took the issue of realism, not abstract morality, as my starting point. My fundamental contention has been that the very logic of Hobbesian realism collapses with the advent of nuclear weapons. Nuclear deterrence is morally so offensive to us for reasons much stronger than the common objection to the amoralism of realism; deterrence is morally abhorrent because nuclear weapons undermine and threaten the very motivation that makes Hobbesian realism plausible—*survival*. Nuclear deterrence pushes Hobbesian realism to its ultimate limits, to the point of becoming incoherent.

We should be reminded, however, how such political incoherence came into being. Nuclear deterrence was conceived initially as a time-buying measure, as an interim policy to be implemented until a grand agreement about delegitimating nuclear weapons would be reached.[51] In the absence of such agreement, nuclear deterrence became a schizophrenic compromise, an attempt to both affirm and deny the uniqueness of the nuclear age. In essence, nuclear deterrence gained its political legitimacy by default, not as a result of some rational decision that the world is better off living under the nuclear shadow. Nuclear deterrence is the by-product of our early failure to ban the bomb and is a living reminder of our inability to avoid the nuclear arms race, that is, to delegitimate nuclear weapons.

Nuclear deterrence emerged as the natural alternative to the prevailing view that only a full-scale revolution in international politics could stop the bomb. Such revolution, as we know too well, did not occur, and as the dream collapsed in the face of the reality of the Cold War, the hope that the bomb could be banned collapsed as well. Nuclear deterrence came instead. It is within the context of that failure that nuclear deterrence is believed by its supporters to demonstrate that no immediate alternative is available. This was Brodie's response to Einstein's nuclear pacifism in the 1946 debate, and this is also the response of the Harvard Nuclear Group to Jonathan Schell in the debate of the early 1980s.

What is wrong with the realistic response? For one thing, it begs the question. The adequacy of realism and its associated modes of thinking is called into question in the nuclear age. We no longer can afford the luxury of living by old-fashioned Hobbesian realism. The risks are morally unacceptable.[52] Hobbesian realism as a framework for international relations must be modified, if we want to survive. Hence standard realistic objections to visionary proposals simply evade the real issue. In addition, realists seem unable to differentiate between the nuclear abolitionists of four decades ago and the present ones.

There is no question, of course, that a common thread unites the nuclear debate of 1946 with the present one. Both debates are concerned with the fundamental question of the legitimacy of the nuclear regime, a question that was forgotten during the years in between these two great debates. The early debate was an immediate response to Hiroshima and Nagasaki and was an acknowledgment of that experience and a harbinger of the forthcoming crisis. The latter is an expression of a deep sense of disappointment with the path we have actually taken and an acknowledgment of mistakes.

However, there are significant differences in attitude and approach between the two debates. In the wake of Hiroshima and Nagasaki nuclear pacifism identified itself closely with the traditional pacifist way of thinking, whose approach addressed the problem of war in general—that is, within the nation-state framework of international politics. For this reason nuclear pacifism insisted upon the establishment of an international authority, a kind of world government, with sovereignty over all decisions concerning nuclear material. Thus, banning the bomb was linked by early nuclear pacifists to a full commitment to the idea of world federalism. To prevent nuclear war one should eliminate the very structural cause of war altogether, that is, the nation-state international system.

Nothing of this either-or attitude, however, is shared by present nuclear abolitionists. Although current nuclear abolitionism calls for the delegitimation of nuclear weapons, this is not a call to abolish national sovereignty. Nor does this abolitionism propose to eliminate the cause of war altogether by creating a regime of *pax universalis*. Here lies the pragmatic novelty of contemporary abolitionists. Their aim is more limited in scope and more specific in purpose: delegitimating the culture and politics of nuclear weapons. In doing so these abolitionists place themselves on the side of practical prudence, not on the side of utopia.

This shift from the question of sovereignty to delegitimation, a shift that is so evident in the work of Jonathan Schell, has some philosophical significance in itself. This shift indicates a pragmatic turn, an abandonment of foundationalism, and a recognition that there is no need to embark on a foundationalist project in order to change basics. To start in a Cartesian fashion by first demolishing the entire framework, the notion of sovereignty, and the nation-state system is utterly unrealistic and would lead to failure. Instead, one should begin by delegitimating the framework from within.

I cannot engage myself here with how the politics of nuclear delegitimation can be put into action within the current political situation. In his recent book, *The Abolition*, Jonathan Schell sketches his own version of delegitimating "living with nuclear weapons"—a "deliberate policy" that would lead to a situation of "weaponless deterrence." There are, of course, other proposals as well. The difficulty with all such outlines is that it is hard, if not impossible, to offer a full conceptual blueprint for such an unprecedented political dynamic. Neither Schell nor anybody else can propose such a vision as a concrete blueprint of how to transcend realism, nor should it be required. At this stage such a vision is not much more than a pledge for the formation of a political agenda that would make delegitimization an explicit, overriding commitment. Obviously, the rise of nuclear consciousness is a necessary step in making the delegitimation project possible.

It is precisely for giving an enormous push to the vision of delegitimation that the Reykjavik summit of November 1986 was so electrifying. Even though no agreement was reached, the summit clearly was concerned with how to bring the vision of delegitimation into concrete reality. Despite the failure to reach specific results, the summit legitimizes the very idea of a nuclear-free world as a realistic project. This in itself is an achievement. The summit was a historically unique meeting because it so fundamentally negated realistic politics.

No one can say a priori whether a politics of hope would succeed or even proceed. It may well die out as the realists warn us it will. There is no question that it would be very hard to undo current deterrence, but we also must remember that it was never tried before.

Notes

A very early version of this chapter was read at the 1984 AMINTAPHIL meeting on War, Peace, and Disarmament at Notre Dame University. Since then the chapter has been revised substantially. I wish to thank Scott Brophy, Ben Frankel, Kenneth Kipnis, Derek Linton, and Diana Meyers for their helpful comments.

1. I use the term *emergent* in a similar way to its current use in the philosophy of biology. For a philosophical account of the notion of emergence, see Joseph Margolis, "Emergence," *The Philosophical Forum* 18, no. 4 (1986):271–295.

2. This point is further investigated in Berel Lang, "Enocide and Omnicide: Technology at the Limits," in Avner Cohen and Steven Lee (eds.), *Nuclear Weapons and the Future of Humanity* (Totowa, N.J.: Rowman & Allanheld, 1986), pp. 115–130.

3. Jonathan Schell elaborates extensively on this point in "Defining the Great Predicament," in his *The Abolition* (New York: Avon Books, 1984), especially pp. 27–35.

4. The political and psychological roots of the denial of the nuclear predicament as a cultural-psychological mechanism of defense is discussed in Richard Falk and Robert Jay Lifton, *Indefensible Weapons* (New York: Basic Books, 1982).

5. I have in mind the Harvard Study Group, *Living with Nuclear Weapons* (New York: Bantam, 1983). See also Leon Wieseltier, *Nuclear War, Nuclear Peace* (New York: Hold, Rinehart and Winston, 1983).

6. Kenneth N. Waltz, *Theory of International Relations* (Reading, Mass.: Addison-Wesley, 1979), p. 113.

7. Michael Mandelbaum, *The Nuclear Revolution: International Politics Before and After Hiroshima* (New York: Cambridge University Press, 1981), pp. 5–6.

8. See, for example, Charles Beitz, *Political Theory and International Relations* (Princeton, N.J.: Princeton University Press, 1981); also see Chapter 1 in this volume.

9. On the impact of Hiroshima and Nagasaki in shaping the sentiment of nuclear pacifism, see, for example, Lawrence S. Wittiner, *Rebels Against War: The American Peace Movement (1941–1960)* (New York: Columbia University Press, 1969). Chapters 5 and 6 narrate the response to the dropping of the bomb and the rise of the scientists movement.

10. Sydnor Walker (ed.), *The First Hundred Days of the Atomic Age* (New York: Woodrow Wilson Foundation, 1946), p. 12.

11. For an historical account of this difference between the new nuclear pacifists and the traditional pacifists, see Wittiner, *Rebels Against War*.

12. American Federation of Atomic Scientists, *One World or None: A Report to the Public of the Full Meaning of the Atomic Bomb* (New York: McGraw-Hill, 1946), p. 79.

13. Eugene Rabinowich, "Five Years After," *Bulletin of the Atomic Scientists* (January 1951):3.

14. Emery Reves, *The Anatomy of Peace* (New York: Harper & Brothers, 1945), pp. 273–274. Interestingly, the book appeared in print in June 1945, just a few weeks before the bomb was dropped. The book became very popular, and by 1949 it appeared in sixteen languages in twenty-one countries. See Wittiner, *Rebels Against War*, p. 142.

15. The quote is attributed to historian Carl Van Doren; see ibid., p. 139.

16. James Franck et al., "The Franck Report: A Report to the Secretary of War, June 11, 1945," reprinted in Donna Gregory, *The Nuclear Predicament* (New York: St. Martin's Press, 1986), pp. 43–52. Also see Robert Jungk, *Brighter Than a Thousand Suns: A Personal History of the Atomic Scientists*, translated by James Cleugh (New York: Harcourt, Brace and Company, 1958).

17. "The Franck Report," p. 51.

18. Ibid., p. 44.

19. Ibid., p. 51.

20. Ibid., p. 46.

21. Ibid., p. 44.

22. Ibid., p. 51.

23. In fact, the Franck Report was never seriously considered by the Interim Committee (who received it from the secretary of war), which already had made its recommendations to use the bomb on June 1, 1945.

24. On the wide popularity of the world government idea within the U.S. public in the years 1945–1949, see Wittiner, *Rebels Against War*, pp. 168–175. For example, "by 1949 seventeen state legislatures had passed resolutions urging Congress to begin planning toward world government" (p. 170).

25. Albert Einstein, "The Real Problem Is in the Heart of Men," *New York Times Magazine*, June 23, 1946, p. 7.

26. On the deep ambivalence that characterized the U.S. attitude to the Baruch Plan, an ambivalence that was a combination of utopianism and cynical realism, see Gregg Herken, *The Winning Weapon* (New York: Vintage Books, 1981).

27. For a survey of the "revisionist" controversy concerning the origins of the Cold War, see Charles S. Maier, "Revisionism and the Interpretation of Cold War Origins," in Charles S. Maier (ed.), *The Origin of the Cold War and Contemporary Europe* (New York: Franklin Watts, 1978).

28. For a historical narrative of how the bomb was legitimated by bureaucratic momentum, see David Allen Rosenberg, "The Origins of Overkill," *International Security* 7, no. 4 (1983):3–71.

29. On the British antinuclear movement, see Christopher Drive, *The Disarmers* (London: Hodder & Stoughton, 1964).

30. For the categorical moral objection to nuclear weapons, see Walter Stein (ed.), *Nuclear Weapons: A Catholic Response* (London: Merlin, 1961); for the just-war revisionists, see Paul Ramsey, *The Just War* (New York: Scribner's, 1968).

31. For a similar historical diagnosis of the early 1980s nuclear debate, see Robert W. Tucker, *The Nuclear Debate* (New York: Holme & Meier, 1985).

32. B. Malinowski, "War: Past, Present, and Future," in Jesse D. Clarkson and Thomas Cochran (eds.), *War as a Social Institution* (New York: Columbia University Press, 1941), p. 22.

33. Ibid., p. 24.

34. The issue of war and civilization generated, of course, a substantial body of historical and anthropological literature. In addition to Malinowski my argument was inspired most directly by the following works: Susan Mansfield, *The Gestalt of War* (New York: Dial Press, 1982); Keith Otterbein, *The Evolution of War* (New Haven, Conn.: HRAF Press, 1970); Harry H. Turney-High, *Primitive War: Its Practice and Concepts* (Columbia: The University of South Carolina Press, 1949); and Kenneth Boulding, *The Meaning of the Twentieth Century* (New York: Harper & Row, 1964). For some further comments on the issue of war and civilization, see my article, (coauthored with Steven Lee), "The Nuclear Predicament," in Cohen and Lee (eds.), *Nuclear Weapons and the Future of Humanity* (Totowa, N.J.: Rowman & Allanheld, 1986), pp. 4–7.

35. Malinowski, "War."

36. Karl von Clausewitz, *On War*, translated by J. J. Graham and edited by Anatol Rapaport (Baltimore, Md.: Penguin Books, 1968), p. 263.

37. Thomas Donaldson, "Nuclear Deterrence and Self-Defense," *Ethics* 95, no. 2 (1985):537–548.

38. Paul Bracken, *The Command and Control of Nuclear Forces* (New Haven, Conn.: Yale University Press, 1983); Ashton B. Carter, "The Command and Control of Nuclear War," *Scientific American* 252 (January 1985):20–27; and Desmond Ball, *Can Nuclear War Be Controlled?* Adelphi Papers, no. 169 (London: Institute for Strategic Studies, 1981).

39. In addition to the work cited in note 38, see Bruce G. Blair, *Strategic Command and Control* (Washington, D.C.: The Brookings Institution, 1985); Aspen Strategy Group, *The Command and Control of Nuclear Weapons* (Wye, Md.: Aspen Institute, 1985); John Steinbruner, "Launch Under Attack," *Scientific American* 250, no. 1 (January 1984):23–31.

40. Donaldson, "Nuclear Deterrence."

41. On our intrinsic uncertainty about the more societal, long-term effects of nuclear war (for example, ecological, economical, and demographical), see Jennifer Leaning and Langley Keyes (eds.), *The Counterfeit Ark* (Cambridge: Ballinger Books, 1983).

42. This is what McGeorge Bundy refers to as "existential deterrence." See, McGeorge Bundy, "Existential Deterrence and Its Consequences," in Douglas MacLean (ed.), *The Security Gamble* (Totowa, N.J.: Rowman & Allanheld, 1985).

43. For a good historical review of the emergence of the theory of nuclear deterrence, see Lawrence D. Friedman, *The Evolution of Nuclear Strategy* (New York: St. Martin's Press, 1981), especially pp. 175–224.

44. This is the line of the current "nuclear establishment." See, for example, the Harvard Study Group, *Living with Nuclear Weapons* (Cambridge: Harvard University Press, 1983); and Michael Madelbaum, *The Nuclear Question* (New York: Cambridge University Press, 1979).

45. For a detailed argument in that direction, see Robert Goodin, "Nuclear Disarmament as a Moral Certainty," *Ethics* 95, no. 2 (1985), pp. 641–658.

46. For a good theoretical analysis of the concept of "deterrence" in general, see Patrick M. Morgan, *Deterrence: A Conceptual Analysis* (Beverly Hills, Calif.: Sage Publications, 1983).

47. On the issue of perceptions and misperceptions, see Robert Jervis, *Perceptions and Misperceptions in International Politics* (Princeton, N.J.: Princeton University Press, 1976); and Robert Jervis, Richard Ned Lebow, Janice Gross Stein, *Psychology and Deterrence* (Baltimore, Md.: John Hopkins University Press, 1985).

48. For a highly skeptical assessment of the actual working of nuclear deterrence, see my "Deterrence, Holocaust and Nuclear Weapons," in Louis Rene Beres (ed.), *Security or Armageddon: Israel's Nuclear Dilemma* (Lexington, Mass.: Lexington Books, 1985), pp. 178–196.

49. See Chapter 2 in this volume.

50. See my review essay "Lackey on Nuclear Deterrence," *Ethics*, no. 1 (1987), pp. 457–472.

51. Jonathan Schell, *The Abolition* (New York: Avon Books, 1984), pp. 35–50.

52. See Goodin, "Nuclear Disarmament."

Selected Bibliography

Boulding, Kenneth. 1964. *The Meaning of the Twentieth Century*. New York: Harper & Row.

Bracken, Paul. 1983. *The Command and Control of Nuclear Forces*. New Haven, Conn.: Yale University Press.

Cohen, Avner, and Steven Lee. 1986. "The Nuclear Predicament." In *Nuclear Weapons and the Future of Humanity*, eds. Avner Cohen and Steven Lee. Totowa, N.J.: Rowman & Allanheld.

Harvard Nuclear Study Group, 1983. *Living with Nuclear Weapons*. Cambridge, Mass.: Harvard University Press.

Morgan, Patrick. 1983. *Deterrence: A Conceptual Analysis*. Beverly Hills, Calif.: Sage Publications.

Morgan, Patrick. 1986. "New Directions in Deterrence Theory." In *Nuclear Weapons and the Future of Humanity*, eds. Avner Cohen and Steven Lee. Totowa, N.J.: Rowman & Allanheld.

Schell, Jonathan. 1984. *The Abolition*. New York: Avon Books.

Steinbruner, John. 1984. "Launch Under Attack." *Scientific American* vol. 250, no. 1 (January).

14

Loyalty and the Limits of Patriotism

Sidney Axinn

War is a relationship among nations, and it requires impressive loyalty on the part of individuals. Without loyalty and a willingness to sacrifice one's life for the benefit of the nation, what we call "conventional war" could not take place.[1] This point was made ironically on posters carried during Vietnam War protests, "Suppose they gave a war and nobody came?" Unfortunately, there is not much bite to that question because almost everyone comes and stays to the end. Odd that they stay. Yet we find that desertion rates are lower during a war than in peacetime. Apparently boredom, not danger, leads to desertion.[2] Wars require loyalty, and loyalty abounds. Trifles can awaken it . . . the Falklands and Grenada as well as great causes and clashes of ideology.

Three obvious questions arise. When is loyalty noble, and when is it stupid? When is loyalty moral and when just the opposite? How ought one to resolve a conflict between loyalty and morality? This chapter offers material that is pertinent to each of these questions. I shall consider the interesting recent analysis of loyalty by Andrew Oldenquist. The strengths and weaknesses of this analysis will bring us to a definition of loyalty and a classification of its four types. Then these four types of loyalty will be applied to some of the issues involved in patriotism.

Oldenquist on Loyalty

In his very helpful article, "Loyalties," Andrew Oldenquist makes a case for loyalties as necessary elements of mental health and of social stability.[3] I will give an outline of his position and then try to sort out its strong and weak features. (Quotations and page numbers are from his article.) The main components of Oldenquist's view are the following:

1. To have loyalty toward something is to view it as a particular and to view it as a possession, as *mine*.

2. An object of loyalty can be shared or "owned" by a number of people, unlike an object of self-interest. Group loyalty or tribal morality lets us speak of *our* family, *our* community, country, team, department, profession, association, and so on.

3. Loyalty is a third category of the normative and is distinct from self-interest and impersonal morality.

4. Our loyalties define moral communities within which we are willing to universalize moral judgments, treating equals equally. This is the crux of Oldenquist's definition of loyalty. One feels an obligation to treat all of one's children equally, but not as mere equals to all other children.

5. We are all tribal moralists. Loyalties are not the enemy of morality, not merely provincial biases, but the requirements for moral judgments and social and personal well-being.

6. A loyalist does not value something simply because it is his or hers. It must have certain features that make it worth having, and it can deteriorate to an extent that kills his or her loyalty.

7. Some loyalties are wide, some are narrow, and most are nested.

8. Each loyalty determines obligations only prima facie. They can be overridden by the degree of harm or good at stake. Loyalties are in limited competition. One is not obliged to accept the expressway that obliterates one's neighborhood just because it is likely to produce an offsetting good for some larger whole. One's own counts for more than do other people's neighborhoods.

9. Persuasion and moral argument are possible only within a loyalty group. The naked declaration of loyalty makes it impossible. So, "whatever kind of patriot we are," we have reason to seek dialogue with the competitor. If the beings I confront are members of one of my communities, it is possible to persuade them that they ought not to enslave me.

10. Three types of patriotism stand out: impartial patriotism, sports patriotism, and loyalty patriotism.

The *impartial patriot* would support any country that had certain very desirable features, "and, as luck would have it, that happens to be his own country." But Oldenquist holds that this is mere rationalization and that "impartial" loyalty is really just plain patriotism.

The *sports patriot* holds that each team ought to try to win and also holds that his own team ought to win, a somewhat inconsistent pair of assertions. He may mask his loyalty by holding that because his team is the best on some scale, it ought to win. But loyalty to sportsmanship is not loyalty to a team. It is loyalty patriotism that Oldenquist defends. He does this by first defending family loyalty and then assuming that what he has shown about this also will hold for patriotism. His case for family loyalty starts with a dramatic situation.

> Suppose that we witness the following scene. A family is vacationing at the beach; as the father walks up on the pier he sees his daughter and her acquaintance fall out of their canoe, swim for a minute in different directions and then both begin to drown. Being sure he can save only one, he lets his daughter drown and saves the other girl. Asked why, he says either (a) he was ever so slightly surer of being able to reach the acquaintance in time, or (b) the acquaintance was well on her way to being a brilliant scientist, bound to contribute more to the general happiness than his daughter, and, given that he could not save both, the choice he made produced more positive value. What do we think of this father? Would we want to shake his hand, or tell the story in the local paper as a moral lesson? Is he not a great fool, an object of pity and contempt? Indeed this is the kind of incident we are embarrassed even to talk about, unlike cases of moral heroism or gross selfishness (186).

Oldenquist takes it that the father owes more to his daughter than to the acquaintance and that we all feel contempt for him if he does not understand and act on this. Oldenquist then extends this reasoning to the view that "the contempt we feel toward traitors" is based on the same notion as our contempt for the father who lets his daughter drown. Oldenquist concludes that "patriotic considerations are . . . genuinely normative . . . partly determinative of what people should do, all things considered (187).

11. Alienation is the name for a situation in which loyalty normally would be expected but does not exist. "The main problem American society currently faces is not so much the competition of group loyalties as their absence." (190) The sense of possession is essential. "It is primarily group loyalties . . . group egoism and tribal morality . . . that have produced the caring and commitment that keep our social worlds going." (191)

Criticisms of Oldenquist's Viewpoint

Although I am delighted with Oldenquist's straightforward defense of the role of loyalties, there are four criticisms that quickly occur.

1. His example of the father/daughter loyalty incident must be balanced by the Mayor Daley/son loyalty case. A number of years ago, Mayor Daley of Chicago was found to have awarded lucrative city insurance business to his son. This discovery struck some observers as so embarrassing to the mayor that they expected him to be defeated in the next election. Not so. The Chicago papers appeared with a picture of the

mayor holding his arm around his son and the quotation, "Can't a father help his son?" No problem with that incident. Well, no political problem for the mayor, but perhaps a bit of a moral problem for those of us who wonder how Oldenquist balances conflict-of-interest cases. Even though Oldenquist says that loyalties determine obligations only prima facie, we need more than this to make serious decisions. Should the father always save his child over any number of other persons? Should the mayor flaunt all the laws in favor of his family?

2. Oldenquist offers no specific criteria for desirable and undesirable attachments. Apparently, any group in which we find ourselves, any community, city, relative, or association deserves loyalty. If we do not give loyalty to our surroundings, we are alienated, and this is personally and socially undesirable. What scope does this leave for the great iconoclasts and social critics? This question does not destroy Oldenquist's work by any means, but implies that we need criteria from some source other than immediate native attachments.

3. Oldenquist presents in-groups, but not out-groups. Can the community members have close and warm loyalties to each other without hating some outsiders, some enemies? I do not understand how a group can be defined without bounds, and those outside the bounds are required to give the group identity, meaning, and purpose. We hardly need each other unless there is a dangerous enemy at the door. But none of this is the case for Oldenquist. His positive loyalty has no negative effect on any group, and that just seems too romantic. Revealingly, he holds that racism is not a proper loyalty "because racism is negative, being much more concerned with hatred of other races than with pride in one's own, whereas loyalty is positive and is primarily characterized by esteem and concern for the common good of one's group" (177). However, the benign, nonracial community loyalties do not remain so innocent. "How can a person maintain community and civic loyalties if he is led to conclude that his community and his city are no better, and deserve no more, than a thousand others" (191)? Wilson Carey McWilliams gives us a more persuasive notion of a group loyalty that depends on contempt (or hate, or at least dislike) for the out-group, in his *The Idea of Fraternity in America.*[4]

4. The fourth objection to Oldenquist, and the most serious in a way, is this: His notion of loyalty has no cost, seems to require no sacrifice. Consider the idea of loyalty in any context, and the test of loyalty will turn out to be the degree of sacrifice involved. A loyal friend stands by, even at personal cost. Apparently, in past civilizations men were supposed to be loyal to their kings (and women loyal to men). To fail one's king was to risk the shame involved in the taunt that King Henry IV (of France) gave to Crillon, one of his captains: "Hang yourself,

brave Crillon. We fought at Arques, and you were not there!" Loyalty refers to a willingness to sacrifice, to risk something for the object of one's loyalty. This element must be added to Oldenquist's analysis.

Definitions of Four Kinds of Loyalty

We get a broad sense of the term *loyalty* in Henry Steel Commager's 1954 book, *Freedom, Loyalty, Dissent*. He defines loyalty as "a willingness to subordinate every private advantage for the larger good."[5] Commager formulates this in the course of a chapter on political loyalty ("Who Is Loyal to America?"), but it reminds us that loyalty is considered a matter of sacrifice. That sacrifice is a three-place predicate. There are three entities involved in the relationship of a sacrifice: the actor or subject who makes the sacrifice, the beneficiary of the sacrifice, and the offering that is given up.

Questions arise about the nature of the occupants of each of these three positions in a sacrifice or loyalty relation. We can imagine various degrees of sacrifice of those desirable things that Commager called private advantages. We also can imagine that an actor or subject might be willing to sacrifice desirables for certain goals but not for any goal that the "larger" entity, the beneficiary, might care to possess. We seem to be dealing with a three-place relationship that involves two quantifiers. We can quantify the amount of the sacrifice of desirable goods, and we also can quantify the amount of the goals for which the sacrifice is to be made. This lets us distinguish four different varieties of loyalty.

1. *Absolute loyalty for any goal.* A subject who is willing to give up *anything* for *any objective* of his or her beneficiary has the strongest kind of loyalty. We will call this loyalty L^1.
2. *Absolute loyalty for some goals.* A subject who is willing to give up *anything* for *at least some goal* of his or her beneficiary has the next strongest kind of loyalty. Call this loyalty L^2.
3. *Some loyalty for any goal.* This is a subject who is willing to give up at least *something* for *any desire* of his or her beneficiary. Call this L^3.
4. *Some loyalty for some goals.* This is the weakest sort of loyalty. He or she is willing to give up *something* for *at least some goal* of his or her beneficiary. Call this L^4.

A common feature of each type is that loyalty requires a willingness to sacrifice, to pay something for the sake of the beneficiary of loyalty. Is there a sense of loyalty that *has no cost*, that takes no sacrifice? The concept carries the notion of consistency, at the least, but that alone will not do. We do say that someone who has read the same newspaper daily for years is a loyal reader. However, this is an abbreviation for the notion that such an individual consistently has paid a certain price beyond the value received, made a certain small sacrifice, in order to maintain that habit. There is a difference between a regular reader and a loyal one. The notion of loyalty includes the idea that the individual gives up more than is received by the benefit of obtaining the paper. Perhaps a once-great paper has deteriorated, but the loyal reader will continue to subscribe even if a better paper is available.

We must distinguish between the term *price*, as used in a free-market trade, and the sacrifice of something of value. In a market trade with a so-called willing seller and willing buyer the individual exchanges something of value for something considered equivalent. In a sacrifice, the individual knows that there is no equal compensation, that more is surrendered than is gained.

As long as loyalty carries the sense of duty, or the intent to do one's duty, it is defined by its cost. (This follows the Kantian notion that moral credit requires cost.) If an individual simply does something regularly—for example, speaks English, draws breath, or says "good morning" at appropriate times—we find no loyalty. However, should he or she pay something beyond the value received for such activities, we have a different situation. When one gives up something desirable without expecting an exchange, pays *that* sort of price, one presents the special relationship called loyalty. Team loyalty in baseball may call for a sacrifice bunt; brand loyalty may cost a higher price. The word *sacrifice* may have originated in the practice of making burned offerings to sacred entities, but it still serves to explain loyalty, perhaps because we still make burned offerings to sacred entities. However, at this stage of human history we seem to take sovereign nations to be the sacred entities, and the burned offerings are called casualties of war.[6] There is a considerable moral distance between the sacrifice bunt in baseball, the biblical Abraham's plan to sacrifice Isaac, and the position of a serviceman in a modern military force, but the existence of a three-place sacrifice relation is common to each example of loyalty. A serious loyalty has a cost; the cost is the subject's sacrifice of something of worth.

There are certain stock questions that arise about any relation and thus about this one. Is it symmetrical?[7] Aristotle's discussion of friendship comes to mind as a parallel. He considers the reflexive and symmetrical properties of friendship, and the contrast with loyalty can be of use to us. The symmetry of friendship is absent here. Loyalty often is taken to be a virtue of followers, not of leaders. We read of loyal followers but wise leaders. Even the well-publicized differences between the arrogant General Patton and the more approachable General Bradley are not enough to give us symmetry between leader and follower, general and soldier. Loyalty approaches but does not reduce to friendship between leaders and followers.

There is no sacrifice if someone else's goals also are mine. (I ignore the trivial sense in which whatever is not chosen is sacrificed.) If an act is understood to be a sacrifice for the sake of an outside beneficiary, I will call it an act of loyalty. If an act is not a matter of sacrifice for an outside entity, then we have other labels available. If I love someone, I take that person's goals to be my own; there is no sacrifice when I pursue my own goals. An act of love might look like a sacrifice to someone else, but if the actor takes him- or herself to be an equal beneficiary, it is more than loyalty. Of course, spectators may differ about the matter; what looks like a loyal sacrifice to one observer may look like love to another. The actor also may have a change of mind about the matter and may revise his or her notion of the beneficiary.

Can we distinguish between love of country and mere loyalty to country? If I am drafted against my will, but I consent to serve honorably, my behavior is loyal. If I volunteer and serve honorably because I am doing exactly what I most desire under the circumstances, then I am making no sacrifice of what I prefer. If I make no sacrifice, I do not act from loyalty. Of course some cases are easy to classify, and some are not. Recall that the derivation of "loyalty" seems to be obedience to the lawful ruler. Such obedience need not be love.

Returning to our four kinds of loyalty, L^1 and L^2 are absolute or complete. In these cases, the subject will sacrifice *anything* for the sake of some or all of the goals of the beneficiary. Can there be individuals that have no ambivalence about the objects of their loyalty and are willing to sacrifice *anything*? I prefer to assume that ambivalence is the normal or healthy state of affairs and that Plato had it right when he had Clinias say and the Athenian agree that "every one of us is in a state of internal warfare with himself."[8] Some other philosophers agree with Plato; Kant also takes ambivalence to be normal and consistency of intentions to be the mark of fanaticism.[9] These kinds of loyalty, L^1 and L^2, are properly called fanatic, according to Kant. A fanatic is someone who has no ambivalence about the goals of his beneficiary, who will do anything, sacrifice anything for those goals. Yet Kant and Plato are far apart on one essential aspect of this matter. For Plato, ambivalence, the "internal warfare," is a mark of weakness to be overcome. For Kant, ambivalence is a requirement for a healthy human and is not to be eliminated.

Let us assume that Kant is right and that a healthy person is forever somewhat ambivalent about the intentions to follow the commands of selfishness and of morality. What becomes of absolute loyalty? Is loyalty to the established government worth any sacrifice? Certainly not. For a

Kantian there must be limits to the sacrifice of people, to using them merely as means to the desires of some other entity.

Patriotism

For a critical view of patriotism, let me now turn to a voice a bit earlier than Oldenquist. Edgar A. Singer, Jr., in "Royce on Love and Loyalty," argues that loyalty is a thing to be outlived.[10]

> There would be no such thing as a demand for loyalty were there no call for a man to deny his wish for home . . . for the sake of organizing himself into a group; which means, as we have seen, sacrificing his purpose for the group purpose. Now, what you think of the value of this sacrifice depends altogether on the esteem in which you hold group minds. If you can find some principal on which to estimate their dignity as something worth dying for in part or altogether, then loyalty may be the last word of virtue. But if you find that at their very best there is something rather primitive, sometimes ameboid, sometimes tigerish about such minds, then you should seriously consider whether your biped soul owes anything more to this polypod entity than the entity owes to it. Merging oneself into something big may not be just the same as reaching for something high.[11]

The sociobiologists might respond to Singer by pointing to the survival value of such patriotism. Singer still might be unimpressed by the need to have particular social groups survive at such cost. He seems to offer us mere anarchism, the denial of any value to group attachment. The sociobiologists, on their side, seem to have only mindless sacrifice of individuals for the power of the community. Obviously we want a synthesis that will give us the advantages of group attachments without the need for absolute loyalty.

The version of the patriotism question that now seems urgent comes at us in apparently absurd form: Is our nation worth the sacrifice of a significant part of humankind? To affirm a patriotism that says "yes" is to adopt the religion of nationalism, a variety of religious fanaticism. Even agreement with Oldenquist that our nation means more to us than other nations does not make a case for using the rest of humankind as means to our political survival. Of course, even this way of putting things is unreal because we no longer can protect ourselves as a nation, however willing we may be to abandon the rest of humankind. Because there is no defense against nuclear attack, we are now forced, despite ourselves, to arrange an international government. This means that patriotism to the nation is no longer a means of physical survival, although such loyalty may continue to have cultural features of great importance to social and mental health. But the needs to possess and to belong do not require sovereign states armed for self-destruction.

What of the status of loyalty, if patriotism becomes an anachronism? Would something of great value be lost? Yes, to Aristotle. In a distinctive passage, Aristotle says, "The good man . . . would prefer one great and noble action to many trivial ones. Now those who die for others doubtless attain this result; it is therefore a great prize that they choose for themselves. . . . They achieve nobility."[12] What a recruiting sergeant he would have made and what a pep talk the night before a battle. But what nonsense. Having served loyally, I find myself thinking, with E. A. Singer, that "I should rather spend my time . . . in wearing away the conditions that make loyalty necessary than in developing a spirit of loyalty."[13]

There are two main attitudes toward loyalty, toward sacrifice. For one group, it is the virtue of the good slave: regrettable even if useful. For another group, it is the only source of value. We owe this second group a little more attention.

Not the absence of loyalty but the impressive availability of it is what needs explaining. If sacrifice were irrational (and humans rational), desertion rates from the military might be much higher. Martin Foss has an interesting answer in his book *Death, Sacrifice, and Tragedy*.[14] He holds that sacrifice is a human necessity,[15] that sacrifice is the core of a person's life,[16] and that it is the way that value is produced.[17] He insists that we "divorce . . . the sublime sacrifice from the various utilitarian activities by which something is given away for the sake of a greater profit."[18] Sacrifice is the means "to bring value into existence."[19] "There is mystery surrounding the giving, a more than rational or utilitarian choice."[20] It is vain, he thinks, to look for a rational basis on which to choose beneficiaries of sacrifice; reason chooses means, and "inspiration" chooses values.[21]

Foss's idea that sacrifice creates value can be traced back to a point that Aristotle makes in his analysis of friendship. The values of friendship and love can be created in a surprising way: "Benefactors are thought to love those they have benefited more than those who have been well treated love those that have treated them well. . . . Those who have done a service to others feel friendship and love for those they have served *even if those they have served are not of any use to them and never will be*" (my italics).[22] The individual who makes the sacrifice creates the value of the friendship; the recipient of the sacrifice has not produced the friendship and may not value it as a friendship (but only as a source of gifts). Foss has (or may have) taken Aristotle's observation and generalized it to reach the view that not only friendship and love but all values are generated by sacrifice (or loyalty to use our synonym).

Is there a rational basis for loyalty, or is "inspiration" our only technique for choice? Even without a satisfying general response to this, we may still find our way to an answer to patriotism. Both reason (with Hobbes) and inspiration tell us that when the king no longer can defend us, we need a new king. Because we now find that with nuclear weapons the system of sovereign states no longer can defend us, we must transfer our loyalty to a still more powerful entity. Which of the four kinds of loyalty will this involve?

I have argued for an end to absolute loyalties, but not to limited loyalties. Aristotle's idea of a "noble" sacrifice seems a vestige of slavery or empty romanticism. Foss's idea of a sublime sacrifice is so mystic that we hardly understand him. However, Foss may be essentially right. We may not be able to do without L^3 and L^4 kinds of loyalty. Without the enthusiasm for risk and the generosity of limited loyalties, there might be no personal values.

Progress in loyalties consists in moving from absolute to partial loyalties. We now can admit that normal people are ambivalent, are not willing to grant dignity to every requested sacrifice for king and country. Likewise, loyalties to individuals need not be "sincere," that is, without *any* ambivalence. Are there sacrifices that are morally or rationally required? There are prices that sometimes are legally and properly enforceable, but not sacrifices. Those are voluntary.

Conclusions

Some of our loyalty must be transferred from the nation to an international government. Perhaps a minimal world government, a Nozickian sort of night watchman government.[23] The familiar Hobbesian arguments for loyalty to the king now must be understood as loyalty to an international king. Mere national governments are in a state of nature and cannot protect us. This is based on the obvious assumption that there is no adequate defense against nuclear weapons.

Absolute loyalty is fanaticism. No beneficiary deserves L^1 loyalty, a willingness to sacrifice for any goal that it may desire. Even the somewhat weaker sort of fanaticism, absolute loyalty for certain goals (L^2), regularly threatens to be immoral. Returning to the questions at the beginning of this chapter, because absolute loyalty is fanaticism, such loyalty to a nation must be replaced by one of the weaker but more defensible loyalties. Absolute loyalty or patriotism is simply not rational. In conflicts between loyalty and morality, morality should win.

I agree with Oldenquist that we need loyalties, that they are presuppositions of morality. As Foss might have put it, only loyalties create values. But I also agree with Sidney Hook that absolute loyalties are misguided.

> I can appreciate and reaffirm the last words uttered by Edith Cavell before a firing squad during the First World War: "Patriotism is not enough." Nor is any brand of theology or religion enough. In this world, of nothing can it be said that it is enough. Patriotism is one value among others, and in the moral economy where right conflicts with right, good with good, and the right with the good, some other value may transcend it. The children who, out of a misguided sense of patriotism, betrayed their parents as secret enemies of the state to the authorities in Nazi Germany or the Soviet Union or Communist China were tearing a rent in the texture of intimate personal relationships much graver than any derelictions against the state of which their parents may have been guilty. A secular democracy worthy of the name would never demand that a child surrender his soul or his moral integrity to the state.[24]

Nor, I would add, should it be demanded of an adult that he or she surrender moral integrity to the state. I expect that progress in loyalties will find us giving new loyalty to an international government. This world government also will threaten us, in its turn, with a demand for fanatical loyalty. Let us try to arrange it so that the benefits will not cost more than the L^3 or L^4 kinds of limited loyalty.

Notes

1. Richard Wasserstrom is quite convincing in his argument that nuclear war would not be war. There would be no time for decisions and strategy, no boundaries, no restrictions on targets—in short, no scope for the Hague and Geneva Conventions on warfare. See his "Moral Issues of the Nuclear Arms Race," delivered at Dayton University, November 1983, and "War, Nuclear War, and Nuclear Deterrence: Some Conceptual and Moral Issues," *Ethics* 95 (1985), 424–444.

2. This point is based on data from Russell Weigley, a U.S. military historian. For example, Weigley reports that 8,800 men deserted in 1871, one-third of the army. That, of course, was peacetime; no percentage that high occurred during any wars involving the United States.

3. Andrew Oldenquist, "Loyalties," *Journal of Philosophy* 79, no. 1 (April 1982):174–193. All the following Oldenquist references are to this article.

4. Wilson Carey McWilliams, *The Idea of Fraternity in America* (Berkeley: University of California Press, 1973).

5. Henry Steele Commager, *Freedom, Loyalty, Dissent* (New York: Oxford University Press, 1954), p. 154.

6. In the classic biblical case of loyalty, Abraham offered to sacrifice Isaac to the wishes of God. The nature of sacrifice as a three-place relation and Abraham's

loyalty are not affected by the question of whether or not God existed at that time. Although something must exist in order for it to be actually sacrificed, the beneficiary of a sacrifice may be a real or a fictitious entity. Isaac was in real trouble, whatever one's theology.

7. The formal logic of relations has a lot to offer a precise analysis of the loyalty relation, although it still needs much more development to serve social philosophy well. Three-place relations have been largely ignored in symbolic logic, perhaps due to Willard Van Orman Quine's mention of the technique of reducing multiplace to two-place relations. See his *Mathematical Logic* (Cambridge, Mass.: Harvard University Press, 1951), p. 201. This reduction blurs features of social importance.

8. Plato, *Laws*, I. 626e.

9. See my "Ambivalence: Kant's View of Human Nature," *Kantstudien*, Heft 2 (1981):169–174.

10. E. A. Singer, Jr., *On the Contented Life* (New York: Henry Holt, 1936), pp. 200–215.

11. Ibid., p. 206.

12. Aristotle, *Nichomachean Ethics*, 1169a.

13. Singer, *On the Contented Life*, p. 207.

14. Martin Foss, *Death, Sacrifice, and Tragedy* (Lincoln: University of Nebraska, 1966).

15. Ibid., p. 39.

16. Ibid., p. 109.

17. Ibid., p. 76.

18. Ibid., p. 74.

19. Ibid., p. 75.

20. Ibid.

21. Ibid.

22. Aristotle, *Nichomachean Ethics*, 1167b. It might be argued that when one makes a sacrifice, one makes a sort of investment in a value. The sacrifice is rational only if something is produced by it. By definition, a sacrifice does not produce "exchange value"; but it may produce nonmarket values such as love, friendship, and art.

23. See my, "The Law of Land Warfare as Minimal Government," *The Personalist* (October 1978):383–384, for comments on Robert Nozick's views as they apply to international government.

24. Sidney Hook, *Religion in a Free Society* (Lincoln: University of Nebraska Press, 1967), pp. 54–55.

Postscript:
Discussing Discussing Peace

Abraham Edel
Elizabeth Flower

In reading the chapters contained in this book we could not help but notice the implicit limitations that are placed on the argument. There is a kind of intellectual substructure that governs the very configuration of problems. Our comments go to a discussion of discussing peace.

Often the moral dilemma is raised in terms of a U.S. response to a first strike, on the assumption that the Soviet Union already has struck. This may be because we want to address a situation that leaves us with the moral initiative or choice. But occasionally it might be helpful to think about the Soviet Union in the context of a second strike in response to an initial U.S. strike.

Some chapters, such as Sterba's are even-handed and pose the problem with an eye on both possibilities. So, too, Child argues that neither the United States nor the Soviet Union can charge immorality if the U.S. population is a casualty of a second strike because there is popular complicity in allowing the first strike to take place. (Compare Sartre's argument that we cannot shed responsibility for a war in which our country is engaged, even if we were children when it began, for we always can be asked what we have done to try stopping it.)

A more likely reason for an "our-side" formulation is the set of assumptions about the current situation: for example, that the United States would not go in for a first strike. There is general agreement on the immorality of a first strike, but fear that bit by bit conventional war might lead to use of tactical nuclear weapons and so open the door for the loser to take the desperate step.[1] (For a plethora of scenarios see Chapter 5.) But the issue of a first use, at least a first use by the United States, is moot, for in fact the United States did use nuclear weapons first. Other countries may decide on a non-first-strike policy, for they have never struck, but the United States had better speak of a never-again-first-strike policy. If Japan ever toyed with the idea of dropping a nuclear bomb on the United States, it could call the strike a delayed reaction response. This is not semiotic trifling. It raises the question of what is happening to the collective U.S. consciousness, if forgetfulness comes so easily. Can the United States really operate without regard to historical considerations? This makes it even more imperative "to see ourselves as others see us" and to appreciate how from others' perspectives their fears are grounded. This calls for genuine inquiry into the total picture. To build on the consciousness of one country alone is to invite ideological illusion. A formulation that poses the objective as avoiding nuclear war and Soviet world domination, could be posed equally well as avoiding nuclear war and world domination by *any* power.

As the problems should not be framed from the perspective of one nation alone, neither can they be approached successfully from a single discipline. For example, the question cannot be handled as an inside problem of political science alone, no matter how analytically refined its categories. Marshall Cohen shows clearly that issues of foreign policy cannot be insulated within purely political considerations but are entangled with moral considerations throughout. Or in other words, there is no purely political ethics different from ethics generally.

This treatment of peace as a purely political issue flaws even Avner Cohen's subtle argument, for he links war as an historical phenomenon with politics and its relation to civilization, and he assumes that politics is guided solely by the pursuit of power. Now power is one of those general categories that screen rather than reveal what is going on in social life. Is war actually *about* power, or is it about grain and gold and land and oil and natural resources? It is necessary to get behind the power idea that so obsessed U.S. political theory in the earlier part of the century when everything from industry to human needs and ideas was viewed simply as bases of power and power itself seen largely in psychological terms. We must get back to the variety of goals for which power is being sought and exercised. The same is true for such opaque terms as *national interest*, behind which very definite material and institutional forms take refuge. If the problems of peace have become interwoven with all parts of economy, culture, and ideation, then these problems cannot be dealt with through the concepts and intellectual habits of a single discipline.

The questions we raise should be realistic. For example, a number of the contributors find it immoral to threaten what it would be immoral to do. This is discussed with respect to a second strike, but it would apply equally to a first strike. Sterba refines the problem to the point where he would have a nation declare that threatening nuclear retaliation is in the national interest, but under present conditions such threats are immoral; hence, the nation refuses to make these threats. But if that nation has a sizable nuclear force, would this not convey a strong sense of hypocrisy?

Realistically, what is "threatening"? Is it making the verbal hypothetical statement, "If you cast the first stone we will cast the second"? Or is there threat enough in acts and collateral utterances: accumulation of missiles without end, Manichaean attitudes, and talk of "evil empire," not to speak of *sotto voce* jests of bombs on the way? There are real problems of deterrence and real questions of policy in the nuclear freeze, but the making or not making of verbal threats is hardly one of them.

The questions we raise should be constructive. Why does the discussion of deterrence most frequently think in terms of negative sanctions alone? Many positive sanctions operate in human life to continue acceptable conduct. In ordinary life, although prominence is given to punishment, what keeps most people on the straight and narrow path (within limits) is the whole system of goals and institutional means for working toward them. Because these operate systematically, we pay little attention to them and think of sanctions largely as negative threats. In international affairs, to cultivate deterrence may be done similarly by established practices that are rewarding as well as punishing. The history of commerce, the law merchant, and international trade all feed into the same story of the mutually beneficial.[2] Detente properly may be considered a positive mode of deterrence.

Many of the contributors assume the approach to peace through deterrence worked for almost four decades, although it is not wholly clear who has been deterring whom. But the situation gets increasingly precarious as the very attitudes harden that must be dissolved to make progress toward stable peace. If there were time and if the situation were not worsening, there might be less urgency about trying an alternative. But there may be a dynamic of escalation that inheres in present policies of deterrence. In attempting to make nuclear war rational we can adopt strategies that make it more likely.

The question remains whether policies of deterrence have been successful and at what costs. The economic costs are evident, although no accounting has been made of lost social opportunities in this expenditure. There are costs as well in moral deterioration. Ideological considerations enter where the issue should be a scientific matter—for example, governmental discussions about whether the United States could survive a first strike. There also are increasing costs in moves that threaten freedom of criticism—for example, legislative proposals that would allow the secretary of state to designate what is labelled as terrorism and terroristic acts and to provide penalties for supporting what is so labelled. The secretary of state thus would be empowered to determine an expandable category of proscribed beliefs.

Yet for all the costs, if the assumptions underlying the policy are secure, perhaps there is no other option. In fact, however, the assumptions are themselves underdetermined. Werner performs the inestimable service of suggesting that the opposite assumptions in all these cases can muster as formidable evidence. Hence policy is being formed on the basis of uncertainty and in a context of risk. Werner then asks what sort of game we are playing—is it chicken or prisoner's dilemma or what?

Instead of resting on shaky sets of assumptions on which to determine policy, if risks are to be taken—and they are no greater than the risks in present policies—then why not pursue a policy in which goals of peace take a direct and primary place? Peace here means more than the absence of war (including even cold war and the threat of war). Werner compares the approach of William James in "The Will to Believe." Others refer to James's "The Moral Equivalent of War," to Gandhi, to a confidence that people are not unconditionally evil.

Exploration of such a completely different approach has been hindered in the past because it has been regarded as philosophically "soft." James's essay uses the illustration of religious belief and so seems concerned with more remote issues instead of direct practice; and Gandhi often has been taken to represent what can be done if one has no more direct coercive weapons, but why use his approach if we are well armed? But both James and Gandhi claim their views are as pertinent to realistic practice as any envisaged alternative.

James's "The Will to Believe" is clearly a general approach to decision under uncertainty and risk, applying to cases where decision is unavoidable, where matters of great importance are at stake, and where not to act is equivalent to making a choice of one side of the issue. Thus in the present context, an inability to decide whether it is worth trying to reach an agreement with the Soviet Union is equivalent to deciding we cannot reach an agreement. The argument for following the course of our "passional nature"—that is, what we very much would want to accomplish—is that it may release unexpected moral forces. We are advised then to act, not in confident prediction, but not without what Kant regards as "rational hope." (Kant is dealing precisely with comparable problems of regulative principles of history and the likelihood of perpetual peace.)

Pacifist theory has made a great deal of the likelihood of emerging moral forces. Tolstoi, in his *The Kingdom of God Is Within You* that so influenced Gandhi, urges pacifists not to refuse to be drafted but to declare that when they are given guns they will not shoot. His argument is that violence invites counterviolence as a standard and habitual response. Nonresistance puzzles, startles, and awakens; it can awaken basic affiliative tendencies, and these are "contagious." (Even in cases of violent resistance the moral force of guerrilla movements often has upset the calculations as well as the heavy armaments of realpolitik.) Doubtless passive resistance in Gandhi's India and in Martin Luther King's United States accomplished a great deal, although violence broke out in both cases. The most significant case of this approach in our time was certainly that of Sadat in bringing peace between Egypt and Israel. Whatever the complexities of the situation that moved Sadat to make this attempt, the result clearly was positive.

A practical program on such a basis would not mean the immediate plowing of swords into plowshares, although it would involve in one form or another a sharp halt in further nuclear armament and a serious negotiation on peace as such. Instead of name-calling, the program would turn over a new leaf and assume a common intent. Instead of arguing about the agenda and refusing to meet unless certain terms were agreed to, this program would set as its agenda proposals for peace. Hare and Lindgren speak of "genuine research into alternative means of conducting international conflict" and make some suggestions. But why ways of conducting international *conflict* rather than ways of solving international problems or reaching decisions or compromises on matters of opposing interests? A serious approach to peace will reach far beyond political policies and techniques and into fundamental attitudes. For example, Axinn suggests this approach requires the cultivation of a global rather than a national patriotism.

There are also many things we recognize in general but often have not applied. Most fundamental in a changing world is the repeated lesson that conflict about present partition of scarce goods is less productive than common exertion for increasing the sum of goods.

What is the point of such work as ours? We have little more influence than the ordinary articulate citizen. But we do have the power to change perceptions, to change the way issues are framed. For example, there is a tremendous difference between defining (and pursuing) peace as an avoidance of war or the threat of war and peace as a cooperative life in one world with mutual development and responsibility. Perhaps Ralph Barton Perry is right when in *The Moral Economy* (1909) he defines morality as "the forced choice between suicide and abundant life." Perhaps, too, if we do not change our way of looking, there will be no one around to quote the old Greek maxim that those whom the gods seek to destroy they first drive mad (not to be read as MAD. Or should it?).

Notes

1. In an Op Ed column (*New York Times,* Sunday, October 7, 1984) Tom Wicker states, "It's official American policy to use nuclear weapons against an overwhelming Soviet attack in Europe, even if the attack is being waged entirely with conventional weapons. And that's been the policy of all post–World War II Administrations of both parties."

2. For an example of how piecemeal interests maintain a high measure of de facto international law, see Oscar Schachter, *Sharing the World's Resources* (New York: Columbia University Press, 1977).

Contributors

Sidney Axinn is a member of the philosophy and the psychiatry departments at Temple University in Philadelphia. In addition to work on Kant and on applied logic, his publications include "Human Dignity and War" in *The Philosophy Forum* (1971) and "Honor, Patriotism, and Ultimate Loyalty" in *Nuclear Weapons and the Future of Humanity*. His current work is on military ethics and on loyalty and sacrifice as indicators of moral style.

Philip Chase Bobbitt is concurrently professor of law at the University of Texas and fellow in strategic studies at Oxford University. He was formerly associate counsel to the president and is the author of *Democracy and Deterrence* and *Nuclear Strategy*.

James W. Child is senior research associate at the Center for Social Philosophy and Policy, Bowling Green State University, Bowling Green, Ohio. He holds a Ph.D. in the philosophy of science from Indiana University and a law degree from Harvard. He has been a member of the faculties of Brandeis University and the University of California at Santa Cruz and also has taught at Harvard University and Northeastern University. He has published *Nuclear War: The Moral Dimension* and articles in logic and the philosophy of science. Other research interests include the philosophy of law and the philosophy of economics. He presently is working on a book on the moral foundations of capitalism.

Avner Cohen is currently lecturer in philosophy at Tel Aviv University. He received his Ph.D. from the University of Chicago in 1981. He has written articles and reviews on skepticism, philosophy, psychiatry, and metaphilosophy. In recent years he has written on issues raised by the nuclear predicament. He is the author of *The Nuclear Age: A Chapter in Moral History* (in Hebrew) and has coedited (with Steven Lee) *Nuclear Weapons and the Future of Humanity* (1986). Dr. Cohen has held visiting appointments in the United States.

Marshall Cohen is professor of philosophy and law and dean of humanities at the University of Southern California. He also is editor of *Philosophy and Public Affairs* and of the Moral, Legal, and Political Philosophy Series published by Princeton University Press. He has published widely in the area of moral and political philosophy as well as in aesthetics and criticism.

Michael W. Doyle is an associate professor in the Department of Political Science at Johns Hopkins University. He is the author of *Empires* (1986) and coeditor (with Arthur Day) of *Escalation and Intervention* (Westview, 1986). His current work focuses on theories of international relations.

Abraham Edel is research professor of philosophy at the University of Pennsylvania and distinguished professor emeritus of the City University of New York. His recent books include *Analyzing Concepts in Social Science*, *Exploring Fact and Value*, *Aristotle and His Philosophy*, and *Interpreting Education*. He currently is collaborating on books covering the history of ethics and the development of John Dewey's ethical theory.

Elizabeth Flower is professor of philosophy at the University of Pennsylvania. She is the author of "Ethics of Peace" in the *Dictionary of the History of Ideas* and (with Murray Murphey) *A History of Philosophy in America*. She currently is collaborating on books covering the history of ethics and the development of John Dewey's ethical theory.

Leslie Pickering Francis is associate professor of philosophy and associate professor of law at the University of Utah. She received her Ph.D. in philosophy from the University of Michigan and her J.D. from the University of Utah. She is the author of articles on age discrimination, seniority, animal rights, distributive justice and health care, and other issues in law and medicine. She teaches courses in the philosophy of law, professional ethics, and law and medicine.

Russell Hardin is professor of political science and philosophy and chair of the Committee on Public Policy Studies at the University of Chicago. He is the author of *Collective Action* (1982), author and editor with Brian Barry of *Rational Man and Irrational Society?* and editor of *Ethics: An International Journal of Social, Political and Legal Philosophy*. He currently is completing *Morality Within the Limits of Reason*.

John E. Hare is a member of the philosophy department at Lehigh University. He was an American Philosophical Association congressional fellow from 1981 to 1982, on the staff of Lee H. Hamilton, and on permanent staff for the House Foreign Affairs Committee for 1982 to 1983. During this time he dealt mainly with arms control issues, including MX funding and the Freeze Resolution. He has written, with Carey B. Joynt, *Ethics and International Affairs* (1981) and a number of other articles on nuclear deterrence, including "Credibility and Bluff" in *Nuclear Weapons and the Future of Humanity*.

Kenneth Kipnis is a member of the Department of Philosophy at the University of Hawaii at Manoa. He is the author of *Legal Ethics*, and his edited books include *Philosophical Issues in Law: Cases and Materials* (1977), *Property: Cases, Concepts, Critiques* with Lawrence C. Becker (1984), and *Economic Justice: Private Rights and Public Responsibilities* with Diana T. Meyers (1985). He has published articles on legal philosophy and ethics and currently is working on problems of professional responsibility in early childhood education.

Steven Lee is associate professor of philosophy at Hobart and William Smith Colleges. He has edited, with Avner Cohen, *Nuclear Weapons and the Future of Humanity: The Fundamental Questions*. His publications include "The Morality of Nuclear Deterrence: Hostage Holding and Consequences" (*Ethics*, 1985) and "Morality and Paradoxical Deterrence" (*Social Philosophy and Policy*, Autumn 1985), in addition to articles in the areas of social philosophy and philosophy of law. One of his current projects is on the notion of limited nuclear war.

J. Ralph Lindgren is a member of the philosophy department and director of the Law and Legal Institutions Program at Lehigh University. He specializes in ethics, the philosophy of law, and the law of sex discrimination. He was a visiting scholar at the University of Pennsylvania Law School during 1977 to 1978. His recent writings include *The Law of Sex Discrimination*.

Jefferson McMahan is a research fellow in philosophy at St. John's College, Cambridge University, England. He is the author of *British Nuclear Weapons: For and Against* (1981), *Reagan and the World: Imperial Policy in the New Cold War* (1984, 1985) and several articles on moral philosophy, including two on the ethics of nuclear deterrence. At present he is working on a book on practical ethics.

Diana T. Meyers teaches philosophy at the University of Connecticut. She is author of *Inalienable Rights: A Defense, Self, Society, and Personal Choice* (forthcoming) and numerous articles in moral, political, and legal philosophy. She is coeditor of *Economic Justice: Private Rights and Public Responsibilities* and *Women and Moral Theory*.

William Nelson is professor of philosophy at the University of Houston, where he teaches ethics, social and political philosophy, and philosophy of law. He is the author of *Justifying Democracy* (1980) and other articles and reviews on topics in moral and political philosophy. He currently is working on a book on the political philosophy of liberalism.

James P. Sterba is professor of philosophy at the University of Notre Dame. He has a Ph.D. from the University of Pittsburgh and was a liberal arts fellow at Harvard Law School from 1981 to 1982. He specializes in political philosophy and practical ethics. The books he has written or edited include *Justice: Alternative Political Perspectives* (1979); *The Demands of Justice* (1980); *Morality in Practice* (1984); and *Ethics of War and Nuclear Deterrence* (1984). He also is general editor for Wadsworth's Basic Issues in Philosophy Series.

Richard Werner is associate professor of philosophy at Hamilton College. He is the author of "Ethical Realism" (*Ethics*, 1983) and "Ethical Realism Defended" (*Ethics*, 1985) as well as articles on abortion, John Dewey's ethics, and nuclear deterrence. He served as coordinator of the Nuclear Weapons Freeze Campaign for the upstate New York region during 1982. Professor Werner was a recipient of a John Dewey Senior Fellowship while work on much of his chapter in this book was undertaken.

Index

DATE DUE

MAR 30 1989			
OCT 11 1989			
OCT 08 1997			
GAYLORD			PRINTED IN U.S.A.